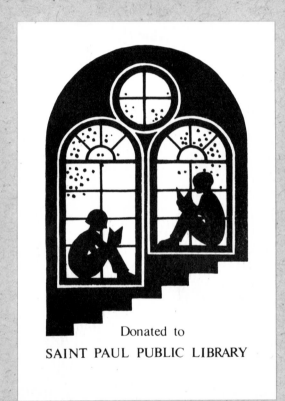

FEAR ITSELF

©80

FEAR ITSELF

THE HORROR FICTION OF STEPHEN KING

Introduction by Peter Straub
Foreword by Stephen King
Afterword by George A. Romero

Edited by
Tim Underwood & Chuck Miller

Underwood-Miller
San Francisco, California
Columbia, Pennsylvania
1982

FEAR ITSELF: The Horror Fiction of Stephen King

Signed edition: ISBN 0-934438-58-7
Trade edition: ISBN 0-934438-59-5

FIRST EDITION

Acknowledgements

The excerpts from Stephen King's works which appear on pages 56, 83, 104,
129, 143, 152, 168, and 181 are reprinted with the kind permission of the
author and his agent, Mr. Kirby McCauley, and are copyright © 1982 by
Stephen King.

"On Becoming a Brand Name" by Stephen King first appeared in *Adelina*,
vol. XIV, no. 2, Feb. 1980, and is reprinted by permission of the author and
his agent, Mr. Kirby McCauley.

Portions of "The Night Journeys of Stephen King" by Douglas E. Winter first
appeared in greatly different form in *Fantasy Newsletter*, copyright © 1981,
1982 by Florida Atlantic University.

Portions of "Horror Hits a High" by Fritz Leiber first appeared in greatly different form in *Locus*, copyright © 1979, 1980 by Locus Publications, and in
Fantasy Newsletter, copyright © 1980 by Paul C. Allen.

The editors wish to express their grateful appreciation to Don Herron and
Jeff Levin for their editorial assistance.

Contents

❉ ❉ ❉

Meeting Stevie

Introduction by
Peter Straub

HE APPEARED IN MY LIFE as a name on a blurb—one of those short comments publishers solicit by sending out galleys to anyone they think might offer a little uncritical kindness. Along with supportive remarks from Dorothy Eden and Robert Bloch, my editor received a paragraph from Stephen King, "author of *Carrie* and *'Salem's Lot*." I had never heard of those two books, nor had I heard of Stephen King, but neither had anyone else. Yet the comment by this obscure author was easily the most insightful of the ten or twelve responses to *Julia*. The others praised, and I was grateful for the praise, but Stephen King showed in a few sentences that he understood what I was trying to do—he had a sort of immediate perception of my goals. So I filed the name away. . . .

Almost a year later I was browsing in a bookstore in London —Hatchard's, this was, one of those wonderful bookstores that get almost everything and display it with care—and saw *'Salem's Lot* on the center table. It had just been published in England. I bought it out of loyalty, with no expectations. That night, I set aside whatever else I had been reading and began

7

on Stephen King. I never went back to the other book. The little town, the Marsten House, Ben Mears and Susan and Mark Petrie, they claimed me and took me out of myself. Occasionally I looked up at my wife and said something like "Christ, this guy is really good." I can still remember the shock of delight when I reached page 158 and saw Mr. Barlow through Dud Rogers' eyes: "The face that was discovered in the red glow of the dying fire was high-cheekboned and thoughtful. The hair was white, streaked with oddly virile slashes of iron gray. The guy had it swept back from his high, waxy forehead like one of those fag concert pianists. The eyes caught and held the red glow of the embers and made them look bloodshot." My God! I thought: a vampire! Nearly everything about this moment took my breath away, and I want to enumerate the reasons why.

1.   In the mid-seventies, I thought it took enormous courage to play this old tired card, and play it seriously. King was not fooling around, he was not even bothering to acknowledge the absurdity of a vampire's appearance in a nowhere Maine town, he was just slapping the card on the table.

2.   And the surprise was timed beautifully; hence it worked; hence it was not absurd. That was a vampire staring down Dud Rogers. Barlow's entrance made sense of all the mystery and at-mospherics of the novel's first section. Everything clicked to-gether like a good lock. The revelation about Barlow was the revelation of the very nature of the book. And King had with-held it for more than a hundred and fifty pages! This was daz-zling.

3.   Because of this wonderfully assured technique, King had disarmed my capacity for doubt. Barlow was there, with every bit of the vampire's questionable and suspect glamour, in the flickeringly firelit dump. The setting was as perfectly chosen as the moment of disclosure: even the landscape had the vampire's illusory beauty.

4.   The style's sloppiness for once did not matter. Surely in the last sentence I quoted it was the eyes, not the embers, which are bloodshot? I didn't much like the awkward passive verb and repetition of "The face that was discovered . . . was, etc.," nor the clumsy mixture of tone, in which the author's voice jostles

the observer's. But compared to the joyful shock of the paragraph, these were quibbles. Anyone could have fixed the writing, but no one could have presented Barlow so completely in so few words.

I suppose that most impressive was the way he had cleared a high fence without even breathing hard. Stephen King became one of my favorite writers on the spot. I read the book as quickly as I could, and then reread it before going on to anything else. The next time I was to read a book like that, twice, without pausing, was when I coaxed an early copy of *The Shining* out of my agent.

By that time I had become evangelical about Stephen King, thinking that here was a writer so good that everybody ought to read him. My little circle of friends in London must have tired of hearing about Stephen King, but once they read him they were converted. I think that three or four of my friends were counting out the bills to buy *The Shining* months before its publication. My own reasons for wanting to see it were more personal than theirs. King had written another blurb, this for my 1977 novel, *If You Could See Me Now*, and it amounted to a mini-essay: two pages of generosity and insight. My publishers thought so much of it that they printed it nearly entire on the book's back jacket. So it was clear that if I had an ideal reader anywhere in the world, it was probably Stephen King; and it was also clear to me that the reason for this was that his aims and ambitions were very close to my own. I have said in other places that the experience of first reading King was like that of suddenly discovering a long-lost family member — of finding a brother, really — and that is no exaggeration.

For he was, very simply, a writer first, and then a writer of horror and fantasy (though he might dispute this); he was serious about the shape and tone of his writing, and he wanted to work with the real stuff of the world, with marriages and hangovers, with cigarettes and rock bands and junk food and rooming houses, as well as with the bizarre and grotesque material of our genre. He invested his characters with feeling; he was tender toward them. Nobody had a funny name and nobody was just a collection of tics and attributes. This was rarer than it should have been in our writing, and still is. I guess what I'm saying is that he put himself wholly into his books, and in the best way: by doing it piecemeal, by spreading himself throughout the book to get between the reader and the narrative. Which is to say that he was a serious storyteller. I responded to the seriousness, to the driven nature of his writing, and saw that he, like myself, was doing his damndest to write books that could be read alongside the best of my contemporaries in the genre, and King seemed the only one who was going for the biggest stakes.

After I read *The Shining* I wrote to him, saying some of this and thanking him for the comments he had written about my work. After *The Shining*, it was *not* possible not to write him. It was obviously a masterpiece, probably the best supernatural novel in a hundred years. He had made a huge leap in quality since *'Salem's Lot*, and was now quite clearly one of the best writers of any kind in the United States. It was the ornamentation of the book that particularly impressed me — his ability to spin out inventive details in such profusion that his story was encased in them, positively encrusted by them. And each detail seemed pumped full of feeling.

Also, he had shown me how to escape from my own education. Good taste had no role in his thinking: he was unafraid of being loud and vulgar, of presenting horrors head-on, and because he was able to abandon notions of good taste he could push his ambition into sheer and delightful gaudiness — into the garish beauty of the gaudy. Before him, only Todd Browning's film, "Freaks," had broken through into that realm of the gorgeously overblown and georgeously garish. For me, this was like a roadmap of where to go: he armored my ambition.

Before moving on, I must mention one other aspect of *The Shining* that impressed me, its style. This was not at all a literary style, but rather the reverse. It made a virtue of colloquialism and transparency. The style could slide into jokes and coarseness, could lift into lyricism, but what was really striking about it was that it moved like the mind itself. It was an unprecedentedly direct style, at least to me, and like a lightning rod to the inner lives of his characters.

He wrote back to me: he and his family were going to England in a short time, and would spend a year there. Could we meet?

Steve arrived in sections, like a caterpillar. First his wife, mother-in-law and new baby, at a party in my agent's office. I remember a vast crowd, a fog of smoke, cheap wine, a crazy meal in a Greek restaurant — also Tabitha King's wit and intelligence. Then a series of telephone calls from the man himself, first from Maine and then from London hotels, as we tried to arrange a meeting. It was raining, and he couldn't find a cab. When he did find one, the driver didn't want to come all the way north to Crouch End. I'd had that problem myself.

Finally we made an afternoon appointment at the bar in Brown's Hotel, the most English and restrained, the most Agatha Christie-like, of London hotels. Patrons of Brown's would prefer their hotel to be a secret to most Americans. It is a red leather and watercress sandwich kind of place. Above all it is genteel.

Steve appeared, not genteel, lumbering toward me down a corridor between the bar and the sedate lobby. "Peter!" he shouted. We went into the bar. He was huge and keyed-up and warm and he laughed a lot; we weren't quite sure we liked each other. I can remember only one thing he said that afternoon: "How can you afford to live in a country with this kind of taxation?" Like every other writer I knew, he talked a lot about money.

A week or so later, he and Tabby came to our house for dinner. They burst in full of energy, on a torrent of talk. It is safe to say that they were completely un-English, which at first was disconcerting — we'd been there ten years, and were used to a less muscular social style — but then finally refreshing. Besides roast beef, we served taramosalata, which the Kings did not eat. Again, there was much talk of money: advances and royalties, strategies. We all drank and drank. I forced them to listen to a lot of jazz. When they left, my wife and I were exhausted.

Other meetings followed; the pressure eased. Meetings of writers are always like the comings together of princes who rule over small, but highly independent countries, and a wrong word, a breath of rudeness, can lead to undeclared warfare;

decorum is as important as affection. In our case, this did not seem to be a problem. From our respective mountain-tops we could speak without shouting. There was a raucous, riotous Thanksgiving dinner in their gloomy rented house when the turkey refused to thaw and we played at spacemen for the amusement of the King children. My agent, Carol Smith, had expected more dignity and gaped in astonishment — besides that, she examined the waxen walls of the King house and muttered about *The Amityville Horror*.

This was the day when Steve and I wandered outside to break up wood for the fire. The air was brisk and cold, more the weather of New than Original England. Steve snapped small branches by propping them against a bench and attacking them with a kick-starting motion of his foot.

"You know," I said, "you and I are the Hammett and Chandler of this genre."

"I know we are," Steve said, kick-starting another branch in half.

I now realize that I was being unjust; pompous too, probably. Robert Bloch and Richard Matheson were there first, and if they were the Dash and Ray of the genre, what was Shirley Jackson? The Dorothy Sayers? It is ridiculous. But he knew what I meant — that our genre had to live in the wider world of literature or it was merely a warped species of children's novel, that it had to be as well written as any other sort of novel to be worth anything. We did not want to be published by the Fantasy Departments of publishing companies (though we had no quarrels with those who did). We wanted to take our chances in the world outside the ghetto of horror-fantasy, and to find also those readers who thought Lovecraft was the author of sex manuals.

He was charitable enough to refrain from pointing out that he was doing this rather better than I.

I saw Steve many times over the following two years. We had become friends, our families had become friends. At some point I began calling him Stevie, partly because that was what I called my friend Steve Miller, and the two of them had some things in common. A little while after that *The Dead Zone* reached the top of *The New York Times* best-seller list. Speaking at the

World Fantasy Convention that same week, Charles Grant said that Steve had driven a huge wedge into the list, and that was the perfect phrase for his effect on publishers and the reading public. He had made other careers possible—his success was magnanimous. But every contributor to this volume, and most who read it, will be aware of that.

It's hard to write in this way about a friend, but this is some of what I know about Stephen King. He is very generous. He is in the first rank of house guests. He takes pills for hypertension and smokes his head off. He appears to be thoroughly monogamous. He is just about the only person with whom I can still be silly. Nothing in a television studio has any power to frighten him, though he won't walk under ladders or light three cigarettes with the same match. He possesses all the virtues of the ideal Boy Scout, possibly excepting reverence, if the ideal Boy Scout drinks a lot of beer and has a taste for fancy cars. He loves rock music but actually bought a Dexter Gordon record, a sign of growth on his part. He would make a terrible housekeeper, a terrible waiter, a terrible soldier. All things being equal, this is what he'd be good at: musician, truck driver, obstetrician. If he were a chef, he'd be like Julia Child, eccentric and great. If he were locked in an elevator overnight, he'd tell stories to himself until the janitor got him out in the morning. Really, you know — and this is easy to say—I love him and don't know what I'd do without him.

On Becoming A Brand Name

Foreword by
Stephen King

WHAT FOLLOWS IS AN ATTEMPT to relate, in a perfectly straight-forward manner, how a young man who knew no one in the publishing world and who had no literary agent became what is known in that same publishing world as a "brand name author."

I would define a "brand name author" as one who is known for a certain genre of the popular novel—that is, Robert Ludlum is the Bird's Eye of neo-Nazi spy suspense, Helen MacInnes is the Listerine of ladies' "international intrigue" stories, John Jakes is the General Motors of popular American historical fiction, and I, perhaps, am the Green Giant of what is called the "modern horror story."

If the title is mine, it is mine by default. Ira Levin has not published a horror story since *The Stepford Wives* (his *The Boys from Brazil* is closer to science fiction than it is to horror), Tom Tryon seems to have repudiated the field and William Peter Blatty has not followed up on *The Exorcist*.

It may well be that the horror cycle that began with *The Exorcist* and *Rosemary's Baby* is ending; the only other brand name horror writer who I can think of off-hand is Frank deFelitta.

But this is not only a piece about being a brand name; it is an attempt to explain how it happened that I made a great deal of money writing novels about ghosts, telekinesis, vampires and the end of the world. But, in the world of publishing, making a great deal of money and being handed the "brand name" tag often go together.

I have written seriously since I was twelve, and to me that means that I always wrote in order to make money, but I have tried to tell my stories with all the integrity I can manage, and with as much honest feeling for the subject as I had. Like Frank Norris, I have always wanted to respond to critics, in my own mind if nowhere else, by saying: "What do I care for your opinion? I never truckled. I told the truth."

There is no particular danger in writing what I will call, for want of a better term, "serious fiction." In writing popular, commercial fiction, there is nothing but danger. The commercial writer is easy to bribe, easy to subvert, and he knows it. I have felt this much more strongly in the last two or three years than ever before. But if this is true, it also means that the commercial writer who can tell the truth has achieved a great deal more than any "serious" writer can hope for; he can tell the truth and still keep up with his mortgage payments.

I wrote my first novel when I was a freshman in college and submitted it to a first novel competition — I believe it was the Bennett Cerf competition. I thought the book had an outside chance, and I was enormously proud to have fathered such a wonderful creation at the age of nineteen. It was rejected with a short "Dear Contributor" note, and I was too crushed to show that book to any publisher in New York. That was Book #1.

Book #2 was a 500-page novel about a race riot in a major (but fictional) American city. At the time — I was twenty — it didn't strike me as either particularly presumptuous or particularly comic that a fellow who had grown up in a Maine town of 900 souls should take a city of millions for his setting, or that this same fellow, who graduated from high school in a class of just over 100, should focus much of the action on a high school with a multiracial student body of 4,000-plus.

A college creative writing teacher found me an agent for this book, Patricia Schartle Myer of McIntosh and Otis. She informed me that she had read the manuscript and liked it a great deal. Mrs. Myrer's husband, by the way, is the author of *Once an Eagle* and *The Last Cadillac*.

Mrs. Myrer shopped the book around to an even dozen publishers, including Doubleday, who later published my first five books. Then she sent it back to me. We lost touch, but I have always thought of her kindly for her efforts. The race riot novel really isn't that good. Book #1 is one I can still take out, read and mourn over when I am drunk. Book #2 is only a badly busted flush.

A year later, when I was a junior in college, I wrote Book #3. And through it, although it was not published, I met William G. Thompson, who edited all five of the books I did with Doubleday.

By the time I was ready to show Book #3, I had finished college and was married. My wife, Tabby, and I had an infant daughter. I was working in a laundromat for $60 a week, having been unable to find a teaching position — and to be fair, I was not even sure I wanted to teach; I was afraid it would be the first large step on the road to giving up my writing ambitions. Tabby worked nights in a Bangor Dunkin' Donuts and came home smelling like a cruller. A pleasant smell at first which eventually became quite depressing.

At about the time I was getting ready to send Book #3 on its appointed rounds, I happened to borrow a novel titled *The Parallax View* from the Bangor Public Library. I didn't take it out because it looked particularly good; I took it out because the old ladies with the blue rinses had, as usual, gotten to the library earlier in the day and taken everything that was good. *The Parallax View* just looked better than anything else. As it turned out, the book — by Loren Singer — was pretty damn good. And it had a slightly surrealistic flavor that reminded me of my own work.

So I sent a query letter on my book — Book #3 — to "The Editor of *The Parallax View*." But that wasn't the only reason I went to Doubleday. Doubleday editors will probably groan and hold their aching heads when they read this, but I would advise any unknown, unpublished writer with a completed novel in hand to think very seriously about going to Doubleday. I went to them because they are gigantic; they are the nearest thing New York's "Publisher's Row" has to a book factory. I figured that they had to be more interested in new products than some of the other houses, and so far as I know, the situation still obtains — although the slushpile, sadly or otherwise, is no more.

In querying Doubleday about Book #3, I was fairly confident that I would be invited to send the novel for a reading, and I felt it was at least possible that they might publish it. I was twenty-two, the age at which Ira Levin had published the classic *A Kiss Before Dying*, three years older than John Farris had been when he finished the remarkable *Harrison High* (and to which, I should add, my unpublished 500-page race-riot epic owed a great debt). I thought it was possible that Doubleday might publish it, but my attitude was light-years away from the insane cockiness with which I had mailed out Book #1 three years before.

On the day that my letter came in, the fellow who had edited *The Parallax View* was ill, and my letter went to Bill Thompson, who had written a positive supporting opinion on the Singer book when it was before the Doubleday publishing board.

Thompson wrote me what is probably the most heartening sort of letter an aspiring novelist can receive, although it prom-ised nothing but a fair hearing — which is, after all, everything. It was an open-minded sort of letter from a man who obviously thought that there just might still be a good unsolicited novel somewhere out there in America.

I sent him the book. He liked it a great deal, and tried to get Doubleday to publish it. Doubleday declined, a painful blow for me, because I had been allowed to entertain some hope for an extraordinarily long time, and had rewritten the book a third time, trying to bring it into line with what Doubleday's publish-ing board would accept.

Thompson delivered the blow as kindly as possible, but it was still a blow. When a teaching position opened up in a nearby high school I applied for it and was hired, taking the first step down the other road, and entertaining half-bitter, half-morbid thoughts about all the potential Plaths and Updikes and Mailers and Ross MacDonalds who had ended up spending the 40 years following their graduation teaching the difference between participles and gerunds (or trying to), coaching debate, and — blackest horror of all — editing the school newspaper.

Most of my fears turned out to be completely justified. We were living in a trailer, and my study was the furnace room. I wrote with Tabby's Olivetti typewriter on a child's desk. My writing-time shrank to an hour or an hour-and-a-half a day, and even that time was curiously vitiated by six periods of teaching and the thought of the stacks of themes that had to be corrected later on. We had a second child, and money was very, very tight. I was making $6,400 a year.

During the winter of my first year of teaching I wrote Book #4. Writing it was a fantastic, white-hot experience; the book was written in one month, the bulk of it in the one week of winter vacation. The book, unfortunately, was not fantastic. I sent it to Bill Thompson, who sent it back in a week and told me to try again. I was as depressed as I had been over the failure of Book #1. I began to have long talks with myself at night about whether or not I was chasing a fool's dream.

That was not a good year. I was drinking too much and Tabby was not very happy about that. The money I was making as a teacher was not enough to cover our bills; I was selling a few short stories, most to *Cavalier* magazine (a good angel named Nye Willden was buying them), but they were not enough to pay the phone bill and we finally asked Ma Bell to come and take the telephone out of our trailer, which sat on a lovely, snow-swept hill in Hermon, Maine. If anyone should ever ask you, Hermon, Maine, is not Paris, France. It is not even Twin Forks, Idaho. If it is not the pits, it is very close. Having the phone taken out was our one pitiful act of defiance that year. It was quitting before the Credit Department fired us.

Tabby juggled the bills with the competent but scary expertise of a circus clown juggling tennis racquets; the transmission on our senile 1965 Buick Special began to whine, then to groan, then to chug and hitch; and as winter came in, the snow-mobiles began to buzz across the fields.

To top off everything, I was in the middle of a dry spell. I had no ideas, not even a self-respecting monster for a *Cavalier* story. Now here is an oddity, one of the very few in what is a fairly typical story of the Young Writer Makes Good sort.

Up until that point, in the late fall and early winter of 1972, it had never crossed my mind to write a horror novel. It's odd because I had never actually sold anything *but* horror stories. I sold two to Robert A. Lowndes's *Magazine of Strange Stories*, one when I was a college freshman and one when I was a sophomore (for a combined total of $65), and at that point I believe I had sold something like four to *Cavalier* — one about giant rats, one about an old lady schoolteacher who becomes so sure that her second-grade pupils are monsters that she leads them down to the mimeo room one by one and kills them all, and one about a laundry machine with a demon inside it.

But all of the novels — Books 1 through 4 — had been either suspense or, in one case, a science fiction novel (the s-f from a man who had passed high school physics with a gift C and barely survived Algebra I). I was aware of publishing trends, was aware of the Tryon novel *The Other*, of *Rosemary's Baby*, and of the fact that the Blatty novel had been — no joke intended — a monster seller, but I never made the connection with my own work.

The summer before, I had begun a short story called *Carrie*. I thought it would make a *Cavalier* story; a straight point-to-point tale of an ugly-duckling girl with the "wild talent" of telekinesis, who finally uses her talent to get even with the bitches in her phys ed class who had been tormenting her.

The story had so many strikes against it from the very beginning that it never should have been written at all. The first problem had occurred about an hour after I sat down and began writing. I decided I couldn't write it at all. I was in a totally foreign environment — a girls' shower room — and writing about teenage girls. I felt completely at sea.

The opening scene revolves around the unexpected (and late) arrival of Carrie White's first menstrual period, and as I arrived at this — on page two — I suddenly realized that I (1) had never been a girl, (2) had never had a menstrual cramp or a menstrual period, (3) had absolutely no idea how I'd react to one. On top of that, the entire geography of that first scene was misty to me. I had been in a girls' shower room exactly once — as part of a college summer job as janitor in a largeish Maine high school — and I was aware that there were sanitary napkin dispensers, but I could not recall if the napkins were a dime each, a quarter each, or possibly a freebie supplied by the school as are paper towels and toilet tissue.

I crumpled up my two pages and threw them in the kitchen wastebasket. About an hour later Tabby saw them there, fished them out, read them and pressed me to go on.

In his biography of Dr. Samuel Johnson, James Boswell repeats a comment that the good doctor made, comparing women preachers and dancing dogs; and to this day I believe that Tabby urged me to go on with what eventually became my first published novel in exactly the same spirit. It is not that you expect to see it done well, Johnson said of women preachers and dancing dogs; it is a wonder just to see it done at all. So I went on with the story, mostly to please Tabby, who was amused to find her husband hopelessly mired in the sociological peer-dance of the adolescent girl.

The second problem showed up less than a week later. *Carrie* was not going to make a *Cavalier* story even if the redoubtable Nye Willden did accept a story about girls in a male-oriented magazine. It was simply going to be too long.

When I got the idea, I saw the shower-room incident followed by a fury of telekinetic destruction. As do most of my ideas, this one came almost as a balanced moral precept, two incidents balancing each other perfectly — no muss, no fuss, no loose ends.

But when the shower-room scene was written, I saw that only the end of the fuse had been lit. I thought that, to tell the story properly, I would have to write about 25,000 words.

One brief digression here on the subject of 25,000 words. It is a number to make a short story writer and a novelist shudder. There is no definition of either the novel or short story in terms of word-count (nor should there be), but when a writer approaches the 15,000-word mark, he is edging out of the province of the short story. Likewise, when he passes the 35,000-word mark, he is edging into the province of the novel. The borders of these countries are fuzzy and ill-defined, but at some point the writer becomes aware of which country he is inhabiting; he finds that the currency and the manners have changed, perhaps while he wasn't looking.

But these borders do not lie side-by-side. In between the novel and the short story is a confused, anarchy-riddled, literary banana republic that is sometimes called the "novella" and sometimes (rather more archaic and too cute for my taste) the "novelette."

Carrie was bound straight for that poverty-stricken, under-developed country, and I damn well knew it.

Now, artistically or literarily speaking, there's nothing wrong with the novella.

Of course, there is nothing wrong with circus freaks, either, except that you rarely see them outside of a circus. The point is that there are great novellas, but they traditionally sell only to the ghetto markets (read "genre markets" if you like; in America the two are as one), such as mystery (*Alfred Hitchcock's Mystery Magazine, Ellery Queen's Mystery Magazine*, etc.) or science fiction (*Fantasy and Science Fiction, Analog*, etc.). There might have been a possibility of selling *Carrie* to a fantasy or science fiction outlet had it not been for the story's strong sexual angle; the fantasy and science fiction magazines have been and for the most part remain a stronghold of macho bull-spinster prudery, careful of the female consciousness issue (witness the splendid success of Joanna Russ, Ursula K. Le Guin, and "James Tiptree") but so terrified of any kind of honest sexual story-angle that an effort in that direction usually results in the wildest over-reaction into pornography.

In other words, I was writing a story with absolutely no market.

I persisted, not out of any noble motivation, not out of any glimmerings into the future, not even because my wife had asked me to, but because I was dry and had no better ideas. If I had, I would have dropped *Carrie* in a flash. I pushed my way through scene after difficult, sticky scene, taking little if any pleasure in any of it, only doing the most competent job that I could. When I finished, I had a novella that was ninety-eight single-spaced manuscript pages long. I think it would be fair to say that I detested it. It was neither fish nor fowl; not a straight story, not strictly a fantasy, not strictly science fiction. The length was wrong and the ending was terribly downbeat. My considered opinion was that I had written the world's all-time loser. The only thing I could say about *Carrie* was that it had a beginning, a middle and an end, and that for some crazy reason my wife liked it better than anything I'd written before.

In December of 1972, I began to rewrite the story, simply because I was still dry and still had nothing better to do. I had decided to try to expand it to novel-length. I began by adding a bogus item of documentation for each of the incidents of narration already written — I made up articles from *Esquire*, *The Reader's Digest*, *Life* (in business when I began *Carrie*, defunct by the time I finished). I surprised myself by having a lot of fun. The rewrite, I decided, had a certain amusement value if nothing else. It was fun trying to sound pseudo-hip as the *Esquire* of the Arnold Gingrich era did, piously American as *The Reader's Digest* always has been, stiff-upper-lip-and-you'll-never-know-how-bad-my-hemorrhoids-are as *The New York Times* is and, one hopes, always will be.

The combination of the documentary cast of the novel and several added scenes did carry the story over the border and into the more prosperous and rather more ordered country of the novel, but it was a short one — and another strike against it. Then, as now, any writer aware of market trends realizes that what readers want is a book to get lost in over a summer weekend or during a three-day blow — a *Shogun*, *The Far Pavillions*, or, God save us, that endless Michener polemic, *Chesapeake*.

The finished manuscript sat for about a month after it was finished; I saw no sense in sending out what I considered to be a certified loser. But my friend at Doubleday, Bill Thompson, had sent me a country music calendar for Christmas, and in early January he sent me a note asking me if I was doing anything. I decided to send him *Carrie* so he would know that I was still in there pitching, if only in the bullpen.

About three weeks later I received a letter (a cautious one) saying that he thought *Carrie* might work if the last quarter of the book could be brought into line with the rather low-key development of what had gone before. I knew what he was talking about: tired and anxious to finish, the last 50 pages of the original draft bore a strong resemblance to a best-forgotten John Agar horror picture called *The Brain from Planet Arous*.

Still dry of ideas, I rewrote along the lines he had suggested, and found that his ideas worked well. No, that is not really fair; on that occasion, Thompson's ideas worked so well that it was almost dreamlike. It was as if he had seen the corner of a treasure chest protruding from the sand and had unerringly driven stakes at the probable boundaries of the buried mass.

That was my first experience with what editors are supposed to do. I think that on subsequent occasions, Thompson's advice has been good or better, but in that particular case, it was inspired. The ease with which his suggestions reinforced the book's main thrust was exhilarating.

I received an even more hopeful letter from Thompson after he had read the rewrite, and in February of 1973 I borrowed $75 from my wife's grandmother (with our expected income tax refund for collateral) and went down to New York City on a Greyhound to meet Bill Thompson.

The bus left Bangor, Maine, in the early evening and passed our phoneless trailer on its hill in deepest, darkest Hermon on the way along Route 2. It got to the Port Authority Terminal in New York around four A.M. and I sat there in a contour chair in front of a blank coin-op TV for about two hours, afraid to go out. The terminal seemed to be filled with an amazing and ominous assortment of whores, hypes and muttering shopping-bag ladies.

I was wearing an outfit that I hoped looked at least moderately authorly—a corduroy jacket and a bulky red turtleneck sweater. The jacket, unfortunately, had no leather patches on the elbows. I had ten dollars and a return Greyhound ticket in my wallet. I parted with fifty cents for a Flash map of Manhattan (being too poor to cab from place to place) and around six A.M. began walking toward Doubleday and Company on Park Avenue. My appointment was for lunch.

Publishing people are famous for their "lunches," a grotesquely modest word for a meal that could sometimes, even in those pre-energy crisis, pre-runaway inflation days, run to better than $120 for four people. That day, we (Thompson, myself and Bill's secretary, a darkly lovely woman named Nadine Weinstein) ate quite modestly at a restaurant called Onde's, not far from the Doubleday offices. In many ways that was the best "publishing lunch" I ever had; in many other ways it was the worst. It is certainly the most memorable.

I had blisters on both feet because I had foolishly worn a new pair of shoes purchased especially for the trip. My neck hurt from doing the famous out-of-town country-boy, my-look-at-them-tall-buildings crane. I had not slept on the bus the night before, ordered two gin-and-tonics and was almost immediately struck drunk. I had never been so determined to make no glaring social *gaffe* and never so convinced (at least since the night of my high school junior prom) that I would make one. To top off everything, I ordered fettucini, a dish bearded young men should avoid.

In spite of all that, Bill and Nadine put me as much at ease as I could be. Although there has always been a rap against New Yorkers about their coldness, aloofness and oftentimes downright rudeness, and the charges have some truth, the other side of that coin is the practiced and natural-seeming hospitality of the native long-time New Yorker. In spite of the fettucini in my beard and the gin buzzing around in my head, I felt good about that lunch — and still do, five years later.

I asked Bill, who turned out to be even broader-shouldered than I am and an inch or two taller than my six-three, to estimate the chances that *Carrie* would be published by Doubleday. He told me he thought they were 60-40 in favor. I learned later that the chances had actually been a good deal better than that, but he didn't want to chance putting a jinx on the deal.

A month later, Tabby called me during my free period at school. I went up to the office to take the call, aware that it was necessary for her to go next door to make the call, and quite sure that one of two things had happened: Either Doubleday had decided to publish *Carrie* or one of the kids had fallen down the front steps of the trailer and fractured his or her skull.

It turned out to be the former. Bill had sent a telegram (and later that day I called him from the phone booth outside Hermon's one and only store). *Carrie* was a Doubleday book. After about 1,500 pages of unpublished manuscripts, I was a bona fide "first novelist."

Doubleday was offering an advance of $2,500, a very respectable advance for a first novel (I would not have felt slighted if they had offered $1,500, which at that time was more the norm). That night Tabby and I had a long heart-to-heart about the windfall, and the fact that the book was going to be published. I told her not to expect another cent from the sale. First novels have a nasty habit of dropping dead-bang in the street. Advances on them are calculated in terms of sure sales potential — which means sales to libraries and the one little old lady in Wheeling, West Virginia, who will take a chance on someone who is not a "brand name" and lay out $5.95 for an unknown quantity.

I suggested we retire our extremely sick Buick and use the advance money to buy a new car — a compact — free and clear. Tabby asked about a paperback sale, and I explained the Doubleday policy that finally led to our parting of the ways four years later. The Doubleday policy on paperback money is a 50-50 split, a policy that is non-negotiable. I told her that a great many first novels never sold to the paperback market at all, and that the big paperback sale of that day (Mario Puzo's *The Godfather*, which had sold to Fawcett the year before for the unheard-of price of $420,000 — a new world's record, but peanuts stacked up against what later happened to Doctorow's *Ragtime* and to Puzo's follow-up, *Fools Die*), was an isolated bolt of lightning.

I had revised my opinion of my own book enough to believe that its true market would be a mostly-young market that was "consumer programmed" to buy paperback books but not hard-covers, the same market that is "consumer programmed" to accept the price of a record album, which is comparable to a hard-cover within a dollar or so. But I told my wife that there was no reason to believe that any paperback buyer in New York would see things that way. I believed then (but to a lesser degree now) that editors along Publisher's Row are extremely skilled at recognizing excellence—even plain old competence—when they see it, but that they have less idea of what will sell than the lowliest newsstand vendor in America.

On the hardcover side, this situation still remains. It seems to me that all of the large hardcover houses almost willfully promote inaccessible books at the expense of others which are written in English. I am not speaking here of excellent books; I am not a writer who is going to tell you that there are unsung Thomas Pynchons and William Kotzwinkles and Dom DeLillos going begging in America while publishers chase junky, sensationalist writers with their checkbooks, because I don't think it's so. If anything obtains, it is the exact reverse; E.L. Doctorow wrote *Ragtime* with a grant, Thomas Williams had a grant-in-aid to help him as he wrote his wonderful, National Book Award-winning *The Hair of Harold Roux*, and I believe that almost any house in New York would be happy to publish a new Thomas Pynchon, no matter how maddeningly abstruse and obfuscatory. But William Peter Blatty had to suffer through countless turn-downs before he found a publisher for *The Exorcist*, and Puzo had much the same experience with *The Godfather*. Excellence is something that publishers and editors, with their excellent university grounding in English literature and their wide range of reading experience, seem to have no trouble at all recognizing. But there are people still kicking themselves because they didn't recognize the commercial potential in *Jonathan Livingston Seagull*.

The paperback people have always been more attuned to what is commercial, which is why paperbacks sell out of all proportion to their higher priced brothers. On the basis of my own reading, I'd say that the two hardcover houses that are best at sensing commercial potential are Putnam's (the publisher of

The Godfather) and Doubleday — my book was published two
months after Peter Benchley's *Jaws*, and I had an opportunity to
watch the publicity and sub-rights department at work on that
book. Doubleday swatted the novel onto the bestseller lists the
way Jim Rice can swat a fastball that gets up and over the plate.

I told Tabby that I thought we could hope for a paperback
deal, maybe for as large a sum as $60,000. Our half of that
would be $30,000, and if it happened I thought I could quit
teaching for a couple of years and write full-time; it might even
give us three years if we averaged our income tax back a few
years and lived close to the bone.

To this day I am not sure exactly what happened with the
novel and how it happened to be read first by New American
Library, which eventually issued the paperback edition of *Carrie* under its Signet imprint; I have heard stories, but I am not
going to offer hearsay here. What happened, happened. The
company got a manuscript of the book early and made a pre-
emptive bid of $400,000, bettering my best-case estimate by
$340,000 and proving that *The Godfather* paperback sale was
not an isolated bolt of lightning but the opening shot in an
escalating paperback price-war — the same price-war that has
forced the paperback houses to make quantum leaps in matters
of cover art, promotion, distribution and cover price.

To say that Tabby and I were flabbergasted by this news
would be to understate the case; there may be no word in
English capable of stating our reaction exactly. Thompson called
me with the news on Mother's Day of 1973, and I called him
back that night, at his home, convinced that what he had actually said was $40,000. And for the next two or three weeks I lived
with a constant, nagging fear that somebody would call and tell
me that it had all been a mistake or a misunderstanding.

After *Carrie*, Book #5 was finally finished, the dry spell ended
and I went through one of the most prolific six-month periods in
my life. I wrote Book #6, a psychological suspense novel. But it
wasn't a horror novel, and I think that is important to the subject under discussion.

In early March of 1973, with Book #6 barely done in first

draft, I began Book #7. Book #7 began as a result of an idle dinner-table conversation among Tabby, myself and a long-time friend of mine named Chris Chesley. I was teaching an elective course at school, the title of which was Fantasy and Science Fiction. Among others, I was teaching Bram Stoker's great vampire novel, *Dracula*. I had read the book first when I was eleven, about fourteen years before, and since then my only contact with the legendary Count had been his incarnation (through Christopher Lee) in the Hammer films.

The book was a delightful and powerful rediscovery. It is the most teachable book I ever used in a literature class — there are dozens of things that can be talked about — and I was impressed with many of the facets of the book; the powerful sense of blood-consciousness, Stoker's childlike enjoyment of fledgling turn-of-the-century technology, his effortless grasp of plot and character. More than anything else I was impressed by the way he made the Count seem more fearsome by keeping him offstage — after Jonathan Harker's encounter with him in the first three or four chapters of the book, the Count is always behind the scenes.

The creation of Count Dracula was Stoker's great *trompe d'oeil* — he created him in the same way a child can create a monstrous rabbit on a movie screen just by wiggling his fingers. In that one book, if no other, Stoker grasped the fact that shadows always stand taller than flesh-and-blood.

The dinner conversation that night was a speculation on what might happen if Dracula returned today, not to London with its "teeming millions" (as Stoker puts it with such purely Victorian complacency), but to rural America. I said jokingly that such a vampire would survive perhaps three weeks before Efrem Zimbalist, Jr. and the FBI showed up and dragged him off, a victim of wiretaps and God knows what other modern surveillance.

My friend Chris responded immediately by saying, "You haven't been through Cumberland Center lately."

Tabby caught his drift more quickly than I did and added, "Or Eddington," and laughed.

I began to see the point. There are so many small towns in

Maine, towns which remain so isolated that almost anything could happen there. People could drop out of sight, disappear, perhaps even come back as the living dead.

I began to turn the idea over in my mind, and it began to coalesce into a possible novel. I thought it would make a good one, if I could create a fictional town with enough prosaic reality about it to offset the comic-book menace of a bunch of vampires.

Luckily for me, I was teaching Thornton Wilder's play *Our Town* to another group, and I relied heavily on that along with my own experience growing up in a one-stoplight town. If the town hadn't worked, I don't think the book would have worked. As it turned out, the town did and the book did. Book #7, originally titled *Second Coming*, was eventually published as the follow-up to *Carrie* one week before Halloween of 1975 and titled *'Salems's Lot*.

I finished the first draft of *'Salem's Lot* one day before Thompson called with the news that NAL had paid bushels of bucks for the reprint rights to *Carrie*. At the tag-end of that euphoric conversation, he mentioned that we should be thinking about a follow-up to *Carrie*.

About a month later I wrote Bill a letter and told him that we had a bit of a problem; I had two possible follow-up books and couldn't pick between them. One was a suspense novel and one — please don't laugh — was about vampires overrunning a small Maine town.

That was when the brand name process began, so far as I can tell; the process is not much different than Hollywood typecasting. Not long ago I saw Bruce Dern on one TV talk show, bemoaning the fact that no one would consider him for the Jon Voight part in *Coming Home*; on another, about a week later, I saw Burt Reynolds bewailing the same sort of thing. You will notice that I made the comparison to type-casting and not to "star-making," which, in the book world as in the film world, are entirely different things.

Bill suggested that, in the light of *Carrie*, we look at the vampire novel first. I sent it to him. He wrote back a very positive letter, saying he had lost one entire sunny summer weekend with Ben Mears, Susan Norton and company in the town of Jerusalem's Lot, Maine. He thought that much of the book's structural set-up was bass-ackwards, but that taking care of that would be — in Publisher's Row's pungent phrase — an "easy fix." The other thing that Bill mentioned — almost overlooked in my euphoria over the *Carrie* paperback sale and my pleasure that he had liked the follow-up book — was a possible danger that I might get a "reputation as a spook-writer."

My own response to that was that reputation follows function as much as form does; I would write the things I had it in me to write and leave it to the critics to figure out labels.

As it turned out, I had no reason to worry about critics; like a lace-curtain Irishman who has somehow wangled an invitation to a Boston Brahmin dinner-party. I was almost totally ignored. *Carrie* was reviewed in Newgate Callendar's "Criminals at Large" column in the Sunday *Times* Book Review (and was later dismissed as "an unassuming potboiler" by Pauline Kael in her two-page serio-comic rave review of Brian dePalma's film); *'Salem's Lot* was not reviewed there at all.

Carrie was published in paperback by NAL in April of 1975 (I saw the paperback on sale for the first time in Las Vegas, in whose school systems it was later banned because of "obscene language"), and the richest process that actually makes brand name writers began. It is a process which, I believe, has made Joseph Wambaugh our "police novelist"; Helen Van Slyke our "the-way-we-live-now" women's book novelist; the late Jacqueline Susann our "sex-in-the-media" novelist.

This process works best with writers who can produce on a regular basis. It is not unlike the process that runs a nuclear reactor, except that, instead of an ever-more-rapid bump-and-bounce of atoms tending toward a critical mass, the writer produces a series of books which ricochet back and forth between hardcover and softcover at an ever-increasing speed.

The softcover *Carrie* was published exactly six months before the hardcover *'Salem's Lot*. The idea here is that the relatively cheap softcover (*Carrie* sold in the NAL edition for $1.50) would introduce me to thousands of readers, and that 80 or 90 of each thousand would be so intrigued that they would rush right out and buy *'Salem's Lot* in hardcover, thereby pushing it onto the bestseller lists, thereby generating even more interest in the follow-up paperback edition (if I had a nickel for every person who has told me, "I'm waiting for the paperback," I could retire to Aruba), thereby generating even *more* interest in the next hardcover, and so on until, instead of an operating nuclear reactor, a perfect hardcover-softcover symbiosis has created a money-machine that will continue churning out bucks unto the end of the world — or at least until the writer drops dead of a heart attack in Cleveland while eating Chicken Surprise at an author dinner.

Well, it didn't work out that way at first, but everyone stuck with it. New American Library published its original edition of *Carrie* with a rather puzzling cover. On it was a picture of a girl's face floating against a mystic blue-black background. The name of the book was not on the cover; neither was mine. There was just that girl's face. Later I found out what had happened from Herb Schnall, the president of NAL. The original edition of the book was "double-covered." When the reader turned past the cover, he or she was presented with a two-page photograph of a small New England town in flames. Written vertically down the extreme right-hand edge of the inner facing page was the word CARRIE and the name of its author.

The plan, Herb said, had been to score the front cover (the girl's head) so that the title and author's name would show in a kind of step-like niche. It's a die-cutting technique that is one of many gimmicks (an unkind word, forsooth, but the only one that fits) paperback publishers have used to get over the first crucial hurdle with readers. "If you can get them to pick up the book," Herb told me, "if you can get them to handle it, you're halfway to getting them to buy it."

Anyway, NAL got too far down that road with their plans to back out when their printer called and told them the scoring idea simply wasn't going to work; they would either have to publish the book with no title and author on the front or do an entirely different cover. They elected to go with the cover as it was. The book did quite well for all that; not well enough to get on *The New York Times*' newly-inaugurated paperback bestseller list, but well enough to reach the magic million mark.

In hardcover, *Carrie* was not a total flop but neither was it much of a success. It sold about 13,000 copies, earning back its advance and its production costs, but not much more. That fall, Doubleday published *'Salem's Lot*, which did about twice as well; it sold roughly 26,000 copies at $7.95 each (a bargain for a novel that was over 400 pages long) and did very, very well as a Literary Guild alternate. Being a book club selection is a wonderful thing. As the country of the novella lies somewhere between the country of the novel and that of the short story, so does the country of book club members lie somewhere between that of the hardcover book-buyer and that great legion who are, God save us, "waiting for the paperback." But while the between-country of the novella is habitually famine-swept and under-developed, the country of the book club is like a small, sleek socialist democracy. It's nice to be an alternate, even nicer to be a main selection. The reason it's nice to be a main, of course, is because if the book club member forgets to send back the order form, they mail him the book anyway. When you're a main selection, the members have to *do* something about you, even if it's only to check the DO NOT SEND box on the computer card.

'Salem's Lot had been read at NAL with a great deal of enthusiasm, much of it undoubtedly because they recognized a brand name potential beginning to shape up. Horror was big in those days — bigger than it is now, certainly — and I had showed no signs with my second book of exchanging my fright wig and Lon Chaney makeup for a pipe and tweed jacket and writing something Deep and Meaningful. In a way, *'Salem's Lot* must have looked even better to them than *Carrie* had done; it had been sold to Warner Brothers for a lot of money and it was a *big* book. The only problem — a minor one — was that Doubleday had published it in October. The normal deal is that the paperback can be published a year after the hardcover, so *'Salem's Lot* should have come out in October of 1976. But the buying cycles in the hardcover and paperback markets are as reversed as the seasons are in North America and Australia. The period that runs from October to March are the paperback Horse Latitudes; people are buying oversized coffee table books such as *Rock*

Climbing in South America and *Grooming Your Weimaraner* as Christmas presents after December 25th (not to mention the big fall novels), and after Christmas they're spending money received from aunts and grandmothers and such on the same sort of thing.

From March until October, people buy paperbacks; the great majority of them for the beach and vacations, and hardcovers gather dust on the shelves. *'Salem's Lot* impressed the people at NAL as a summer-type book; big, engrossing, but not terribly demanding. So they made an arrangement with Doubleday to publish it in August instead of October.

In the spring of 1976, Bill Thompson and I were invited to NAL's offices for an advance look at the cover they were planning — we were given to understand that they didn't even want to go ahead without the full approval of the author. Our curiosity was piqued, to say the least. We were ushered into a small room where a tripod had been set up. Something was on the tripod, but it was covered with a small gray dropcloth — the whole thing was like a scene out of a Madison Avenue novel.

I had visualized everything from another two-cover die-cut to some sort of three-dimensional effect. As the NAL art director began to outline their thinking on the cover of a novel about modern-day vampires, I said — a bit nervously — that anything would be okay as long as it had my name on it this time. The art director and Herb Schnall exchanged a look, and my heart sank. Shortly, the small dropcloth was whisked away and the cover was revealed: It was a dead-black embossing of a girl's head. With her damply-curling hair and her blank, pupil-less eyes, she looked a bit like a Grecian bust. The only spot of color in the whole thing was a single drop of blood at the corner of the girl's mouth. The title and author's name were both on the back of the book.

I gave my approval — a little uneasily, but I gave it. Later editions of the book retained the girl's head, but the title and author were both printed in silver on the cover. What a relief.

The black cover worked extremely well. *'Salem's Lot* went to number one on the *Times* bestseller list, and to number two on the *Publishers Weekly* list.

In the late summer of 1974, the whole family had moved out to Colorado. There were two reasons. One was that I knew by then that I would be publishing two novels with Maine backgrounds, and I thought it was time to research a new setting. The other reason was that we just wanted to go to Colorado and see if it was as nice as we had heard.

In late September of 1974, Tabby and I spent a night at a grand old hotel in Estes Park, the Stanley. We were the only guests, as it turned out; the following day they were going to close the place down for the winter. Wandering through its corridors, I thought that it seemed to be the perfect — maybe the archetypal — setting for a ghost story. At that time I had been trying quite hard to write a kidnap novel, this one loosely based on the Patricia Hearst-SLA business, which seemed to have almost every dramatic aspect in it known to man. It is a story that Shakespeare could have hit a mile — that is, if you can imagine Shakespeare somehow couching "fuck all fascist pigs" in iambic pentameter. But the story just wasn't marching. I went on nuzzling it apathetically for the next few weeks and then decided to put it aside and try what I was thinking of as "the haunted hotel story."

I never have written a book that went so smoothly. I have always been a fairly rapid writer, but have always believed that the speed at which you're writing has very little to do with the problems you are solving or not solving — you can write as slowly as Joseph Heller and still produce a bad book. My own feeling about problems in matters of plot or theme — even something so vague as the general feeling a work-in-progress is giving you — is to write my way through them; if necessary, to attack them with my bare hands the way a miner might attack a cave-in.

This is not to say that hard work and determination always carry the day, because they don't — and you don't have to be a novelist to know that. All I have ever been able to hope for is that when the words are down on paper I'll be able to tell good work from bad, and I've made plenty of mistakes that way. But those are perhaps only lapses of taste, and that is surely not a problem any writer should concern himself or herself with, at least not if he or she wants to remain sane for long.

There were none of these problems with Book #8. The story unspooled itself without a hitch or a snag. I never had that depressing feeling that I had lost the way. The writer is a pilgrim, and that particular trip went very smoothly.

But the countryside was dim and drear. The book, to me at least, seemed to be primarily a story about a miserable, damned man who is very slowly losing his grip on his life, a man who is being driven to destroy all the things he loves. For much of the three or four months it took me to write the first draft of the novel I was calling *The Shine*, I seemed to be back in that trailer in Hermon, Maine, with no company but the buzzing sound of the snowmobiles and my own fears — fears that my chance to be a writer had come and gone, fears that I had gotten into a teaching job that was completely wrong for me, fears most of all that my marriage was edging onto marshy ground and that there might be quicksand anyplace ahead.

By the time I went to New York from Colorado that January to go over the copy-edited manuscript of *'Salem's Lot* (due for publication eight months later), I told Bill Thompson that I had written a new book and outlined the plot for him. I have heard that some authors are excellent summarizers — just as good at oral story-telling as they are at writing them down — but I am not one of those. I spilled the plot of *The Shine* over roughly 2,000 beers in a pleasant little hamburger place called Jasper's.

Bill wasn't terribly enthusiastic. He thought the idea of the book sounded quite a bit like Marasco's *Burnt Offerings*, which he knew I admired immensely, and that a long novel about a family trapped in a haunted hotel would only reinforce the "spook novelist" tag. Editors, of course, are paid to be schizos: the part of Bill that was the company man liked the idea of a third horror novel — it would help the brand name ricochet to pick up speed — but the part that was just Steve King's friend seemed to think that I might be hurting myself, and maybe my future.

Writers themselves are paranoids about "the future." Of course, it's a tremendous glamour job; who wouldn't want to be Youngblood Hawke if he had the chance? No boss, no nine-to-five grind, no shaving in the morning with one eye open, scarf-

hours are regular but quite short, and in my case the pay has been good. The major financial and psychic drawback is the uncertainty. If you're making good money, the critics usually don't like you. If the critics do like you, there is a fair chance that you and your family may sit down some night to an Alpo-and-noodles casserole. There's no social security; you have to have enough foresight to provide you own retirement program — Keogh or something similar — if you can afford it. You have to resign yourself to the fact that you're just not going to have the security of a regular paycheck, and that if you're making a great deal of money, IRS is going to take a lot — although you may not work at all the following year.

All of which proves very little, except that the concept of "the future" for a writer is a very tenuous thing — as my agent keeps reminding me, you're only as good as your last book, or maybe your last two, if you've got a track record. And it seemed to me that the only true north I could steer by was whether or not I thought the book was good, not whether it was going to "type" me as a horror writer. I thought that the book was like *Burnt Offerings* only in that they were both haunted house stories, a sub-genre of the supernatural tale that, by its very nature, has as many similarities as Westerns do.

When Bill Thompson saw the book, he was much more enthusiastic, and that book, of all the novels I've published was the one that required the least rewriting.

Doubleday's formidable sub-rights department went to work on it, and the book built up a great deal of steam before publication — undoubtedly because it could be neatly categorized by this time as "a Stephen King novel" (just as when you say "Hellman's," most everyone knows you're talking about mayonnaise). The flap-copy referred to me as "the master of the modern horror story," neatly ignoring the likes of Shirley Jackson, Richard Matheson, and Ira Levin, none of whom I have yet approached.

Warner Brothers again bought the book, this time with Stanley Kubrick in mind to direct, with Jack Nicholson in the lead and Shelley Duvall as his wife. Then a problem came up about the title. They wanted it retitled *The Shining*, because "shine" is a pre-World War II pejorative for black, as in "Hey, shoeshine boy." This would not have been a problem had not one of the main characters been a black cook named Dick Hallorann. Someone in Warner Brothers title department (perhaps the same half-wit who suggested — seriously or in jest, I don't know — that *'Salem's Lot* be retitled *As Maine Goes, So Goes the Nation*) felt that people would think the title a half-satirical gibe at my black character. So we changed it to *The Shining* (the original title had been suggested by a John Lennon song, *Instant Karma*, the chorus of which goes, "We all shine on . . . like the moon and the stars and the sun . . ."), which I have learned to live with but which still strikes me as rather unwieldy and thudding. It has also been used before, by a good writer named Stephen Marlowe.

Besides the movie sale, *The Shining* had been chosen as a lead selection of the Literary Guild, and the paperback rights had been sold to NAL for a goodish sum. Shortly after NAL published *'Salem's Lot* — only about ten weeks after, as a matter of fact — United Artists released Brian dePalma's film of *Carrie*, and NAL released their "movie tie-in" edition.

My novel had sold just under a million copies its first time out, but when the movie was released, it sold another million-and-a-half and legged it up the *Times* bestseller list to Number 4. It undoubtedly says something — a not very flattering something — about our reading habits as a nation when you examine the fact that these days people are driven to read books as a result of having seen a film. When I was growing up in the 1950's, the slogan was, "read the book, see the movie"; nowadays it seems to be "See the movie, read the movie novelization that some journeyman knocked out in four days from the shooting script."

With *The Shining*, Doubleday really cashed in for the first time on the ricochet-action that creates a brand name. My first two books sold approximately 35,000 copies in their hardcover bookstore editions; the same two books had sold 4.5 *million* copies in their softcover reincarnations. Statistics are no one's answer to the world's problems, but that one may help to explain why the paperback industry is now the giant of the publishing world; it may also go a ways toward explaining why a good many people (including myself) believe that the hand-writing has gone up on the wall for the hardcover book.

To the above I should add that *The Shining* was my first hard-cover bestseller; it went to Number 8 on the *Times* list (then promptly dropped off the list altogether), to Number 7 on the *Publishers Weekly* list, to Number 6 on the *Time Magazine* list. I got to be a popcorn celebrity one week in *People* magazine — a two-page spread sandwiched in between Bjorn Borg and Larry Flynt. Brand name-making undoubtedly played a major part in the book's moderate hardcover success. It sold roughly 50,000 copies, twice as many as *'Salem's Lot*, and while that may not be such great shakes, compared to another Doubleday novel, *Trinity*, that was in the running at the same time, it seemed that I had finally begun to develop a hardcover readership.

I began by saying that commercial writing was dangerous writing — as cigarette smoking may be hazardous to your health, so may popular writing be hazardous to your integrity. It's all too easy to begin producing the literary equivalent of frozen TV dinners. I believe that, after a string of half-a-dozen brilliant suspense novels, Alistair MacLean was busy selling frozen dinners for a good many years; and the late Ian Fleming as much as admitted the same thing following the publication of his last three rather lame James Bond novels.

But the writer's job is to write: after years of hit-or-miss, slap-dash promotion, the publishing industry — spearheaded by the paperback sector — has apparently made up its mind that its job is to sell books. In a world that has gone made for bush league celebs such as Farrah and Chér, the brand name author is the result, and as I conclude, I hasten to add that I am one only fair-ly minor example of that phenomenon. There's Robert Ludlum, Rosemary Rogers, Katherine Woodiwiss, a score of others. Not even so-called "serious" novelists are immune; Gore Vidal is certainly a brand name, as to a lesser degree are Kurt Vonnegut, Jr. and Paul Theroux. Others, such as paperback-originals writers John Saul, have been tooled up in the work-shops along Publishers' Row. But the writer's job is to write, and there are no brand names in the little room where the typewriter or the pen and notebook sit waiting. There are no stars or brand names in that place; only people who will try to create something out of nothing, and those who succeed and those who fail.

Perhaps the first brand name writer was Charles Dickens. In America people used to line the docks when the ship bearing the next installment of *Little Dorritt* or *Oliver Twist* was due. If his reputation as the first "star" novelist hurt him, it does not show in his later work. Nor is there any reason for anyone to think it might or expect it should. The idea that success in itself can hurt a writer is as ridiculous and as elitist as the commonly held belief that a popular book is a bad book — the former belief presumes that writers are even more corruptible than, say, politicians, and the latter belief presumes that the level of taste in the world's most literate country is illogically low. I don't — and perhaps can't, as a direct result of what I'm doing — accept either idea. Being a brand name is all right. Trying to be a writer, trying to fill the blank sheet in an honorable and truthful way, is better. And if those two things ever change places on me (and it can happen with a creepy, unobtrusive ease), I'm in a lot of trouble.

FEAR ITSELF

Cinderella's Revenge

Twists on fairy tale and mythic themes in the work of Stephen King

by Chelsea Quinn Yarbro

MOST CHILDREN HAVE A TASTE for the gruesome; comic books and Saturday morning cartoons reflect their fascination with mayhem. This is not new to this culture or this century, as a quick glance at children's books, to say nothing of those books traditionally called "The Classics," will show. The myths and fairy tales that are progenitors of most literature are tales of the most dastardly, violent, despicable, treacherous behavior, and require heroic, though often unpleasant remedies. This is the source of much of the suspense in literature, and it is an easy thing to assume that the need for suspense generates the need for ghastly deeds and events in modern fiction, horror and otherwise. Judging from the recurring popularity of the scarey/gothic/supernatural/horror/shudder tale, it may well be that the case is the other way around — suspense is the means to achieve the *frisson* that is sought by the reader.

No contemporary writer is more in tune with this literary resonance than Stephen King, and the great general appreciation of his work is ample proof of this. King knows how to evoke those special images that hook into all the archetypal forms of horror that we have thrived on since earliest youth. He often puts menace in stodgy settings: not for him the "Once upon a time in a land far away from here" approach to a story. He shows us the beloved malignant forms not in castles and caves but high schools and condominiums. He does not rely on the exotic for his tension, but the mundane, everyday world. Yet the figures he puts there are known and familiar to anyone who shivered in blissful fright at those ominous words: "Who's been sleeping in *my* bed?". He has not turned away from the Handsome Prince, or the Poor Woodcutter, or the Little Mermaid; he has transformed them, but we recognize his characters as old friends (we always knew they were).

Nowhere is this more apparent than in *Carrie*. Although Carrie lacks the Ugly Step-sisters, she has more than enough to contend with in her mother, who is so rejecting and unlike her that Carrie's mother serves the function of a step-mother better than most real ones could. Carrie is, as is only mythically proper, the ugly duckling, caught up in a home that is no shelter and protection to her, but a terrifying prison where she is at the beck and call of a mother who neither understands her nor wishes to, because of her own warped personality and rigid religious thought. Carrie is not in a position to find comfort from her peers, because in a very real sense, they are not her peers; they mock her for her manner and appearance, their derision not unlike the Step-Sisters. It is not a fairy-Godmother and mice who come to her rescue, but a classmate feeling guilty who lends Carrie her Prince Charming to alleviate her shame for the dreadful way Carrie has been treated. There are conditions to her gift, as all fairy tales have conditions. In this case, she will not have a pumpkin coach and mice footmen to return, but she will have to give back Prince Charming, who is not truly her own. So far the material is not unlike the story we all read when very young. But just as the original mythic versions of the story have been softened over the centuries, so this story returns to the more somber tale. In one of the original versions of Cinderella, when she is given the chance to be revenged upon her family, she has their noses and hands cut off. Carrie goes further than that; she wrecks the entire town in a display of psychokinesis that smacks of Jovian rage. It is the right of the Queen of the Fairies to punish erring mortals, and Carrie, being psychically gifted, reflects not only the beautiful and beneficent nature of fairy-folk, but their malignancy and caprice as well. This is not the Cinderella of later days when virtue and humility were supposed to be their own rewards, but an earlier manifestation of that figure, taking much more than an eye for an eye. Although destroying herself, Carrie exacts a terrible price for such riddance.

To say that Stephen King deliberately set out to do a modern-day Cinderella story with a nasty end would be both silly and misleading. Few writers are quite so academic in their approach to their work, and certainly King is no different in this respect. But he has the same resonances as the rest of us, and for that reason it is not strange that he would use a very strong archetypal conflict for his little morality play. Certainly the miseries of high school are as agonizing as anything suffered by sweeping ashes from the hearth and running errands for an ungrateful and unfeeling family. The anguish Carrie feels has been experienced by almost anyone who endured high school America this century. The plight of honest servants is not as strong a subject for most of us because few of us have been or have been raised with servants. King has taken one set of intolerable circumstances—servitude—and substituted another that is equally ghastly—high school.

However, in some respects, with this and several other of his works, where he might have had his greatest strength, King reveals a telling weakness. Part of the Cinderella myth is concerned with the proper programming of women in western European society, and a good case can be made for Carrie that she was treated as she was because she was a girl, not a boy. I find it hard to believe that no one in that book ever was troubled by the neglect Carrie was subjected to because as a girl she was expected to submit to the will of her mother. No one pointed out that the girls in the school were treating her badly, and that as girls they had an interest in how Carrie was abused. And there was a tendency to avoid the uncomfortable feeling that perhaps some of the other girls might have made as sweeping devastation of the town if they had the chance because of the frustrations being female often evokes. No other girl is able to stand up for Carrie, though most of them must surely have had some difficulties in high school that might cause anger, if not on the scale of Carrie's wrath, at least as intense as hers. There was no element of sympathy invoked with the horror.

In *'Salem's Lot* there was a more obvious archetype to deal with: the vampire. Again, the setting is ordinary to the point of dullness, and the townspeople are not foreign and strange, but very familiar. King takes the most movie-land Lugosiad, 20th-century baroque representation of the vampire menace and introduces him with all the trimmings to this ordinary little town. This is the malignant version of the Prince from Another Land; instead of showing wonders he brings death and the most vile resurrection to people unprepared to deal with them. In this book, there is a deliberate recognition of the *reality* of fairy tale and mythic figures in the life of children, for it is the children who have the quickest understanding of the source of danger that has come to town. They are the most unusual prey and they appreciate the risks being taken. The fact that to all intents and purposes the vampire wins only adds to the mythic power of the story, since it not only emphasizes the power of the Undead but avoids the glib reassurances that are often found at the end of the most hair-raising penny dreadfuls. Unlike Stoker, King is not afraid to let the evil figure triumph when he logically would win, given the book's circumstances. The malign Prince (a title that is given to vampires somewhat less often than "Count") is the victor because he has not only the power mythically conferred on him, he also has the tactical advantage that most of the townspeople do not believe in him and take no precautions whatever to protect themselves from his predations. Myths and fairy tales abound with cautionary tales of the men who learned, but learned too late, and paid for their ignorance and obstinacy with any combination of their lives, their souls, and their fortunes. By the time King is through with it, 'Salem's Lot is a ghost town in every ironic sense of the word, and much of this comes about through the stubborn resistance of the townspeople to the notion that they might be dealing with a great danger.

The dubious advantages of gods or demi-gods living among mortals is one of the most persistently recurring themes in myth. Certainly a vampire figures as demi-god, as well as highly ambivalent archetype. Giving such a creature haven, no matter how unwittingly, openly invites disaster. Fairy tales far more often warn of entertaining demons unaware, than angels. King has a fine sense of the hazard and plays upon it, mixing in just enough social paranoia to make the course of the action compelling, and far more important, convincing.

In *The Shining*, King comes closer to a fairy tale setting; that huge pile of an empty hotel in the isolated mountains of Colorado is as exotic a locale as the castles of medieval romances. In this case, however, the unused and dangerous house is also a metaphor for Jack's mind, filled with closed rooms that may contain things he does not wish to look at. Who can blame him? Those are the very forces that at last destroy him. This castle is inhabited by dangerous spirits — Jack and his family — and is therefore slated for destruction. Castles of evil wizards almost always fall, and often through the use of the owner's own twisted powers. King's skill in story-telling disguises this so that the reader is more caught up in the victimization of the family than in the manipulations of the mind that is the source of the trouble. In this context it is not important whether the things Jack sees are actual or invented or past events in the hotel's history. Jack's state of mind calls these demons forth, just as the fate of his son Danny is to be the blessed spirit or pure soul that sees the fall from grace and all that it entails and can do little or nothing to prevent or change the destruction taking place, within the house and within his father. Sadly, this complex mythic element was one of many aspects of the book that the subsequent film did not develop. What could have been a tremendous accomplishment of the psychological sense of reality would also have sustained the cinematic version.

But back to that lamentable flaw in King's perceptions. It is disheartening when a writer with so much talent and strength and vision is not able to develop a believable woman character between the ages of seventeen and sixty. Jack's poor, troubled wife has little to do but worry about her child and husband. She takes action only when the danger is so omnipresent and so obvious that to deny its existence would be true madness. While King effectively shows a gifted and intelligent child and a ruined human being of a father, he is stymied by a woman. Why does she remain inactive for so long? Is she one of those who freezes when frightened? Is she blinded by love? Is she in fear of retribution or retaliation? With the general excellence of King's work and solidness of characterization, this blind spot is particularly disappointing. In a less accomplished writer it would be unnoticeable or understandable, but Stephen King is too good to make this kind of mistake. While it is true that there are fewer mythic figures of the sort that makes for the best of stories, King has shown a great capacity for invention and mythic appreciation, and it is unfortunate that this is one area where he has not yet shown the range and force that are the hallmarks of his work. Perhaps in balance I should point out that few writers have been able to show the relationship of fathers to their children, and to integrate that relationship with the development of the plot so effectively, as King has.

Of all King's work, the most clearly mythic in structure and intent is *The Stand*. Here King is using the post-catastrophic landscape as the setting for a final confrontation of Good and Evil. Beginning as a survival novel, it quickly shifts into gear for a proper Armageddon, complete with a very diabolical symbol of evil going to and fro in the earth and walking up and down in it.

The mythic derivations are so demanding that the narrative develops along lines that allow for little ambiguity; the one character, Nick, who is the embodiment of ambiguity, is eliminated before the final confrontation of the book, so that the lines are clearly drawn from the first to the last of that confrontation. Since there were substantial cuts in this work, it is not entirely fair to criticize it in the same light as his other works, which are intact. With much material missing from *The Stand*, many of the usual subtleties are not present that would increase the strength of the work. The post-disaster landscape in which *The Stand* takes place has many mythic resonances that add to the focus of the work, so that the action is already highly colored by the setting and location. King has a keen sense of the power of environment evinced in *The Shining*, but it took *The Stand* to bring this perception into full flower. King presupposes a world in ruin which makes it possible to achieve a world cleansed of evil and destruction. This is not unlike the Hindu teachings of the Dance of Shiva which occurs on the Burning Gound. Shiva is spirit, free from the degradation of the flesh. Shiva dances on the Burning Ground, trampling the dwarf of ignorance and beating the drum which is the pulse of time. The pacing of the evil being in *The Stand* through the ruined world is not unlike the dance of Shiva on the Burning Ground. While this may not have been King's specific intention, there are enough similarities to make the Burning Ground a persuasive reality for the setting of *The Stand*.

There is also the question of the figure of God, who in this case is the answer to the riddle: "Well, to begin with, She's black." King has taken the figure of an elderly black woman, Mother Abagail, who acts as deity and compassionate judge in the middle-to-middle-end of the book. She serves both as oracle and god, and for that reason has strengths far beyond her immediate characterization. King shows an appreciation of the extended power of the individual in this woman, and leans on her heavily to keep positive characters moving against the negative ones.

After *The Stand* comes *The Dead Zone*, which is in many ways King's most successful book. King does not often deal with Everyman so clearly as in *The Dead Zone*. To pit a man, something of an innocent, against the casual brutality of his villains shows an increasing depth to King's work. Johnny is out of synch with the rest of the world, as is Everyman, and has to deal with his uncanny awareness of evil as best he can. At first this is merely inconvenient and awkward, but as the presence of the evil grows stronger and attracts reinforcements, Johnny is made more and more aware of the need for action. This is not unlike the story of Grimm's Everyman, Faithful John, who to avert great travail must act in ways that will earn him the punishment and the odium of his peers and superiors. Like Faithful John, Johnny does as his conscience and perceptions require, and he is prepared to pay the price. As Johnny with his paranormal gift devotes his attention to the needs of mankind, so Faithful John, in overhearing the ravens talking, realizes that if he is to be a worthy servant, he must ignore the immediate commands of his Prince and dedicate himself to preserving the Prince's family. Faithful John becomes a stone statue for his efforts; Johnny is almost a murderer; both of them set aside considerations of personal safety and the good opinion of those around them for the greater good of their countries. Selflessness is not a virtue often espoused in literature these days, but pitting selflessness against the Neo-Nazi destruction in *The Dead Zone* shows how that choice must be clearly made by all of us at one time or another, with or without the benefit of psychic insight. As Faithful John had the ravens, so Johnny has his precognition, and both of them are required to pay the price of what they and they alone understand to be a deadly threat. As fairy tales often deal with the question of moral responsibility, so Stephen King often broaches the subject through his characters, in situations where moral and civic good must be weighed against personal advantage. This sort of double bind is not only the stuff that great fairy tales are made of; they are also the issues that make for compelling literature of any time, any culture, any century.

In *Firestarter*, King once again returns to children, to one special child for his focal point. Charlie is one of those very wise children who populate myths, in a special niche all her own. Charlie is a mutant, which gives King the chance to change the usual rules of childhood in order to show the persuasive strength of the gifted kid more sharply. This is the fairy child, the changeling, brought into the Twentieth Century and into modern parlance. Charlie is not just a bright little girl: she is a kid with the power to (dare I say it?) rule the world. We know from relatively early in the story that Charlie is able to make a great many changes in the world around her with relatively little danger to herself. What brings her into hazardous positions are the expectations of others.

Like a great many of the demi-gods of mythology, Charlie is tested by circumstances and escapes peril through the use of her inborn abilities, not unlike the infant Hercules or the child Jesus (see the *Apocrypha*, Infancy Books I and II). As is often the case, the single biggest threat that this wonder-child faces comes from the king, or in Charlie's case, the government, the modern equivalent. The minister of the king, or the men of the Shop who attempt to use and subvert Charlie, have their parallels in fairy tales and myths, in the sinister figures of plotting viziers and zealous lieutenants, in treacherous dukes and malignant guardians. That one of them is basically well-intentioned but misled is a device often found in Greek myths, most familiar as the minister to the King of Arcadia who acts on his king's orders, unaware that he has only half of them, and thereby makes several fatal mistakes. Charlie, in remaining true to her father, also remains true to herself, for in myths and fairy tales the denial of family and heritage is one of the most reprehensible and damning of actions, for which there is rarely any forgiveness; if pardon comes at all, it is after the expiation of suffering and trial. In myth and fairy tale, the wonder-child must never deny his or her humanity, for that leads to destruction and the utmost rejection. King was canny in *Firestarter* because he pitted Charlie against a wonder-child gone wrong, a wonder-child who had denied his heritage and his past in a way that Charlie had not and could not. Rainbird is her mythic antithesis, the demi-god who perverted his gift. In true mythic fashion, he is now the servant of the king, who has the mark of his betrayal on his face. Most failed demi-gods are scarred or crippled in some way, and Rainbird is no different.

Firestarter, in the grand tradition of heroic fairy tales, starts with an ordeal and persecution, and ends with implied revenge of a sort that every demi-god from Brunhilde to Samson to Loon Brother understands: justice will triumph or the world will end.

King's iconography is not that of Medieval and Renaissance Europe, nor that of ancient and Imperial Rome, but rather of the late 20th century America. Some of the changes are obvious — chariots and horses become automobiles and motorcycles, hymns and prophecies are transformed into popular songs, demi-gods into mutants and medically-altered people. Again, it would be too simplistic and absurd to say that this is done academically or deliberately, but the structure of much of King's writing draws on those archetypes, and it is no disservice to his work to examine it in this light. Even much of King's style is mythic and fairy-tale-like in tone. In general, his narrative style is low key and conversational, as if he were speaking to you, quite literally telling you a story. This conversational tone allows him to use these archetypes most effectively, since almost all of them come from the oral traditions. Today's tall tale is tomorrow's immortal myth. King has hooked into this sequence in a way that makes his writing doubly persuasive, giving it the force of good story-telling and neatly paranoid plot, and adding to it the whole weight of those well-known figures from our past. From the stories heard in childhood comes part of the impact he creates.

Cujo is perhaps the farthest from this fairy-tale world of any of King's work, but there is still that persistent sense of a larger reality. Plenty of myths warn that those creatures you trust may not be all that trustworthy. The whole book has a miasmic sense of uncertainty, as if the characters were already on their way to madness and despair before the horror actually hits them. There is something particularly hideous about rabies; few of us can think of that disease without a very real shudder. In this case, it serves as an evil spell, a malignant force that accelerates and enhances a decline that is in progress before the terrifying events begin. That the instrument of destruction is "man's best friend" is not only appropriately ironic, it serves to point up the assumptions of the characters in general, so that the fear engendered extends beyond the immediate threat.

King has a real appreciation and sympathy for monsters, so that even at their worst, they never go beyond the bounds of a rough kind of compassion. In *Cujo* he uses this more directly than in his other work, by making his monster — poor old sick dangerous beast that he is — pitiable. At no time does Cujo cease to be the dog we were all made to like; he is as much a victim as anyone else in the story. Fairy tales are full of monsters with wounded human eyes, the most obvious being Beauty's Beast. Although Cujo is not in that metaphor, there is much of the Beast tragedy touching him, just as it touches all those possessed and transformed creatures in myth — the Ondine does not intend to drown her Knight, she seeks only to love him; the Fool does not mean to send all the tsareviches over the precipice, but he knows no other answer to give them and they have no chance to question him; there need be no malign intention for things to go terribly wrong. In many ways, Cujo keeps the readers' sympathy because he is so much an object of terror (and the power, in this case from a disease, he has is no more in his control than anyone else's).

Just as myth and fairy tales are much concerned with the use and misuse of power, so King often balances his critical moments on that issue. When all the trappings are gone, King shows the difference between strength and tyranny, between persuasion and manipulation. He often makes sure that his characters have powerful gifts, but turns the plot on how those gifts are to be used, including the power of fear. In this, he is drinking from the same potent well as Euripides, Racine and Cervantes, who also drew heavily on the myths and folk tales of their people and cultures. It would be misleading to say that there must necessarily be a mythic correlation between popular fiction and the mythic archetypes of a society, but writers, being products of their society, will tend to be sensitive to these constructs and use them. Almost all horror fiction, no matter who writes it, relies on these earlier images to some degree to create the environment required to move its readers. That King is especially sensitive to these archetypes is evinced in the quality of his work and its wide popularity.

With Stephen King, you never have to ask "Who's afraid of the big bad wolf?"—You are. And he knows it.

In the darkness the booming noises grew louder, louder still, echoing, everywhere, all around.

And now he was crouched in a dark hallway, crouched on a blue rug with a riot of twisting black shapes woven into its pile, listening to the booming noises approach, and now a Shape turned the corner and began to come toward him, lurching, smelling of blood and doom. It had a mallet in one hand and it was swinging it (REDRUM) from side to side in vicious arcs, slamming it into the walls, cutting the silk wallpaper and knocking out ghostly bursts of plasterdust:

Come on and take your medicine! Take it like a man!

—from THE SHINING

Horror Springs in the Fiction of Stephen King

by Don Herron

I. The Bestseller

STEPHEN KING IS THE FIRST *living* horror writer consistently to place one novel after another on the bestseller lists. Yes, a few horror writers have been successful from the underside of the grave — Edgar Allan Poe, H. P. Lovecraft — and a few living authors — Peter Straub, Ira Levin — do well. And single titles such as *Dracula*, *The Exorcist*, *The Other* or *The Amityville Horror* may enjoy terrific sales. But King's success is phenomenal. With novel after novel selling millions of copies, he has captured so vast an audience that a large part of it surely ought to be watching television at night instead of reading books.

King scares hell out of even the hardcore horror fan, who reads not only Poe and Lovecraft, but also J. Sheridan Le Fanu, M. R. James, Algernon Blackwood and other writers scarce heard of by the television generations. What makes *'Salem's Lot* or *The Shining* a bestseller while *The House on the Borderland* or *The Three Impostors* sells modestly? Why does King raise the hackles of millions while Le Fanu, James

and company titillate the exclusive few? Is King truly an important writer in the literature of supernatural horror?

Some basic reasons for his success are apparent. King is a
capable author who writes clearly and mostly uses as characters
"ordinary" people — couples with children, small town cops,
teenagers — while most horror fiction writers have followed Poe
into a literary style so exotic and opulent that the average reader
seldom lasts more than a few pages. Until recently, characters
in horror fiction all seemed to be pale-blooded librarians cata-
loging the occult or aged recluses living alone in crumbling
mansions filled with sarcophagi, tomb rubbings, and rats. After
considering the stories of such fabulist stylists as M. P. Shiel,
Clark Ashton Smith or Arthur Machen, the reader might believe
that Stephen King is the first horror writer to use an everyday
high school in his fiction.

Also, the novels in which King places his believable sort of
characters are generally quite *long* — the fat kind of book which
bestseller readers seem to prefer, from *David Copperfield* to
Gone With the Wind to *Hawaii*.

King performs another rite common in contemporary best-
sellerdom: he breaks social taboos. Here the seasoned horror
reader may chuckle evilly to himself. What taboos have not
been violated in the horror story by this late date? At the very
start Poe catalogued seemingly every type of aberration, death,
rictus and torture. Poe's characters were incestuous and necro-
philiac, and it is not pleasant to dwell on the sexual implications
of such tales as Le Fanu's "Schalken the Painter" or Clark Ashton Smith's "The Nameless Offspring." *Dracula* is today considered a novel of repressed Victorian sexuality, and who would
doubt the genuine perversity of Stevenson's Mr. Hyde or Wilde's
Dorian Gray? If these stories are not as graphic as the writings of
De Sade, they still make their points. In the horror story at least,
sex and death are not new subjects.

King's books deal with sex and death in modern terms, but his
major contribution toward reader shock has been detailed realism, not unlike De Sade's, in picturing acts of violence, in re-
cording language, in describing reactions to horror. King's creations swear as profanely and believably as the next fellow on the

street. His characters defecate in fear, wet their pants — things anyone might do when confronted with a source of horror, but which King's predecessors have not been so explicit in mentioning. It's difficult to imagine a character in an M. R. James ghost story fleeing the scene (as Corey Bryant does in *'Salem's Lot*) with "the smell of his own shit satcheled in his trousers."

In a radio interview in Berkeley, California, and later on NBC television, King explained what he tries to accomplish: "First I try to terrify my readers. If I can't achieve terror, then I try for horror. And if I can't manage horror — I'm not proud — I try at least to gross 'em out." In order to gross out his readers King will break any social taboo.

Past supernaturalists such as H. P. Lovecraft, M. R. James or Algernon Blackwood tried almost exclusively to evoke *terror*. Terror is defined in the field of supernatural fiction as fear eating at the imaginative faculties, usually developed in storytelling through subtle hints and happenings which worm their way into the reader's subconscious mind and later emerge, dragging all manner of phobias and unconscious phychological dreads out with them. *Horror*, on the other hand, is a reaction to unpleasant physical details or peril — such as witnessing the slow, detailed dismemberment of a fellow human being. Grossness, in the King manner, is simply horror material which is not necessarily scary, but is piled on to the point where many readers become nauseated.*

To understand *why* King became a bestseller, it is important to recognize the market for horror which he tapped with *Carrie* and subsequent novels, and the connection of this readership with horror films. However great his talents, King did not create his market — neither did Poe for that matter: grotesque tales

---

*A speech by Dr. Jimmy Cody in *'Salem's Lot*: "When the coffin is opened, there's apt to be a rush of gas and a rather offensive smell. The body may be bloated. The hair will have grown down over his collar . . . and the fingernails will also be quite long. The eyes will almost certainly have fallen in. The corpse will not have begun radical mortification, but enough moisture may be present to encourage growth on the exposed cheeks and hands, possibly a mossy substance called — I'm sorry. I'm grossing you out." (Chapter 11, section 4.)

were in demand at the time Poe wrote, and he turned them out for money, as well as by inclination.

King has said that by the late fall and early winter of 1972 he had several horror stories published, but "it had never crossed my mind to write a horror novel." He added that he "was aware of publishing trends, was aware of the Tryon novel *The Other*, of *Rosemary's Baby*," and of the fact that *The Exorcist* had been "a monster seller, but I had never made the connection with my own work."

Carrie appeared in 1974, the very year *The Exorcist* drew record-breaking crowds into theatres. According to King, the Doubleday hardcover sold a respectable 13,000 copies; the Signet paperback issued in April, 1975, sold "just under a million copies its first time out." The paperback carried the legend, "a novel of a girl possessed of a terrifying power" over a painting of a girl's head. The ready-made market for this package had been waiting in line to see *The Exorcist* not long before.

King's next published novel was *'Salem's Lot*, selling 26,000 hardcover copies. In August, 1976, the paperback version appeared, featuring a girl's head on the cover with a drop of blood on her lips (according to the *Kirkus Review*'s blurb, "A super exorcism . . . Tremendous!"). Ten weeks later the Brian De Palma film of *Carrie* exploded in the nation's theatres. *'Salem's Lot* hit #1 on the *New York Times* paperback list.

From this point on, trying to unravel the interdependence of King's success and the popularity of contemporary horror films would be impossible. If King's brand of shocking horror is disturbingly unfamiliar to the connoisseur of James or Blackwood, it must seem relatively tame stuff to an audience which watched *Texas Chainsaw Massacre* and remained unsated. Indeed, film has catered to — and in part created — an audience for horror of which American publishers were unaware. Ghetto kids who might consider a charmingly creepy M. R. James tale pointless or irrelevant, housewives who can't be bothered reading Lovecraft's large words, stentorian narrative voice and complex sentence structure, all manner of people who have had no affinity for "literary" horror patiently wait in line to see *The Exorcist*, *Alien*, *Halloween*, *The Boogeyman*, and *Carrie*.

Why does *'Salem's Lot* or *The Shining* outsell William Hope Hodgson's *The House on the Borderland* or Arthur Machen's *The Three Impostors* or any other classic supernatural horror story you would care to name? Simply because King has reached an audience which has no interest in classic supernatural horror. His readers want the frights of classic horror without intellectual baggage attached. When King's readers aren't reeling under a barrage of horrors, they apparently prefer interludes featuring characters pretty much like themselves, worrying about work, finances or personal relationships, drinking beer and watching television, not puttering around ancient cathedrals or rambling in some London backwater as characters in James and Machen are wont to do.

King's long novels, as violent and raunchy as horror in the local movie house, act as a codicil to mass-market tastes, refining and expanding them. King has broadened the audience that came to his early work out of *The Exorcist*. King is a law unto himself, because he breaks accepted rules of supernatural fiction at will and gets away with it — and has a host of imitators follow his every move. Have you noticed titles like *The Glowing* on the paperback racks, the dozens of obvious King imitations now stacked in the new "occult and horror" sections in the bookstores?

In the marketplace, the bestseller is King, and he certainly is king of horror fiction in America today.

II.   The Horror Fan

POPULARITY AMONG HARDCORE horror fans is more difficult to gauge than acceptance by bestseller readers. Yet King was guest of honor at the Fifth World Fantasy Convention and was given a special award the following year for outstanding contributions to the field. His books are often praised in the fan press, in such citadels of horror *aficionados* as the Esoteric Order of Dagon. I think it's fair to say King is popular with horror fans.

I suspect the overriding reason for King's popularity with this inner circle is his commercial success. For the first time an author of horror, instead of starving, is actually making a fortune; for the first time a horror fan can buy books by a writer his neighbor or his dentist may be familiar with.

Except for his persistent appearance on the bestseller lists, I would never have read a Stephen King novel. Like a mountain, King is there. If you're interested in the field you are forced to give his work a reading (just as any modern hard-boiled detective fan cannot forever ignore the novels of bestseller Mickey Spillane).

And once the horror reader comes to King, he'll find a great deal in the novels and stories that will appeal to him as a *fan*. King clearly has a wide knowledge of horror in literature and film: see articles such as "The Fright Report" or King's own survey of horror in *Danse Macabre* or his introductions to various collections of supernatural fiction — obvious research-reading, hours in darkened theatres, late nights before the tv screen, and much thought went into these writings.

King's familiarity with his field surfaces in his books in many ways. As an example, we know King is aware of Shirley Jackson's (1919–1965) status as one of the few horror writers to be recognized critically and commercially by the mainstream audience. He modestly complains that dustjacket copy on *The Shining* ". . . referred to me as 'the master of the modern horror story,' neatly ignoring the likes of Shirley Jackson, Richard Matheson, and Ira Levin, none of whom I have yet approached."

King begins part one of his novel, *'Salem's Lot*, with a quote from Jackson's *The Haunting of Hill House*, and in the course of the novel itself King has the hero, Ben Mears, ask Susan Norton:

"Do you know *The Haunting of Hill House* by Shirley Jackson?"

"Yes."

He quoted softly, " 'And whatever walked there, walked alone.' " (Chapter 5, section 3.)

King gets double usage out of this same quote — by using it as an introduction, he lets his readers know that *he* himself is familiar with the Jackson novel; by having it turn up in the conversation of Ben Mears and Susan Norton, he lets us know that *his charac-*

ters are also familiar with the book, that they live in the real world too.

King reworks traditional material to the delight of the horror fan, who is always on the lookout for new tales of lycanthropy or necromancy. In *The Shining*, King's haunted hotel is the main source of supernatural horror, but he has another haunted house in *'Salem's Lot*, where vampirism is the star attraction. In his essay "The Fright Report," King calls *'Salem's Lot* "my *Dracula* look-alike." So it is. The use of telekinesis (Carrie's power to affect things with her mind) is not new either—T. K. has been used as a staple in science-fiction novels for decades, even in comic books such as *The X-Men* from Marvel. Likewise, the ability to foresee the future, used so well in *The Dead Zone*, has been seen in fiction often before. And the end-of-the-world novel, which *The Stand* represents, is a sub-genre at least as large as the vampire novel.*

(This reworking of material, by the way, is done even within the body of King's fiction. Elements from his short stories appear later in novels, and King has a definite propensity toward characters with extranormal mental abilities—*Carrie*, *The Shining*, *The Dead Zone*, *Firestarter*, the story "I Know What You Need." *Firestarter* is largely a reworking of ideas originally set forth in *Carrie*, and thematically may be considered a sequel; the child Annie Jenks, mentioned in the last paragraphs of *Carrie*, could well have been used instead of Charlie McGee as the heroine of *Firestarter*.)

The vampire is one of the most popular embodiments of terror. For the knowledgeable reader, *'Salem's Lot* serves as a virtual *catalog* of vampirism and kindred horrors. Consider the following:

> One was taught that such things could not be; that
> things like Coleridge's "Cristabel" or Bram Stoker's

---

*The end-of-the-world novel flourished particularly in *fin-de-siécle* England, with M. P. Shiel's *The Purple Cloud* emerging as the classic from that era.

evil fairy tale were only the warp and woof of fantasy. (Chapter 7, section 5.)

He remembered it both from Stoker's *Dracula* and from the Hammer films starring Christopher Lee. (Chapter 8, section 4.)

"How much of this Count Dracula stuff do you believe?" (Chapter 10, section 4.)

"It's rather like something by Boris Karloff out of Mary Shelley. Someone snatched the bodies from the Cumberland County Morgue in Portland last night." (Chapter 11, section 4.)

. . . she had seen enough Hammer films at the drive-in on double dates to know you had to pound a stake into a vampire's heart. . . . (Chapter 11, section 8.)

"Did he remind you of anyone?"

"Yes," Jimmy said. "Van Helsing." (Chapter 14, section 6.)

And suddenly a line came to him from *Dracula*, that amusing bit of fiction that no longer amused him in the slightest. It was Van Helsing's speech to Arthur Holmwood. . . . (Chapter 14, section 15.)

At one point the group of people combating the vampire plague round up all the literature on the subject they can find. "He read the titles aloud as he put them back. '*Dracula. Dracula's Guest. The Search for Dracula. The Golden Bough. The Natural History of the Vampire. . . . Hungarian Folk Tales. Monsters of the Darkness. Monsters in Real Life. Peter Kurtin, Monster of Düsseldorf.* And . . . *Varney the Vampire, or The Feast of Blood*'" (Chapter 13, section 1.) They even have a copy of a *Vampirella* comic magazine!

These allusions, combined with pages upon pages of characters discussing vampirism; the familiar scenes of coffins being brought into a basement by unsuspecting workmen; vampires being done in with hammer and stake as they lie in their boxes; even Barlow the vampire forcing Callahan the priest to drink from an opened vein in the vampire's throat and so become his slave, just as Count Dracula forced Mina Harker to drink from a wound in his chest — *'Salem's Lot* is made to order for an *aficionado*.*

These references are all overt, but King gets in others: when Ben Mears and Dr. Cody are waiting in the morgue to see if Mrs. Glick will rise as a vampire, they fashion a cross, say a prayer over it, and — "The cross was glowing. The light spilled over his hand in an elvish flood." (Chapter 11, section 10.) Surely an allusion to J. R. R. Tolkien's *The Lord of the Rings* and the vial Galadriel the Elf Queen gives the hobbits, which glows when evil is near. What is this doing in a vampire novel? Just another example of King's readiness to use *any* device that might work in a scene. Later, much of the plot and thematic material of the Tolkien trilogy became the basis for *The Stand*.**

The Shining has in-genre references and allusions too — to Poe: a long quotation in the front of the book followed up by "(*The Red Death held sway over all!*) He frowned. What left field had that come out of? That was Poe, the Great American Hack" (Chapter 18); and to *The Haunting of Hill House*:

> There was a little boy to terrorize, a man and his woman to set against the other, and if it played its cards right they could end up flitting through the Overlook's hall like insubstantial shades in a Shirley Jackson novel, whatever walked in Hill House walked alone, but you wouldn't be alone in the Overlook, oh no, there would be plenty of company here. (Chapter 33.)

That this allusion turns up in the stream-of-consciousness mus-

---

*Horror fans also may take delight in finding that young Mark Petrie has "the entire set of Aurora plastic monsters — wolfman, mummy, Dracula, Frankenstein, the mad doctor, and even the Chamber of Horrors." (Chapter 3, section 18.) King also gets in a reference to Roman Polanski's "The Fearless Vampire Killers" and even mentions Frank Frazetta and Gahan Wilson, two popular contemporary artists identified with the macabre.

**King, in an interview in *College Papers*, winter 1980, said he wrote *The Stand* because ". . . I wanted to do *The Lord of the Rings* with an American background."

ings of Jack Torrance, edging toward madness, is important. Torrance obviously has some knowledge of haunted houses, and in the Jackson novel he has literary forewarnings of What Might Happen—this only increases his horror: he *knows* damn well he's going crazy, *knows* the Overlook is haunted, but is powerless to acknowledge or deal with either fact. He's a victim, but not an unwitting victim. He knows what awaits him.

A final example of King's special appeal to horror fans—by popular consensus, the most terrifying chapters in *The Shining* seem to be those featuring a dead woman in a bathtub—a bathtub with shower curtain drawn shut. And who can think of a drawn shower curtain in a bathtub without remembering *Pyscho*? Consider this scene, when Jack Torrance realizes the Overlook is not interested in him; it wants his young son, Danny, and Jack is just another pawn like the ghosts surrounding him in the bar:

> He suddenly felt closed in and claustrophobic; he wanted to get out. He wanted the Overlook back the way it had been . . . free of these unwanted guests. His place was not honored, as the true opener of the way; he was only another of the ten thousand cheering extras, a doggy rolling over and sitting up on command. (Chapter 44.)

The Opener of the Way was Robert Bloch's first book, a title well known among *aficionados*, yet not as well known as Bloch's later novel, *Psycho*.

What purposes do these references serve? They tell the hardcore horror fan that *Stephen King himself is also a hardcore horror fan*—"one of us." For the general reader they may say much the same thing: that King is truly knowledgeable about literary and cinematic horror, and that if they finally are going to read "a horror book," at least they're in good hands.

By extension, this pervasive use of references may offer something else to the general reader. King obviously has read all these books, seen all those films. The reader who is not especially interested in horror can read *'Salem's Lot*, then, and get an effective *Reader's Digest* overview of the vampire novel (though considering the sheer length of King's books, "digest" isn't quite the appropriate word).

The bestseller reader may not care to read Bram Stoker's *Dracula*, written in a leisurely epistolary style, but he can read *'Salem's Lot* and get the same sort of thrills in contemporary language and style. King's scenes cut and dissolve like those in film or television, the camera-like point of view shifts suddenly between different actors.* When Stoker wrote *Dracula*, letters and newspaper articles were standard means of spreading news; hence the developing information about Count Dracula related by extracts from Jonathan Harker's journal, Mina's journal, newsclippings, letters. . . . Today we often get news *as it is happening* — the Kennedy assassination in 1963, the Chicago political riots of 1968, the attack on Reagan in 1981 serve as classic examples.

King's storytelling is as immediate. Whatever its merits as a work of fiction, *'Salem's Lot* does for the modern audience what *Dracula* did for the Victorians, in a style as appropriate today as letters were in Stoker's own time.

This reworking of classic scenes from *Dracula* and familiar situations from Hammer horror films makes *'Salem's Lot* a novel of a type James Blish pointed to some years ago, in connection with science fiction, that a certain tale ". . . is a prime example of the incestuous science-fiction story — that is, a yarn which depends for its effect on overt cross-references to science fiction itself." Blish stated that "few trends [are] more dangerous to the field both artistically and financially. An increase in the percentage of yarns of this kind would be the quickest imaginable way of turning science fiction into a closed circle of mutual ap-

---

*From comments King has made in essays, interviews, and in his recent history of horror, *Danse Macabre*, it is apparent that he has been influenced greatly by visual horror — films such as "The Creature from the Black Lagoon," "Invasion of the Body Snatchers," and so forth, even by the E.C. Comics of the 1950s. It is no surprise that King's work is visually oriented, as if written with the idea that later this book must translate effectively into films, for theatres and television.

preciators, speaking a jargon comprehensible only to themselves. . . . In short, a form of fandom."

Obviously, what Blish thought of as a trend dangerous to science fiction "both artistically and financially" is in the case of *'Salem's Lot* certainly *not* a financial disaster for supernatural horror. If anything, King's immense popularizing of standard horror themes has been a major economic boost for the field, perhaps the greatest since Hollywood began optioning horror novels for film. Whether or not the example of *'Salem's Lot* will prove to be an artistic disaster remains to be seen.

Blish's observation makes a point about *'Salem's Lot* and about other books outside the field of science fiction, such as the horde of mystery novels about Sherlock Holmes meeting Mr. Hyde, Dracula, Sigmund Freud or Jack the Ripper. These books are not *serious* novels, because their effectiveness entirely depends on the reader being familiar with the characters and clichés of that particular genre. Try to imagine the various books about Sherlock Holmes being written *without* Holmes as the hero. Not one would have appeared. They are "a form of fandom" and are profitable only because of the enormous worldwide popularity of Holmes and Dr. Watson. I contend that *'Salem's Lot* is not a serious novel about vampires — rather, it is a *horror fan's* novel about vampires.

A serious modern novel about the undead is Anne Rice's *Interview with the Vampire*, published in 1976, one year after *'Salem's Lot*. Since it is a contemporary of King's novel and also was a bestseller, it serves as a good book for comparison. Anne Rice does not rely, as King does, on refried scenes from *Dracula* or Christopher Lee's Hammer films to carry her novel. Yet her vampire is just as aware of the literature and film lore about his kind as are the King characters — witness this exchange:

> "Oh, the rumor about crosses!" the vampire laughed. "You refer to our being afraid of crosses?"
> "Unable to look on them, I thought," said the boy.
> "Nonsense, my friend, sheer nonsense. I can look on anything I like. And I rather like looking on crucifixes in particular." (From part I.)

Rice quickly gets away from the cliché about crosses, but King is content to use it to the point where Dr. Jimmy Cody, in need of a cross, ". . . brought out two tongue depressors, stripped off the protective cellophane, and bound them together at right angles with a twist of Red Cross tape." (*'Salem's Lot*, Chapter 11, section 10.)

In contrast, Rice creates original scenes of horror. The instance where the vampire Lestat brings two prostitutes to his and the narrator's rooms, slays one, then drains the second of some blood and places her in a coffin while she's still partly conscious is a moment of sadistic horror *you won't find in Dracula*. She screams inside the coffin. Then:

> It opened, and the girl sat up astonished, wild-eyed, her lips blue and trembling. 'Lie down, love,' he said to her, and pushed her back; and she lay, near-hysterical, staring up at him. 'You're dead, love,' he said to her; and she screamed and turned desperately in the coffin like a fish, as if her body could escape through the sides, through the bottom. 'It's a coffin, a coffin!' she cried. 'Let me out.'
>
> 'But we all must lie in coffins, eventually,' he said to her. 'Lie still, love. This is your coffin. Most of us never get to know what it feels like.' (From part I.)

The scenes in the Theatre des Vampires in Paris are memorable moments of horror, *not to be found in Hammer films*. But you'll find the death of the vampire Barlow in *'Salem's Lot* pictured in many films — trapped in his coffin, a stake driven through his heart as he struggles, then quick dissolution into a rotting corpse and finally a skeleton.

Simply put, you may read Rice's *Interview with the Vampire* and encounter new scenes and new insights about vampires, but all *'Salem's Lot* offers as a vampire novel is the utterly familiar: scenes and insights dating back to Victorian England, re-cast in an immediate style more appropriate for our times — a grand catalog for horror fans.

III.   The Supernaturalist

Is Stephen King truly an important writer in the literature of supernatural horror? Certainly, he has netted more book sales than there are dead people in a George Romero film. He has made a largely good impression on horror fandom. But to make any lasting evaluation of King's position at this time would be impossible. King is still in his thirties, and may well turn out dozens more novels and hundreds of stories.

But if King were to die tomorrow, what then? His work has made an impact. Scholars of the supernatural will not be able to look at the fiction of the 1970s and 1980s without taking King into the account. Obviously, he's been influential.

King has some excellent supernatural scenes in his fiction. The two chapters with the dead woman in the bathtub from *The Shining* constitute a high water mark of pure terror, as frightening as William Hope Hodgson's (1877–1918) best efforts. Young Danny pursued through the concrete tunnel in the Over-look's playground is unnerving. Three of King's short stories stand with the best in the genre: "Children of the Corn," while owing something to Ray Bradbury, is King at his finest — real people, believable action, a perfectly developed setting and a freightload of horror. "Sometimes They Come Back" is in form a classic ghost story, with personalized King touches, and I wouldn't balk at placing it with the best of M. R. James (1862–1936). "The Boogeyman" is quintessential King — it has his major concerns out front, and delivers a supernatural punchline of pure evil.

But to get to the scary and effective chapters of *The Shining* we are forced to read page after page of Jack Torrance worrying about his history of alcoholism. (I had the idea firmly in mind the third or fourth time it was mentioned, and didn't need the other couple of hundred hits in the head.) I had read *Dracula*, so *'Salem's Lot* offered nothing new, and lacked the power of the original's early scenes set in Dracula's castle in Transylvania, the best part of Stoker's novel. And with *The Stand*, *The Dead Zone*, and *Firestarter*, King has left the supernatural arena for other areas: science-fiction and the thriller. His only long recent supernatural work is *The Mist*, a short novel — very well written, without the padding obvious in every novel since *Carrie*, yet offering little that a seasoned horror reader has not encountered before, in one book or another.

The people who are calling King "the Twentieth Century Poe" seem to be grasping for an over-all quality that is not there. However good King is, he has yet to write a weird tale comparable to "The Fall of the House of Usher." In fact, King has not been even a *developmental* force in supernatural literature, as were Poe and H. P. Lovecraft. Lovecraft (1890–1937) took the supernatural completely away from Satan and his minions and invested it with beings from cosmic space — essentially, he made the supernatural meaningful in the Twentieth Century, now that Science speaks with the authority once commanded by Religion. J. Sheridan Le Fanu (1814–1873) used characters' psychological breakdowns as a prelude and partial reason for supernatural intrusions in the 1800s. Jack Torrance's breakdown in *The Shining* cannot be considered a startling development. Nor is King the first to use believable characters and real-life situations in the genre — in *Conjure Wife* (1943), Fritz Leiber had characters as real as any later found in King's books, used as effectively. King himself has said the title of modern master of horror was his only "by default." It seems clear enough that King's role in supernatural horror to date has been that of a *popularizer*, a writer capable of making the supernatural interesting to the modern bestseller reader.

In doing this he has done *some* things supernaturalists have not done much before. His characters swear. They excrete. They often act crudely, grossly. The hot-rodder Billy Nolan in *Carrie* is described as having the "unfailing ability to pinpoint the vulgar." King has this ability in spades, and uses it often. It is a kind of honesty, and I suspect it is one of his greatest commercial assets.

It's obvious that King's fiction is a direct product of our times. Horror in films and horror on the evening news paved the way for King's steamrolling bestseller machine. The books depend heavily on film for their reference frames, and certainly without the cultural and social loosening-up in the past two decades,* King's scenes of excretion and profanity would have crashed against a brick wall of censorship — at least, if he had insisted on staying in the supernatural genre.

King initially was not interested predominately in writing about horror, though that is the fiction he has had the best luck in selling. His first four novels, still unpublished, were not horror. His fifth novel, *Carrie*, is horror, but not *supernatural* horror. *Carrie*, like *The Dead Zone* and *Firestarter* to follow, is science fiction, if you wish to put it in a genre.**

But whether you consider *Carrie* and company science fiction, thriller, plain horror or mainstream, to criticize them in terms used for a supernatural novel is laziness on the part of the critic. A stodgy English professor (imaginary, of course) might wish *not* to acquaint himself with the literature of supernatural horror in order to maintain his opinion that *The Shining* stinks. On the other hand, a horror fan might wish to label *'Salem's Lot* one of the greatest novels of all time, without having any accurate notion of just what kind of novels people have written around the world for the past couple of centuries.

Of King's eight published novels only three — *'Salem's Lot*, *The Shining* and *The Mist* — are supernatural horror. Slightly more than half the stories in *Night Shift* are supernatural; the others are sf, mainstream, thriller or have a maniac instead of a

---

*I suspect that a great deal of H. P. Lovecraft's current popularity is related to the emergence of the drug culture in the 1960s. The cosmic perspective Lovecraft often took in his fiction seldom has been seen in literature, and Lovecraft felt that there would "never be more than a minority" sensitive to such writing. He reckoned without realizing that L.S.D. would one day take the mundane intelligence into outer space at bargain rates. The entire field of horror, King included, probably owes more of its popularity to the drug culture than can ever be gauged.

**King withdrew *The Dead Zone* from the best novel competition at the Sixth World Fantasy Convention held in Baltimore, 1980, stating it was not fantasy but science fiction.

ghost for the menace (thus, Robert Bloch's *Psycho* is psychological horror, not supernatural horror).

Contrast this sporadic supernatural output with the work of two writers who *were* serious supernaturalists, (though neither believed in ghosts). H. P. Lovecraft devoted *all* his fiction to portraying fantasy, horror or the supernatural, and all his mature fiction toward provoking cosmic wonder and dread in the reader. Though philosophically he was a mechanistic-materialist, Lovecraft today is remembered as a supernaturalist and his fiction is taken as genuine unveiling of the mysteries in some occult circles. M. R. James, now considered by many critics to be the best of all ghost story writers, wrote *one* fantastic children's tale; the rest of his fiction was in the supernatural genre. His spectral tales are not overt moral fables. They do not make a commotion about social consciousness. They are not political. James wrote his supernatural stories for only one reason: so that his ghosts could leap from the page and claw the reader's hackles.

From what supernatural work he has done so far, it is unimaginable that any of King's creations will ever assume the mythic proportions of those of Lovecraft. Where James created ghosts, one after another, like none that came before him, King seems content to rework well-worn material. The Overlook Hotel surely is a noteworthy creation, but no more so than Shirley Jackson's Hill House, which came before. Barlow in *'Salem's Lot* is at best a shadow of Count Dracula. Rarely in King's stories are there supernatural creations that do not at least *suggest* earlier work in the genre; usually they are borrowed outright.

Why should a writer of King's obvious talents settle so often for reworking such ideas as haunted houses or vampires? One reason, of course, is that he is a *horror fan*, and takes some pleasure in what he can do with traditional horror themes. But a greater reason exists: *The wellspring of horror in Stephen King's fiction has nothing to do with the supernatural.*

If *'Salem's Lot* is not a serious vampire novel, neither is King a serious supernaturalist. King says he got the idea for *'Salem's Lot* after teaching *Dracula* in a fantasy and science-fiction elective course at a high school. His wife and a friend suggested that he set the vampires down in a small town rather than in a metropolis such as London or New York. King thought the idea might make a good novel, *if* he ". . . could create a fictional town with enough prosaic reality about it to offset the comic-book menace of a bunch of vampires."

The comic-book menace of a bunch of vampires. . . .

King says of *The Shining*: "The book, to me at least, seemed to be primarily a story about a miserable, damned man who is very slowly losing his grip on his life, a man who is being driven to destroy all the things he loves."

What about the Overlook Hotel? What about the dead woman in the bathtub? In the novel itself King wrote:

> . . . Danny was thrashing again, twisting in his bed and rumpling the blankets. The boy was moaning deep in his throat, a small, caged sound. What nightmare? A purple woman, long dead, shambling after him down twisting hotel corridors? Somehow he didn't think so. Something else chased Danny in his dreams. Something worse. (Chapter 32.)

Yes, something worse *as far as King is concerned*: Danny's insane father, Jack Torrance. What really could be more terrifying for a child than to see his parent go crazy?

The wellspring of horror in King's fiction has nothing to do with the supernatural, so one more old-fashioned vampire or haunted house is adequate for his purpose; now that King is so firmly identified with horror fiction, he may need a weird element to make his books distinct from those of other bestsellers, but the horror does not have to be new. It's just icing the cake. Horror springs in King's stories from contemporary social *reality*, and I'd say it is this quality more than any other which has made King a bestseller. King doesn't take vampires seriously, and neither do most of his readers, but you would have to be a fool or a saint not to recognize and react to the pervasive horror in everyday life. Just turn on the evening news.

✳ ✺

Four stories appear for the first time in *Night Shift*. Presumably King especially wanted these stories published. The book is thick enough without them, and King had other published but uncollected stories — in Lowndes' *Magazine of Horror*, for instance — which could have been used instead. But these four tales accomplish things the other fiction in the book does not.

One of them, "Jerusalem's Lot," is a direct imitation of H. P. Lovecraft — a nod to horror fandom. As the first tale in the book, it serves as a familiar welcome mat for *aficionados*, as an announcement that King likes Lovecraft just as much as the next fan.

"The Last Rung on the Ladder," on the other hand, demonstrates that King can write straight mainstream fiction. In his introduction to this collection, John D. MacDonald called this story "a gem." King may write about monsters, he may even imitate Lovecraft himself at times, but if you don't like monsters or Lovecraft, King has something else to offer. MacDonald suggests that "Stephen King is not going to restrict himself to his present field of intense interest."

"Quitters, Inc." is a grim fantasy about giving up smoking, most likely having some personal meaning for King. In his foreword King writes: "In the last year I have been able to reduce my cigarette habit from the unfiltered brand I had smoked since I was eighteen to a low nicotine and tar brand, and I still hope to be able to quit completely." How important this fantasy may be in terms of revealing King's own fears about smoking is up for debate.

The last story in the book is about a woman in a hospital. She's gutted with cancer. I wonder why John D. MacDonald did not point to *this* story as having "nary a rustle or breath of other worlds in it," as he did with "The Last Rung on the Ladder." "The Woman in the Room" has nothing supernatural in it. It is horror, but an all too real horror millions of Americans face every year: seeing a loved one dying of metastasizing cancer . . . or contracting cancer yourself.

I can understand why MacDonald ignored "The Woman in the Room" in favor of the only other mainstream story in the book. "The Last Rung on the Ladder" has one dramatic scene: kids jumping from a beam down into a haystack, the rickety ladder to the cross-beam suddenly breaking under a girl's weight — then, as she hangs by a single rung, her brother desperately stacks hay where she will fall to the plank floor of the barn. "The Woman in the Room" has nothing as overblown to offer. It's not exciting. I can't imagine a single person who would *enjoy* reading it, but it says something important, it deals with real problems and emotions. A son *hates* his dying mother, and loves her too; he thinks of killing her to put her out of pain. He does not make much of a hero. An old woman dying of cancer is not a subject for *clichéd* action-adventure fiction.

Why have this story as the *last* offering? Surely not just to say, hey, America, I'm afraid of cancer too. If "Jerusalem's Lot" announces King as a horror fan, a writer who knows the in-jokes, this story does just the opposite. It says, after other scares have come and gone, that King is *serious* about horror, *real horror* like cancer.

In his foreword King puts it clearly enough: ". . . something *bad* is also going to happen to *you*, and it may be cancer and it may be a stroke, and it may be a car accident, but it's going to happen." He does not suggest a vampire is going to bite you, because he knows better:

> When you read horror, you don't really believe what you read. You don't believe in vampires, werewolves, trucks that suddenly start up and drive themselves. The horrors that we all do believe in are the sort that Dostoyevsky and Albee and MacDonald write about; hate, alienation, growing lovelessly old, tottering out into a hostile world on the unsteady legs of adolescence.

Real horror and a sense of disgust pervade King's fiction. Cancer is mentioned frequently, hospitals are places of dread. Car wrecks even form a literary motif of sorts: the crash in *Carrie* of the hot-rod carrying Billy Nolan and Chris Hargensen, both killed; the car accident in *The Dead Zone*, John Smith thrown into a coma for four and a half years; the motorcycle wreck in *'Salem's Lot*, Ben Mears' wife killed; the Jaguar carrying the drunken Al Shockley and Jack Torrance running over a bicycle in *The Shining — was a child killed?* King never says. (Child abuse, too, forms a connecting link of concern between King stories.)

Why be afraid of vampires, then, when there are more immediate horrors about, in our everyday life? King suggests that mock fear is for emotional release, and that ". . . only the writer of horror and the supernatural gives the reader such an opportunity for total identification and catharsis" — a cathartic purging of the fear of death, the Big Fear.

Frankly, this idea is debatable. Mainstream writers have had their say on death, often to more effect than horror writers. And writers, whether of horror or mainstream, only reach *readers*. Compared to what the various established religions have been doing about assuaging fear of death among the populace, the best efforts of Poe and Lovecraft seem pitiful. And for people who actually believe in Hell, King's horrors must seem pretty lightweight, mere piffles. I daresay the heights of terror to which a good Fundamentalist minister can drive his flock never have been equalled by King. The minister has belief for a whip, but King doesn't — or does not think so. . . . "*When you read horror, you don't really believe what you read.*" (*Night Shift* introduction.)

One reason King does not impress me as a great supernaturalist is because the true horror in his fiction is so firmly based in the material world. Once you die a horrible death in a King story, that's it. The potential *spiritual* horrors are sketched in quickly or not mentioned at all. When Susan Snell tunes into Carrie White's dying thoughts, "She felt that she was dying herself and did not want to see this preview of her own eventual end." (*Carrie*, Prom Night section.) For King, horror fiction acts as a rehearsal for death, as hinted here in *Carrie* and explored in King's introduction to *Night Shift* and in King's non-fiction book on the subject, *Danse Macabre*. Yet death for Carrie is ". . . the final horror — that last lighted thought carried swiftly down into the black tunnel of eternity, followed by the blank, idiot hum of prosaic electricity." (Prom Night section.) In a word, oblivion — not some fiendishly conceived Hell and further horrors.

Even in *The Shining*, King's best supernatural novel, the ghosts don't have much power. The dead woman in the tub, King's most terror-laden creation, does not have the power to *kill*; all she accomplishes in the physical world is some light strangulation. The Overlook ghosts can't get rid of Wendy and Danny without Jack's help. The animate hedge creatures cannot even prevent the cook Hallorann from reaching the hotel in his cavalry charge.

King's serious interest in horror unmistakeably is grounded in American social reality. Vampires and haunted houses are thrilling, lots of fun. Wife-beating and child abuse are more horrible and disturbing. Cancer and car wrecks are deadly.

IV.   The Writer

KING'S BASIC CONCERNS ABOUT everyday horror are put forth seriously, even when fanged monsters are loose in the story. Too many critics have torn apart his work, *dismissing it simply because of its fantastic trappings*. Other points being equal, a supernatural tale should be able to work effectively toward evoking terror and at the same time be as good a piece of fiction as *any* modern story. Many mainstream critics seem to miss the point that King's work is top-notch *noir*, that it deals *regularly* with important social problems such as child abuse, that it unrelentingly details the many facets of horror in everyday life for all to see (especially in small-town U.S.A.), even those who may prefer to ignore it.

Yet it is only recently that King has gained control of his fiction. He ended *Carrie* by burning the town down, *'Salem's Lot* by burning the town down, *The Shining* by exploding the hotel and burning it down, *The Stand* by blowing up the citadel of the evil forces. (Dark clouds of Evil shoot skyward after the explosions in *The Shining* and *The Stand*.) If the early tales in the *Magazine of Horror* are now considered King's apprentice work, the skill he is showing in new books such as *The Dead Zone* or *Cujo* suggests that it won't be long before King's early novels also are looked back upon as fledgling efforts, instead of the milestones of horror some people are calling them even today. King himself has few kind words to say for *Carrie*, and undoubtedly felt an artistic compulsion to rewrite the novel as

Firestarter, to show what he can do with similar themes at this point in his career.

The Dead Zone is the starting point for any recognition King will get as an important mainstream novelist. The weird aspects are subdued, the human elements brought more fully to the front. In *'Salem's Lot*, for all the value King attached to creating a fictional town full of prosaic reality, the vampires necessarily assume much of the action. Small town reality and real human values command half the plot, but then some concession must be made so that a character can be menaced by a vampire: the horrors of everyday life and the horrors of the vampire plague pull the narrative in different directions, with neither getting the upper hand.

King's major problem as a supernaturalist and simply as a writer has been the balancing of the real and the unreal elements in his plots. In many cases, *the failures of the supernatural forces are obvious concessions by the author to prolong the action:* Surely the Overlook Hotel's hedge animals could swallow Hallorann and spit him out with no trouble at all, if King had *allowed* them to live up to their potential. The woman in the tub—*she* could have done in a child. King sacrifices *overall* believability in plot in favor of *believability for the moment*. He sacrifices *rationality* for intensity. Fritz Leiber pointed out this problem when he wrote:

> Faced with the need to bolster up an impossible or near-impossible situation, he'll not use up space in cobbling together explanations; he'll employ the wordage instead to intensify the situation itself, and his characters' reactions to it, make this so real-seeming that we just have to believe. Aim at convincing . . . the feelings, not the mind.

Catering to emotion at the expense of the intellect is useful for writing intended for a single reading. Most *popular* writing—in markets such as *People* magazine, *The National Enquirer* or most books on the bestseller lists—is read once and then tossed away in favor of next week's issue or next week's bestseller. These lack sufficient intellectual content to merit another reading, and in any case are meant only as entertainment, as diver-

sion. (I know one man who has read every new John D. Mac-
Donald novel on publication since the 1950s. He has never reread one of the books. He thinks MacDonald is *the best*.) It surely
is difficult to imagine the bestseller reader going through all
those fat Stephen King books two or three times.

If King is writing only for pure entertainment, giving people
a chance to escape into his fictional world for awhile, then obviously any extended critical evaluation of his work is beside the
point. I recall Mickey Spillane once saying in an interview: "I
don't care what the critics say about me as long as they don't
take away my money."

King, however, is very much aware of critical recognition
and approval. In *College Papers*, winter 1980, interviewer Abe
Peck said to King: "I heard you once said you were afraid *Firestarter* might be received as 'Carrie II.'" King replied: "Yeah. If
you're taken seriously as somebody who's practicing literature
as art, you're allowed to return to what you've done before;
you're amplifying previous themes. But if you write popular literature and you repeat a theme, the idea is that your head is so
empty it's produced an echo." Peck prefaced the interview with
some notes on King, including a paragraph of negative comments on King's work by critics Pauline Kael and Leonard
Wolf. Peck them states:

> King is stung by such criticism, but admits he is less
> than great at plot. Still, he values what he calls "the
> Plain Style" of storytelling, which stresses accessibili-
> ty to the reader, and counter-attacks by criticizing
> more cerebral writers, such as Thomas Pynchon and
> John Updike, as elitists who appeal to "preppies."

This line of thought suggests that King wants to be taken seriously, that he wants his books to be considered as literature
rather than as pure escapism. King has said:

> The idea that success in itself can hurt a writer is as
> ridiculous and as elitist as the commonly held belief
> that a popular book is a bad book — the former belief
> presumes that writers are even more corruptible
> than, say, politicians, and the latter belief presumes
> that the level of taste in the world's most literate coun-

try is illogically low. I don't — and perhaps I can't, as a direct result of what I'm doing — accept either idea.

King has the ability to write books both the critics and the readers may approve. He may well come into his share of serious critical attention, but it won't be based on the novels which have made him such a hit with the horror fans and the bestseller readers; at least, none of his books prior to *The Dead Zone*.

Today King is sitting on the imaginary rail which separates pure mainstream fiction from supernatural horror, with a leg dangling into either field. John D. MacDonald has suggested that King may jump from that rail fully into the mainstream, drop his affection for *monsters* and get on with writing about *people*, which seems to be his serious interest. The risk is that he might then find his brand name as a horror writer of no commercial value at all. He *might* lose his audience.

No matter how fully he controls the narrative in *The Dead Zone* or how believably he works in his favored motifs of extranormal mental powers, some critics aren't going to take King seriously until he comes out from behind his facade as a "horror writer." And they may have a valid point: that monsters may be gimmicks King *needs*, instead of writing simply about death or insanity — the cake may not be palatable without the icing. King may not have what it takes to succeed without the added titillation offered by vampires or evil forces.

The next major step for King will not be to write another variation on *Firestarter* or to haul out more vampires or build another haunted house or sketch another scenario for the end of the world. We all know he can write these books. We have good reason to suspect that he *could* write an interesting novel about a small Maine village or about a family disintegrating without isolating them in some ghost-ridden hotel. Now that his craft is honed and his name known, King should write another straight mainstream novel like those first ones that never sold, to show what he can (or cannot) do. If he wants to be ranked with Albee, Dostoyevsky, Pynchon or Updike, that is the step he must take.

If, however, he's content to remain a "brand name horror writer," then I for one want to see *more* spectral horror and less talk about alcoholism or small town life for awhile. Anyone who could write the dead woman in the tub from *The Shining* should be able to turn out a *great supernatural novel* without a lame moral ending, a novel wherein the monsters are not "comic-book menaces," one in which the supernatural is not hamstrung repeatedly so a few characters can escape with their lives.

In fact, in the *College Papers* interview (1980) King mentioned a novel on burial customs he finished some time ago: "I have no plans to publish it in the near future. It's too horrible. It's worse than *The Shining* or any of the other things. It's terrifying."

Consider that. A novel *too terrifying* to publish. *Exactly* what the field of supernatural horror has needed for about two hundred years.

Bring it on!

Charlie turned toward them. As she did so, half a dozen other men, John Mayo and Ray Knowles among them, broke for the porch's back steps with their guns drawn.

Charlie's eyes widened a little, and Andy felt something hot pass by him in a warm puff of air.

The three men at the front end of the porch had got halfway toward them when their hair caught on fire.

A gun boomed, deafeningly loud, and a splinter of wood perhaps eight inches long jumped from one of the porch's supporting posts. Norma Manders screamed, and Andy flinched. But Charlie seemed not to notice. Her face was dreamy and thoughtful. A small Mona Lisa smile had touched the corners of her mouth.

She's enjoying this, *Andy thought with something like horror.* Is that why she's so afraid of it? Because she *likes* it?

—*from* Firestarter

Horror Hits a High

by Fritz Leiber

I.   Reluctant Admiration

I DON'T READ ALL THAT MUCH SCIENCE FICTION, fantasy and supernatural horror. Sometimes I'm afraid it'll interfere with my own writing. I can skim if I have to, but not very well, and I don't enjoy it. Yet every once in a while I run into a kindred writer who touches my fancy and pushes my compulsion button so that for the next few months I'll read everything of his I can lay may hands on. But that's so rare I can count them on my fingers: Henrik Ibsen, H. P. Lovecraft, Robert Heinlein, Nigel Balchin, Dashiell Hammett, C. S. Forester, Robert Graves, Ian Fleming, Nevil Shute. And, most recent, Stephen King.

In 1978 a magazine editor slipped me a hardcover copy of *The Stand*. I don't believe I promised him I'd review it, but I think I sort of promised *myself* I would — which can be an even more dangerous commitment. Heretofore I'd read only *The Shining* by King and had been of two minds about it. I'd put it down somewhat as a book written with the films in mind, and now wondered guiltily whether that hadn't been because I was jealous of the author's ability to evoke fear.

The Shining is a supernatural novel about the power of evil, in which the forces of good are mostly outmatched. It has a lot of strong stuff in it, enough to hold our interest without the supernatural element.

The central and pivotal character is a brilliant young English teacher, superficially liberated but with a savagely moralistic religious background, who has just lost his job at a prestigious boys' school because of his alcoholism and rare but terrible rages. He *may* have killed a child in a drunken hit-and-run accident. His book of short stories has been a critical success, and he has a great novel in him. To complete it and so rehabilitate himself, he takes a job as winter caretaker of a deluxe old Rocky Mountain resort hotel which is snowbound most of the year.

He brings his family with him to this solitude: a sensitive wife, well intentioned but weak, forever tempted to flee back to her devouring mother; and his highly imaginative young son who has a poetic streak and an imaginary playmate. Pretty good, huh?

But when you add the supernatural element — ! The boy has "the shining"; in other words he is prescient; he dreams future events in a jumbled way, especially the repeated scene in which he is fleeing through long hotel corridors from a drunken figure who is calling to him threateningly, obscenely, and carrying a roque mallet. Trying to aid the boy is an old black cook with a little bit of "the shining" too. While menacing them all is a host of monstrous ghosts — suicides, murderers, hedonists, power maniacs, sinister celebrities from the hotel's illustrious and notorious guest register — trembling on the brink of materialization.

In my review I'd grudgingly admitted the book's power to push my panic buttons, while at the same time putting it down somewhat as "written for the movies."

So look at another of King's efforts, eh? I told myself — fair is fair. Though *The Stand* was twice as long, dammit! a monster book almost three inches thick, supposed to be science fiction in part and blurbed as "a story of dark wonders and irresistible terror, an epic of final confrontation between Good and Evil."

Two or three months later, on an empty tired evening, I rather aimlessly took up the massive tome and read six or eight pages without getting hooked. It seemed to be science fiction, all right, all about a terrible plague that breaks out in the near future, nothing I could easily set against *The Shining* and make points, and it looked longer than ever. (Why, oh why, did people have to write 800-page books? And why should I read them when there were all sorts of unread 200-page books at hand?) Feeling guilty, I closed it and laid it carefully on the top shelf of my closet.

From time to time I'd take another look at this cigar-box-size book in the heights of my closet, generally without opening it, just savoring the guilt-pang. I became very familiar with the exterior of that book. The jacket art by John Cayea shows a wasteland where a medieval beaked monster in motley with a single-pointed pick — a gink straight out of Breughel — duels drunkenly with a frightened blond man in white doublet and hose gingerly wielding a two-handed shining sword. Good and Evil confronting, all right, all right.

Also, a picture of the author on the inside back flap — not the one I later became familiar with of the eyes in black glasses staring out piercingly over a muff-size black beard, but a clean-shaven, grinning, lowbrowed one that looked like nothing so much as a blarneying Irish comedian. A man with a face like that might write anything, and I wouldn't trust him for an inch of print, either.

And there was a fascinating back-cover excerpt about "Randy Flagg, the dark man, the Walkin' Dude, the man with no face, the living image of Satan, his hour come round again. . . ."

I suppose this deplorable game with myself might have gone on indefinitely, except that after about a year the Fifth World Fantasy Convention came along. It was in Providence, H. P. Lovecraft's city, and I felt I just had to go. It turned out that Stephen King was co-guest of honor along with Frank Belknap Long, while King's most recent novel, *The Dead Zone*, was number one on *The New York Times* bestseller list. Moreover, he behaved modestly and said several sensible things on panels and in the course of his winningly brief guest of honor speech.

He also told us that his publishers had cut some 100,000 words from *The Stand* — 200 pages, that'd be — and he vowed some day to reinstate them. Despite this horrendous thought of *The Stand* 1,000 pages long (thick as it was wide, almost), I had to face it; my ridiculous charade with the book in the closet just couldn't go on. I broke down and bought *The Dead Zone*, got King's autograph on it, and before the busy convention ended I was fifty pages into it.

Soon I'd written the first draft of an enthusiastic review. I got more and more interested in how King gets his effects, what rules he follows in horror writing, for these are methods worth serious consideration by any horror writer.

In *The Dead Zone* Stephen King has constructed a well-nigh perfect novel of supernatural terror out of notoriously hard-to-handle material. It's a big and gripping novel, emotionally rich, imagination-bending, very frightening, and as real as today's headlines.

The Dead Zone is successful because it has enough situation and feeling for a workable novel even if the supernatural element were left out. This seems to me an obvious ingredient in "mainstreaming" the horror novel. *The Shining* had punched my panic buttons too, but it did so with the aid of a lot of supernatural paraphernalia: the old hotel, the vicious ghosts, the straining boiler (a reasonable materialistic fear), the malignant topiary, vicious wasps, and the half-explained clouds of guilts which blur the protagonist's brain.

The Dead Zone achieves the same thing with far simpler, leaner, clear-cut materials. This is the sort of stuff you know is close to the heart of reality. There's nothing artistically *wrong* with darkly atmospheric paraphernalia, but it has to be handled and justified very carefully.

John Smith is a likeable young Maine high school teacher who because of two brain fractures develops a sporadic and uncertain gift for reading character and future dangers from touching a person or some object that person has handled. The messages are sometimes obscured with missing details, because of the "dead zone" in his brain (scar tissue). When the messages do come through they pack an emotional punch, both for sender and receiver.

The problem is how to make a fictional psychic convincingly believable and generate a story from his gift of foresight.

Well, for one thing, the writer should ground the psychic phenomena in the physical, in the life-and-death realm of the medical, the world of hard fact and pain. King does this with Smith's brain injuries and long coma, and all the tortures involved with rehabilitating atrophied muscles. John Smith spends a long time in intensive care in a hospital, under laboratory conditions and close scrutiny, as it were — so we're more apt to believe what happens.

His predictive flashes should cause him effort and pain. He must work against strong resistance — in line with the feeling that real achievement comes only through hard work and suffering and that the working of true magic involves exhausting effort and great danger.

As to the kind of flashes our psychic gets, they should all involve very serious matters — accidents, fires, lightning, strokes, murders, wars. Then they'll generate tension, suspense and plot, which psychic stunts like spoonbending wouldn't. King doesn't talk much about other psychics in his novel, but one he does mention is Peter Hurkos, with his impressive police work. *The Dead Zone* is rooted in the real world of proclaimed psychics and ambitious politicians, where the fakers outnumber the honest performers ten to one. King convinces us that John Smith is one of the genuine ones.

Finally, the author should take a good hard look at how people would actually feel about a psychic who occasionally predicted catastrophe accurately. King does, and discovers they'd be much more apt to fear and shun than to lionize him; each of John Smith's danger-flashes poses him the problem of *whom* to warn and *how*, and how to endure being hated for his prediction. Knotty moral problems are bound to arise.

When you add to these concerns the ordinary problems of putting a life together after a gap of four and a half years (the coma), you can readily see that John Smith's plight is not an enviable one.

I don't say that this is the only good way a novel could have been generated from the same materials, but it is Stephen King's way and it works! It keeps the surprises streaming from his pen far beyond the point at which I thought he'd exhausted them. It's as though he'd dipped his pen in a magic ink of moment-to-moment futurity. And I certainly sympathize with King's intention, if I've surmised it correctly, to underline the point that this novel in no way depends on traditional and often movie-clichéd sources of terror (vampirism, werewolfery, Satanism) or even on the religious supernatural. That's most true and makes his action in part a declaration of independence from the stale, crude, and often moralistic concepts of horror movies and horror comics. As you might expect, *The Dead Zone* is King's most restrained novel, and, I think, the best of King's novels so far, well thought out, plotted soundly and carefully, no holes I noted, a sympathy-rouser with strong feelings, no flamboyant supernatural trappings, but a chilling area of inner space at its center.

In the course of *The Dead Zone*, King punched my compulsion button, for instead of running to my closet to grab down *The Stand*, I decided first to read everything else available by the author. For starters, *'Salem's Lot*, his vampire novel, where I discovered that King wasn't afraid of overwriting or of common editorial no-no's such as having a young writer the protagonist of your book. King writes a good deal of the book from the viewpoint of the Lot, the people in that Maine town. He clearly likes these quirky folk: the Amazonian landlady who makes herself four-egg breakfasts, the teenage mother who bats her brat in the eye when he yowls or dirties because she simply can't contain herself, the bitter and kinky-minded old schoolbus driver, who puts kids off the bus for whispering. He enjoys writing about them. He trusts his supernatural story is strong enough to carry this excess material.

Next I tackled his first novel, *Carrie*, and would you believe it? — was acutely disappointed when I found it was short, less than half the length of *The Shining* or *'Salem's Lot*, one-quarter that of *The Stand*. I felt deprived. Also, the structure at first seemed alien and overtly quiet, almost half the book consisting of pretended quotes from newspaper stories, scientific journals, occult encyclopedias, pop bios of Carrie White by classmates, teachers, pop occult writers and the like, with the third person omniscient author taking up whenever the going warranted it. I'd seen the film, of course, and understood the movie-effectiveness of the shocker "first menstruation" opening in the girls' showers and locker room. The quotations device hadn't cramped King's all-out writing style.

Meanwhile I'd been reading King's early stories in his collection, *Night Shift*. Several of these stories are early handlings of the themes of his novels, first developments of incidents which reoccur in them, or otherwise offshoots of his longer works. What most impresses me about these apprentice stories by King is the vigor and recklessness of the writing, the all-out, no holds barred imaginings he performs as he works new variations and intensifications on old themes. Most, but not all, hinge on supernatural explanations, and mostly it's King's sort of supernatural, a highly energetic and mostly unstoppable force, outrageous in one way or another.

The first of them, the novelette "Jerusalem's Lot," is positively Lovecraftian, with mention of Yog-Sothoth and Ludwig Prinn's *Mysteries of the Worm*. It might well be the beginning of the novel about a survival of the witch cult in Maine that the character Robert Blake is said to have been writing in Lovecraft's "The Haunter of the Dark."

But it's when he gets to the stories in the style of the magazine *Unknown* that King really shows his bubbling inventive power — *Unknown*, with its unique blend of logic and the irrational, the mod and the morbid, the scientific and the scatty. No question but he'd have hit *Unknown* easily if he'd been writing in the early 1940s, the thought of which fills me with sentimental joy, as a contributor to that publication. He's especially good on those tales of machines that come catastrophically alive — "The Mangler," "Trucks" — jiggering their controls by a steely telekinesis (of which the best example is Theodore Sturgeon's "Killdozer"). "The Mangler" is the best of King's, a tale of an ironing machine that that runs amuck in a commercial laundry. His characters rediscover the mathematics of magic to stop it, but as the story ends the machine is still heading out to destroy the universe.

Films make their premises visually. They show instead of explain. It becomes a "like it or lump it" technique. The camera says, "There they are right before your eyes. Don't you see them? Don't you believe? It's so vivid." I seem to find a similar technique in the stories in *Night Shift*. Tales such as "Sometimes They Come Back" in which the evil dead return to flesh and do havoc occur with no explanation. In "Children of the Corn" the children in a Nebraska town kill all the adults and live for ten years worshipping a corn god without a soul in the rest of the U.S.A. catching on and living to spread the alarm. Faced with the need to bolster up an impossible situation, King will not use up space in cobbling together explanations. He'll employ the wordage instead to intensify the situation itself and his characters' reactions to it. He makes this so real-seeming that we just have to believe.

King aims at convincing the eye and the other senses and emotions, before the mind.

So I was ready for *The Stand*. Fortunately I caught a feverish sort of cold just then, so I could lose myself with a dreamlike absorption in the book without feeling too guilty about other tasks undone. I had a couple of uncomfortable moments when my symptoms seemed to parallel those of the folk being struck down by the great pandemic during the first quarter of the book.

I was to page 200 or so before I caught on to the full grandiose magnificence of his initial concept. He was assembling the cast of his novel by the sweeping method of killing off everyone else in the world. This developed into what was for me the strongest part of the novel, as the author follows the survivors in their wanderings by singles and pairs and triplets and quadruplets of most very disparate people, all of them forced to build up thier beliefs and their values from scratch. There's a wonderful electric loneliness in this section, as the survivors' dreams begin to come back and strengthen in the great silence.

Some of them develop psionic abilities, and an awareness grows of principalities and powers striding about or lurking and luring and enticing them. They themselves become as mythic figures, demigods almost, as humanity dwindles away. There is inevitably a choosing up of sides here, roughly between those who drift toward the influence of Mother Abagail, and those who accept the leadership of that eternal terrorist, the Walkin' Dude.

Here the language of the novel becomes more poetic, and there is feeling on both sides that mankind is shaping toward some great swift change. And King gets hold of a strong suggestive idea: He questions the common Twentieth Century notion (Jung, etc.) that everyone carries in his or her subconscious the seed of every evil possible and shares the thinking guilt — maybe this is only one more last gasp of anthropomorphism, an attempt to soften the horrors that may lurk in the unknown. Maybe man is not the measure of all things, and in particular evil.

In *The Stand* we soon find Boulder, Colorado (Good) pitted against Las Vegas, Nevada (Evil). The former spends most of its time burying the plague dead and clumsily trying to work out a kind of town-meeting democracy with representation. The latter concentrates on keeping the casinos open and every last light bulb burning as it was before the plague — they have atomic power.

At this point the story line begins to follow various individuals who set off on half-planned, half-impulsive quests. The question arises: Why then was it necessary to build up the two communities? I think the answer is to keep the story real, to prevent it from turning into pure fantasy. To this degree *The Stand* is science fiction.

Firestarter, King's sixth published novel, also is science fiction, a suspenseful and well-thought-out work. It's about a girl with a wild talent for starting fires — but there the similarity to *Carrie* ends. Charlie McGee is an attractive child able to make moral choices, not a creature of ignorance emotionally swamped by an antisex religious maniac of a mother. The book is rooted in the topical realities of the notorious CIA drug experiments — here it's an establishment outfit called The Shop. It has the nitty-gritty reality we've come to expect of King — a baby able to start little blazes in her crib and sear bad teddy bears would have to be fire-trained by her parents, just as ordinary children are toilet-trained. The large and small catastrophes caused by the pyro-telekenetic girl and the set-ups for studying her safely are thoughtfully envisioned and described — and with considerable of the engineer's feel for large scale material phenomena that is so useful to the science-fiction writer. Charlie's own subjective awarenesses are well handled too, the answers to the question "What's it really feel like to be able to start fires by mind-power?"

It has an Indian hit man reminiscent of the Walkin' Dude in *The Stand* — another memorable death-god figure. And the ending has rather more of the science-fictional "We can do something about it," than the traditional horror story's "We can only be terrorized and run."

Firestarter and *The Dead Zone* both fulfill John D. Mac-Donald's prediction that King would get away from writing books about "spooks and spells and slitherings in the cellar" and all the rest of the Saturday night horror movie repertory. And unlike her foreshadower, Carrie White the victim, Charlie McGee emerges from this novel as an admirable and well-rounded character, able to show initiative and accept responsibility, an achiever, fit compatriot of her partial namesake, John D. MacDonald's own Travis McGee. It's very understandable that King should have wanted to rework the *Carrie* material and he makes a good job of it. A meaty book.

King's recent short novel, *The Mist*, despite its hanging ending, continues impressively in the science-fiction vein, while his most recent full-length novel, *Cujo*, achieves memorable suspense and horror without any resort whatever to science fiction or the supernatural, except for the suggestion that some dreams may be predictive and that a dim telepathy may exist between sympathetic people, which hardly counts as supernaturalism at all in these credulous times.

King is the sort of writer who follows where the story leads. In *The Stand* he needed loneliness and the plague gave him that. Then he needed the feeling of community and so brought back cities. Then he needed loneliness again, and brought it back by sending out some characters on solitary quests. Undoubtedly there were more succinct ways of doing these things, but I don't think King sets that much store by concision. He doesn't mind over-writing, both as to quantity and quality of prose, so long as it stays gripping.

Take the old resort hotel in *The Shining,* a real cesspool of evil. Its psychic residue includes lewd and perverse ghosts of various suicides, murderers and murderees, cafe society degenerates, a shot-gunned Mafia boss, the entourage of a presidential scandal and all manner of sinister types. While outside broods a malefic topiary zoo of hedge animals that move when you are not watching them. Add to this the fact that the hotel must be kept heated by a huge boiler which has to be nursed very carefully to keep it from exploding. . . .

Don't mistake me. All this strong stuff *works.* But with so many horrendous elements working together, there is a sort of horror-comics blatancy. I certainly saw the last scenes as a double-page spread on pulp paper: the burning hotel with its evil escaping, bat-like and triumphant in a great thick smoke cloud.

Several effective modern horror writers and scenarists show the effects of their exposure to the horror comics, perhaps inevitably. These modern authors have the advantage of being able to be explicit about sex and its sauces, while writers like Arthur Machen and Oscar Wilde had to depend on hints.

Likewise is the advantage of having mostly a soft audience, inclined, at least for amusement purposes, to believe in witchcraft and demons, all sorts of psychic powers, and in flying saucers with extraterrestrial crews. They see it all the time on TV and in films.

Aside from the workmanlike physical realism of their stories, the new writers can devote most of their effort to mixing the most potent supernatural brew from existent raw materials rather than spend time asking the basic question, "Can such things be?" as did writers such as Ambrose Bierce, Algernon Blackwood, M.R. James, Machen and Lovecraft.

I miss the intellectual engagement with which the earlier authors provided me, the finer textured terror of speculating about the truly unknown.

Which makes me ask myself whether I'm just boasting about

my taste, saying that my horrors are more intellectual, more stylish, more elegant than the common garden variety. But I think there's a real point. Take the evil hotel and the hedge animals — why are they haunted, how do they work? Basic questions aren't answered. How much throughout the story is subjective, how much objective? That's never clear either.

The truth seems to be that the hotel and the hedge animals were introduced into the story for their *effect*. They frightened the reader at that point of the story, and that was all they were ever supposed to do. There was no need to explain them. They *worked*. One of King's rules seems to be: *Write! Write it with the most color, the most feeling, the greatest intensity possible, using whatever you need: filthy language, clichés, kookie images and word formations. Don't be afraid of being melodramatic AND SCREAMING AT THE READER. Then, if that doesn't work*, try restraint.

In sum, Stephen King has made the horror book bestsellingly popular once more — even when it's nonfiction, meaning his *Danse Macabre*. His appeal is chiefly to the emotions, peripherally to the intellect, but he is always workmanlike. His fiction fulfills the promise of the dedication of *The Stand*: "This dark chest of wonders."

II.   Cinema is a Chancier Medium

ANY DISCUSSION OF FILMS made or in the making from King's novels or short stories can best take off from his rich and remarkable nonfiction book, *Stephen King's Danse Macabre*, which is essentially a celebration and analysis of horror as entertainment in America since 1950: books, magazines, comic books, associative items, radio, TV, and films — especially films. It is at once a loving and personal introduction to the field and a generous bull-session sharing of its obscure wonders and little secrets, written with honesty, shamelessness, demandingness, and humor of a devoted and deeply involved practitioner.

The book is built around two lists, one of 100 horror films worth viewing released between 1950 and 1980, which is essentially King's own lifetime as a movie viewer. The other is of 100 horror novels and collections of short stories published during the same period. In each list King stars his personal favorites, "the best," as it were, but he believes all contributed to the field. So the book is based on and grows from personal experience. King describes with much insight his own childhood introduction to horror as art and entertainment. Occasionally he refers to older books and films when he is searching for examples of basic horror themes, but even here the influence of films is noticeable, for his four horror archetypes are the vampire (*Dracula*), the werewolf (*Dr. Jekyll and Mr. Hyde*), the monster or thing (*Frankenstein*), and the ghost (*The Turn of the Screw* and Peter Straub's *Ghost Story*).

King writes in part as a psychologist searching for the individual's phobic pressure points (the point, for instance, where mythically for the child "death" is "when the monsters get you") and as a sociologist hunting for society's phobic pressure points, which change with the times and elucidate the subtext of a film. For instance, in *Earth Vs. the Flying Saucers* (1956) ugly root-creatures from outer space destroy Washington, D. C. (the text); but the actual fear involved here, King interprets, is that of Russian atomic attack (the subtext). While the classically bad *Horror of Party Beach* (1964) nevertheless plays on the submerged dread of poisoning by radioactive waste dumped in the sea.

But King also writes as a seasoned horror film buff explaining what he finds powerful in cult films such as George Romero's *Night of the Living Dead* and Tobe Hooper's *The Texas Chainsaw Massacre*. He's a mine of lively horror information, which sometimes finds its way into his fiction. For example, take the "desperate gimmicks used to sell bad horror movies. During one imported Italian turkey, the theatres advertised 'bloodcorn,' which was ordinary popcorn with a red food dye added." In his novel *Cujo* a red-dyed breakfast cereal—"Cherrypops," or something like that—causes a brief nationwide scare because the children regurgitating it are thought to have hemorrhaged.

And it's a good thing that King is hardened to the mischances that can occur in the course of horror movie making, aside from purely commercial monkeying, for the films made from his books have so far been of uneven quality. *Carrie*, directed by Brian De Palma and released in 1976, is to my mind undoubtedly the best, and wisely capitalized on the book's strongest points: the shocker scene of the title character's first menstruation in the school shower room with her classmates pelting her with tampons and sanitary napkins; the general tendency of high-schoolers to persecute any of their members who are sensitive, not hip to things, or have an oddball parent; the inability and unwillingness of most teachers to interfere with such rites; the loathsome anti-sex mania of the pitifully naive Carrie's religious nut of a mother; and the swift build-up of the final insult where the victim, dressed in white and with ego inflated for the sacrifice, is drenched with hog's blood. After that, the violence of the electric poltergeist phenomena could hardly have been overdone. The film also benefitted from having a very talented young actress as Carrie — Sissy Spacek — while John Travolta did well as one of her nastier persecutors.

The TV two-part *'Salem's Lot* didn't do a bad job of presenting parts of the story, though it suffered from a tendency to hold back at the stronger moments, while six or eight episodes would have been needed to convey anything like the full flavour of this big novel.

The Shining had the dubious good fortune of catching the interest of one of the really big, mysterious and self-willed (*auteur*'s the art word) talents in the producing-and-directing field, as unpredictable and half-the-time-brilliant as Robert Altman and as committed to superexpensive years-long productions as Francis Coppola: Stanley Kubrick, great on photography, visual effects, and heavily orchestrated *themes*, weak on explanations, justifications, and tidy plotting, whose characters have always been either caricatures or ciphers (the four-star generals and other wonderful nuts of *Dr. Strangelove* and Hal the computer of *2001*; the babyish spacemen and pretty Irishmen of that film and *Barry Lyndon*).

So what does he do with *The Shining*? He seizes on the theme of the snowbound and ferociously haunted luxury hotel high in the Rocky Mountains and makes it vast as the spaceship in *2001*, with its crew (as it were) of three insignificant and powerless mortals forever creeping (or pedalling a tricycle) through its impeccable endless corridors, inevitably going to pieces, cracking up, *dissolving* from the unbearable, dreadfully haunted, isolated immensity of the dismal place.

But three ciphers won't make even the most artistically realized film move. So Kubrick turns the husband, Jack Torrance, into probably the broadest ever of his caricatures, a veritable type of the boastful dumb tenderfoot, a failed and alcoholic schoolteacher who asserts *he'll* never let isolation drive *him* crazy (no matter that a former caretaker went crackers and murdered wife, daughters, self) and who thinks on no evidence whatsoever that he has it in him to write a great novel if only he ever gets the peace, time, and solitude necessary for the task.

All the interesting character weaknesses, emotional traumas, and knotty problems that King inflicted on Torrance in the novel to soften him up for the hotel (and make us sympathize with him in his terrible troubles) are simply thrown out the window by Kubrick, thrown out *in toto*, to be replaced by one master explain-all bedrock character-insight: this guy is a cocky dumb little jerk.

Because Jack Nicholson is a fine actor, highly disciplined and always totally loyal to the production, he follows this interpretation faithfully, employing a marvelous repertory of mad grimaces, double takes, husbandly sneers at little wifey, idiot exultations, rooster preenings, and a rich variety of vacuous looks.

Of course with goings-on like these, it soon becomes clear that Torrance has been crazy as a cockatoo from the very start. Thereafter he is of little use to the picture except to make crazy faces and do crazy things, such as destroying the CB radio linking the hotel with the outside world after the telephone lines go down.

Such a character can't possibly be writing a documentary novel about the evil hotel and the sinister bloody scandals that have clustered about it, researching this material from scrapbooks and records he finds in the basement. And so Kubrick is forced to throw away the background of reality for the terrible hauntings of the hotel that attracted him to King's book in the first place. When he does populate the vast grand ballroom with these ghosts in 1920s garb, they can only stand around and make background atmosphere; we don't learn their horrifying stories; they can't frighten us. We tend to assume they are part of Torrance's hallucinations of grandeur — until late in the picture one of them has to perform a physical act vital to the plot — release Torrance from the storeroom in which his wife has locked him — and by then it's too late for them to achieve any real supernatural stature.

In fact, it comes close to the truth to say that the process of filming *The Shining* was largely one of throwing away effective incidents, either entirely or by giving them a one-shot "once funny" or "once scarey" use, beginning with Torrance's "novel," which turns out to be one sentence typed over and over. These thrown-away incidents are worth exploring in some detail:

In the book the hotel's elevators are cranky, threatening to stall between floors, and the ghosts use them at night, sometimes leaving behind scatters of confetti, party masks and trinkets. In the film blood once leaks from between an elevator's doors, which open to release a red flood so devastating we know it can't be real. (It is passed off as a hallucination of Wendy, Torrance's wife.)

The hotel has a topiary of hedge-animals which have a way of moving threateningly closer while you're not looking at them. I'm told that Kubrick spent a million trying to get this effect before throwing the leaf-beasts out. He replaced them with a hedge-maze that covers what looks like four city blocks. Wendy and Danny apparently find their way to its center and then out again with incredible ease — its scare-possibilities are never tapped. At the end of the film Torrance chases his son through it, but the boy easily escapes.

In a way the hero of the book is the black hotel-chef Hallorann, who gets a psychic SOS from Torrance's son Danny while he is 2,000 miles away in Florida; he races to the blizzarded-in hotel by airplane, car and snowmobile to rescue Danny and his mother. All this happens identically in the film until he arrives at the hotel, when Torrance hops out of a side corridor and kills him with one blow of an axe — bop! thus at one stroke throwing away an emotionally strong part of the novel, a good actor, and a carefully developed plot element in the film. Was ever a director as spendthrift as Kubrick?

A central climax in both book and film occurs when Danny comes terrified to his father and mother with a bruised throat and a frantic story of how a drowned old lady (ghost of a suicide, apparently) in a bathtub in one of the suites rose slopping from the water and tried to strangle him. Torrance goes to investigate. So far, film and book are pretty much alike.

In the book Torrance finds the bathroom apparently all in order, though the bathtub curtains are closed. With some trepidation he opens them, but finds nothing and the tub dry as the rest of the room. He starts to leave but is stopped by a *klirring* sound beind him. He turns to find the curtains have been swept shut, and sees silhouetted a figure rising behind them. He flees. This scared me, and would, I think, have worked equally well in the film.

In the movie Torrance sees a statuesque blonde young woman calmly bathing. He at once begins to grin, leer and slaver with the effect of a demented boy scout saying, "Gee, fellers, Sex!" But all is not lost. The young lady takes note of him, rises gravely from the tub, and approaches him gracefully. But there's something strange about her; her beauty is a sort of combination of Art Deco and Swedish Modern; she's not quite human or alive.

At this point Kubrick, who had been sparing of his apparitions in the earlier parts of the film, still had me, or at any rate I was still willing to be had, in spite of Torrance's imbecile antics.

Torrance embraces her tentatively and sees over her shoulder, in a mirror, his hand and arm that have gone around her back sinking into puffy, unlovely flesh. She transforms into a swollen ancient hag — she looks now like something out of *The Night of the Living Dead* or that gates-of-hell film, *The Sentinel* — and pursues him clumsily as he stumbles off in terror and sexual disappointment.

I think it was at this point Kubrick lost me for good.

Another touch straight out of B-minus horror flicks comes later when the 1920s ghosts haunting the grand ballroom are

shown briefly as skeletons amid draperies and furniture fes-
tooned with cobwebs and dust. (as with the blood-flood, it's
written off as another of Wendy's hallucinations.)

Now I can understand Kubrick being hesitant, and even unwilling, to put in unequivocally supernatural touches, wanting
to keep open alternate explanations dependent on mania and
hallucinatory visions. After all, these are modern times, and
nobody really believes in spooks and devils, do they? — just cruel
death and super-nastiness. But then why the B-minus horror
touches such as bedizened skeletons, and disgusting old female
zombies floundering around, hopping maniacs with axes, unexplained apparitions from King's original hotel of masked people
in animal suits or grinning in evening dress with their heads split
open, and the final touch of a photograph of the hotel's staff
decades ago with Torrance grinning out of the midst of it? Some
critics have said black comedy, but I think that's just clutching
at an Out. No, I think Kubrick saw the film going dead and
rather desperately resorted to these cheap stimulants.

For somewhat similar reasons — and because he's a gifted
director in spite of his incredible blind spots — Kubrick gives
Nicholson one sympathetic scene where Torrance assures his
son that he'll always love him and never hurt him — even as we
see the man's eyes and mind wandering away.

Shelley Duvall, an excellent eccentric actress who's done fine
things for Altman, does her best with the minor and even emp-
tier caricature of Torrance's wife Wendy, forever covering up
inadequately for her crazy dumb husband — and doing, whenever he moodily allows her, all the chores that ever get done
around the snowbound hotel.

The boy who plays Danny pedals and trots obediently
through the film for some time without insulting our intelligence, but then he's terrified into some sort of coma where his
imaginary-playmate alter ego takes over, saying in sepulchral
tones, "Danny's not here." He comes to his senses barely in time
for the final flight from papa, and the picture in its final stages
has to depend on flibberty-gibbet Wendy as its sole viewpoint
character. It's surely a dismal prospect she bears witness to.

Some people may say I'm just an author characteristically complaining "They didn't follow the book," not realizing that books and films are the products of different arts and have to achieve their effects in different ways, by different routes. That may sometimes be so, but in this case I certainly don't think so. Film's a visual art, yes, but that doesn't mean it has to eliminate reasoning altogether. Flashbacks and explanations can sometimes be very helpful, and there were a lot of good films, including fantasies and supernaturals, done with narrative voice-over, especially in the 1940s and 50s, though the *auteur* boys don't go for it much and Kubrick chose not to use those methods of giving reality to the hotel's evil past.

I don't know about that. But I do know that when *The Shining* terminated with Torrance's interminable frozen bellow, I rather surprised myself by adding on two loud boos.

Later I felt a bit ashamed about that — I've watched far worse films without crudely voicing my reaction. I think I was mostly *angry* then, as I am now, at the *waste*. A big young writer, a big actor, and a big big director: all of them contributing so much and achieving so little; leaning solicitously and clumsily, like unhappy elephants, over a big derailed film, while big successful recent films — like *The Exorcist*, *Jaws*, and *Alien* — orbit around them silently.

King had provided all the materials for a good horror film, but most of them were thrown away and the rest given an unfortunate satiric slant. Hopefully something better will come of the projected film, *Creepshow*, with King writing directly for the screen and George Romero directing.

❀ ❀ ❀

Tommy nodded, then smiled. He leaned forward and told her that he hated to dance. Would she like to go around and visit some of the other tables? Trepidation rose thickly in her throat, but she nodded. Yes, that would be nice. He was seeing to her. She must see to him (even if he really did not expect it); that was part of the deal. And she felt dusted over with the enchantment of the evening. She was suddenly hopeful that no one would stick out a foot or slyly paste a kick-me-hard sign on her back or suddenly squirt water in her face from a novelty carnation and retreat cackling while everyone laughed and pointed and catcalled.

And if there was enchantment, it was not divine but pagan

(momma untie your apron strings i'm getting big) and she wanted it that way.

— from Carrie

The Movies and Mr. King

by Bill Warren

IT WAS ONLY NATURAL that the movies and Stephen King would get together. His books are not only laden with references to movies, his writing is intensely cinematic. And he loves horror movies; he even knows something about them. King has said that *Carrie* somehow derived from *The Brain from Planet Arous*, a bizarre SF film of 1957. In *'Salem's Lot*, the characters learn how to combat vampires from Christopher Lee movies.

The thickest of King's books often seem like richly detailed novelizations of films. King constantly uses filmic devices, or literary devices in a cinematic way, his favorite being the flashback. In the middle of scenes set in the "present," King's characters will suddenly recall a drama from the past, and we see it in bits and pieces or in full, in a manner much like movie flashbacks. And as in cinema, when we return to the present, no time has passed.

He uses the equivalent of voice-over narration at times, typically in italicized phrases which pop into the middle of otherwise complete sentences. These sometimes have the feel of what's called a "shock cut," as a dissimilar and suprising shot "bursts" into another scene. In Chapter 1 of 'Salem's Lot, writer Ben Mears is daydreaming along a turnpike when a motorcycle suddenly cuts in front of him. One can imagine King playing this scene out in the movie theatre of his mind; it reads like script description.

Fractured elements of settings are used for narrative description by King, exactly the same kinds of elements that a skilled director might use for emphasis in movie story-telling. Later in the same novel, in the heroine's house, King begins a paragraph: "the windows were up, and a lazy forenoon breeze ruffled the yellow curtains in the kitchen." This is not only cinematic in style, it has much of the same effect that a similar scene element, glimpsed behind the characters, would have in the film; there's even a hint of sunlight ("forenoon," "yellow") that sounds like directions for a lighting cameraman.

King's frequently-shifting points of view, in his earlier novels, are also cinematic, functioning as a form of "intercutting," a device that King used in *The Shining,* when the three central characters lie awake in the Overlook Hotel, each thinking the others asleep.

King has also used a "camera pullback," and he almost literally describes it that way. In 'Salem's Lot, Ben Mears imagines a scene of a fish swimming around placidly: "Draw away for the long view," says King, "and there's the kicker: It's a goldfish bowl."

King's use in his books of brand names, real locations and authentic TV shows is well known; he does the same with films, often inventing phony movies to make points. The non-existent *Abbott and Costello Meet the Monsters* is mentioned in *The Shining*; in 'Salem's Lot, several phony Republic serials are referred to. Those "films" function simply as types; when King has need of a real film, he mentions it.

There are two qualities to King's writing that are distinctly non-movie, in different ways. First, of course, is the great length of his major novels (which are sometimes too long for the story King is telling). This made 'Salem's Lot notably difficult to translate into film; not only is that novel very long, it has an especially large number of characters. Few directors other than Robert Altman have shown any ability at following a large, shifting group of intersecting characters. In the case of *The Shining*, virtually all of the background material for the various characters, including the hotel itself, had to be jettisoned from the film; including it would have made the film far too cumbersome.

The other central element in most of King's novels which presents problems in filming is his emphasis on children as central characters (*The Stand* and *The Dead Zone* are exceptions).

But with *'Salem's Lot* and *The Shining*, adjustments were necessary, and they were not always successful. Lance Kerwin play's Mark in the 3½-hour TV movie of *'Salem's Lot*; this actor is at least 16, whereas in the book Mark was 12 (and either tall for his age, Chapter X — or small, Chapter X). In the book, Mark's devotion to his Aurora plastic models and monster movies is necessary to the plot and makes perfect sense; that's certainly the age that most monster movie fans become fascinated with the stuff (including me and, I presume, Stephen King). But to be so engrossed at 16, Kerwin, despite a good performance, seems almost retarded; his father's suggestions that he drop this passion seem like good advice in the film, but not in the book.

In Kubrick's film, *The Shining*, the changes were beneficial. The boy, played by Danny Lloyd, is much more like a real child in the movie than in the book. Having telepathic powers would make a child mature awfully fast in some ways, but for a five-year-old to use dialogue like "I swear to God," "I passed out" and "I came to" is not believable. King is much more successful treating Danny's internal life and his conflict with the hotel than he is in handling the dialogue. In the film, Danny says almost nothing, a wise decision and entirely believable.

I suspect that one of the primary reasons for King's enormous popularity is the movie-esque qualities of his books. He's a storyteller, not a stylist, and I would be anything but surprised to learn that he "sees" his books as movies while he's writing; as I said, they certainly read that way. His excellence as a writer of horror fiction is in getting us to see these "movies" ourselves; his weaknesses are almost always movie-like weaknesses, such as over-use of stereotyped characters. King is improving and maturing as a writer, and the stereotypes are becoming real Characters; But I can only hope that he retains this movie-like quality to his prose. He's the first major writer of horror fiction to adopt this approach.

Before I get into discussions of the films adapted from King's works, a mention of two screenplays I've read recently is in order. *Nightshift* is a script by George P. Erengis, written for Martin Poll Productions. Despite the title, it is not an anthology film drawn from King's fine collection of the same title. Instead, it is a perfectly dreadful script based on just one story from that book, "Strawberry Spring," by far the most conventional and, as far as I am concerned, least interesting story in the collection.

King's story, told in the first person, is about a series of gruesome, apparently motiveless murders taking place on a college campus. The story is only ten pages long, and is primarily a mood piece concluding with the narrator realizing that he himself is the killer. (Oddly, King uses "Springheel Jack," the name of a real London mass murderer.) The story isn't bad, but it is slim and is far from King's most successful piece of short fiction.

The screenplay is reprehensible, and we can all feel relieved that it wasn't filmed. Ergenis' script is also about multiple killings on a New England campus, but he populates it with trite conflicts (newcomer vs. established athlete; East vs. California; professor and student romance), lame comedy (a college reporter straight out of Archie), and absolutely no suspense at all. The killer—or killers—are obvious from the beginning. And he throws in black magic to no good end, plus a reference to the town of Jerusalem's Lot which violates the history King created for that town. This *Nightshift* would have been a standard, commonplace killer-with-a-knife film, and would have done King's reputation no good.

Contrasted with that screenplay is King's own *Creepshow*, which finished shooting late in December, 1981. King wrote this to be directed by George Romero, who made *Night of the Living Dead* and *Dawn of the Dead*, among others. King and Romero apparently became friends, and King appears as a bit player in Romero's interesting but overlong *Knightriders*. King is a gross, crude spectator at the mortorcycle jousts, and seems to be greatly enjoying himself. He also has a part in *Creepshow*.

The structure of *Creepshow* is the most interesting and amusing thing about the script; the series of stories are good but somewhat conventional. The stories are found in a comic book of the same title, tossed out by an overbearing father of a comic-loving kid. The camera moves in on an illustration, which becomes a scene from the next story. King has fun describing the ads in the comic.

He intended the film to be something of a tribute to the horror comics of the 1950s, especially those published by E.C. Comics. (There were two previous films adapted directly from those comics, "Tales from the Crypt" and "The Vault of Horror.") But King makes an error; except for "Something to Tide You Over," the stories he includes would not have seen print in E.C. Comics. They have no E.C. *comeuppance*. A common theme in virtually all the horror stories published by E.C. is revenge. The bad guy always gets his comeuppance — by fate, a walking corpse, or some detail he overlooked. Revenge is the main feature in the film, but it is usually enacted on the wrong character. The stories are good otherwise, especially "The Crate," a tour de force of grisly humor.

It's impossible to evaluate a film before it is even in rough-cut form, but "Creepshow" has the potential for being a scary and funny movie. Geroge Romero may not be the right director for this project; he's far too literal in his style, but his dogged realism may pay off. Time will tell.

The three novels of King's that have been filmed have had very different treatment. Two of the directors, Brian De Palma and Stanley Kubrick, are highly skilled craftsmen with distinctive styles (even if De Palma's seems heavily derivative of Hitchcock). The other film, *'Salem's Lot*, was made for TV by Tobe Hooper, an erratic director at best, and it is by far the weakest of the three.

The screenplay for *Carrie* was by Lawrence D. Cohen, and within the budget allowed by producer Paul Monash (who later scripted *'Salem's Lot* himself), it is an excellent adaptation of the novel. With a few minor changes (Carrie was fat in the novel), the film comes as close to *being* the book as any I have ever seen. De Palma's direction is among the best of his career, topped only by that for his finest film, *Phantom of the Paradise*. *Carrie* is a stunner, helped immeasurably by Sissy Spacek's perfect (and Oscar-nominated) performance in the lead The great success of the film helped make the book an even bigger seller in paperback; King's fame from the novel helped De Palma and Spacek, and the high quality of their film helped King's later novels reach greater sales. It seems unlikely that he would be so enormously popular if *Carrie* hadn't been such a worthy showcase, such a huge hit — the film broadened King's audience.

The opening scene in *Carrie* is among the most dreamily erotic ever in a mainstream film (topped perhaps only by the more romantic but somewhat similar opening scene in Peter Weir's *Picnic at Hanging Rock*). In *Carrie* the scene behind the titles is set in a high school girls' locker room, and surely must fulfill the wetdream fantasy of almost every boy who went to high school in the United States. Maro Tosi's slow, graceful camera drifts over these healthy young bodies (the scene is in slow motion). Breasts bounce gracefully by as the camera slowly moves in on Carrie herself, dreamily soaping in the shower. She is not well liked — a brief previous scene showed that — and it's clear that the shower is the only thing about gym class that she really enjoys. Until blood pours down her leg.

Spacek's all-out panic is deeply affecting. She is completely terrified and puzzled, she has no idea what is happening to her, she thinks she is dying. When she clutches helplessly at other students, she's only desperately seeking out assistance. But Carrie White is not liked, and all the students begin flinging Kotex and tampons at her shouting "Plug it up." Even Sue (Amy Irving), the "good girl" in the story, joins in but almost immediately regrets it.

The scene could have been comic, but Spacek's torment is too real, too deeply-felt by the character; we can't ignore it, we empathize with her. The rapidly moving camera and the swift intercuts as well as closeups of Carrie's tormentors and long shots of Spacek herself, emphasize the mob mind at work as well as Carrie's terror and isolation.

The flawless handling of this scene sets the tone for "Carrie." Throughout the film, Carrie's expectations — here, the thoughts of a lingering shower (no doubt waiting for the other girls to leave) — are completely upset, almost always by nasty Chris (Nancy Allen, who later married De Palma). It is as if Carrie really doesn't have the right to expect anything good for herself, it will always end in pain and humiliation. As King's sympathetic and cynical novel tells Carrie's story (in news clippings, interviews, etc.), this is simply the truth.

Poor Carrie has the deck stacked against her. She thinks she's not attractive, she's shy and not very bright, she's awkward, she's late in getting her period (and hadn't been told what to expect), she has one of the most hideous mothers in literature or film. It's no wonder that she develops telekinetic powers. King did his research well; "poltergeist" phenomena, such as those surrounding Carrie, traditionally occur in the homes of troubled adolescents. Carrie is far more troubled than most of those, so it's no wonder that her poltergiest manisfestations are so much more potent. In the film, De Palma's storytelling is clean and precise; at no point does Carrie ever say to anyone that she can move objects with her mind. We simply see Spacek doing it so convincingly that most viewers never even bother to look for the wires controlling the flying objects.

The only faltering in the story-telling is near the end. Sue, the good girl, has urged her boyfriend Tommy (William Katt) to take Carrie to the prom. Partly for reasons of his own, partly to comply with the request, he does. Sue, who didn't go, sneaks into the back of the gym to watch the results of her request. Unfortunately, until the scene in which she discovers the rope leading to the bucket of pig's blood that Chris plans to dump on Carrie, most audiences felt that Sue herself was in on the plot. De Palma failed to establish clearly enough that Sue was genuinely contrite about her part in tormenting Carrie. When she asks Tommy to take Carrie to the prom, it comes out of left field, Her affirmation later to the girl's P.E. teacher that she really is acting out of kindness is unconvincing, and feels as though it was meant to be.

Although the story of *Carrie* is basically well told, it is primarily a film of *sequences*, which I suppose is how De Palma prefers to work: most of his films are like that. In themselves the sequences are often very good, but they usually fail to coalesce into a whole. De Palma uses connective tissue between scenes — sounds, camera positions — but usually fails to think out and realize his films as a unit. Probably because he grew out of American "underground" filmmaking, and because his model is Alfred Hitchcock (whose films are also often made of great scenes), De Palma is not concerned with creating a unified whole.

There's a scene on a residential street in *Carrie* in which a little boy (De Palma's son) on a bike torments her. In a flash, Carrie knocks him over with her power. It's obvious that De Palma spent much time setting up the shot, with the trees stretching off into the background. But there's also extraneous material: the boy is riding in and out between the trees, even though we don't need to see so much of him. De Palma simply liked the looks of the scene and kept it.

The religious elements found in the book are treated in a similar iconographic way. Spacek and Piper Laurie (excellent as her repressed mother) have a good early scene in which the mother's domination and Carrie's growing rebellion are both well established. But that's all De Palma does with the situation. The visual element predominates in the rest of the scenes, not the character relationships. It isn't even clear that Carrie's mother comes to hate and fear her, once Carrie has established herself in control.

Carrie is put in a closet where she prays to a statue of Saint Sebastian which is full of darts and arrows. At the climax, Carrie's mother stabs her, and Carrie responds by telekinetically filling her mother full of knives. The result, of course, looks exactly like the statuette of Saint Sebastian; the camera pulls back slowly from Piper Laurie, pinned to a doorway, and later from the statuette to re-emphasize this (the hair on both is the same color). But what does this have to do with anything? Because Carrie remembered the statuette, she had to fill her mother full of knives the same way? We never see Carrie showing any real religious feelings herself, and she clearly hates being penned up in the closet; it seems out of character for her to exact such a matching form of revenge. This device amuses the director rather than providing further insights. It's an effective scene, but gimmicky.

De Palma is one of the few directors to pay homage to himself. In *Greetings*, one of his earliest feature-length films, there's a scene in which three friends try on clothes in a store (one is Robert De Niro); in *Carrie*, there's a very similar scene in which three friends pick out clothes for the prom. It has nothing to do with anything else in the picture; It adds nothing to our view of Tommy as a nice guy — that's clearly established in the scene in which he comes to Carrie's house — the scene exists solely for De Palma to play with it, and should have been left out of the film.

The interior of the White's house resembles a church, with peaked archways and dark wood. Why? Did Mrs. White make it look like that? Over the years did the house grow to resemble a church? This is not from the book and feels affected. It might have been more interesting if the house was a thoroughly typical ranch-style suburban home, but full of religious paraphernalia. In a church, one expects religious feelings: it's as if the house forced Mrs. White to act as she does.

There are amusing touches throughout, although there's less humor than in most of De Palma's other films. After Carrie uses her telekinetic powers to reassemble a mirror she had just shattered, her mother enters the room and the face of Jesus can be glimpsed in the mirror. Later, in a classroom, there is a deep focus shot: Tommy is in extreme closeup on the left, in clear focus; Carrie, also in focus, is in the back. This establishes a link between them before we know one will exist, and Spacek's eloquence shows at once that she has a tremendous crush on Tommy.

John Travolta, excellent as Chris' boyfriend Billy, is seen driving her around one night in a scene clearly inspired by *American Graffiti*. This adds little to the film, but the scene does go on to establish the peculiar relationship between Billy and Chris; he hates being dominated by her, but her sexual favors and the fact that she's a class act and he's a hoodlum make up for her repeatedly calling him a "dumb shit."

A major difficulty in *Carrie*, the novel and film, is the clichéd characterization, starting with Carrie herself. The despised person in class must be ugly, must be insecure, must come from a weird background. This is dictated by melodrama. Chris is a cliché, the richbitch brat who loves sensual pleasures. Minor characters, such as Sydney Lassick's poetry teacher and Chris' flunkies, are often total stereotypes. Norma (P. J. Soles) wears a baseball cap all the time, even to the prom, and whatever Chris does is okay with her. That's all the characterization she's given. But the film rises above these faults.

De Palma's emphasis on cinematic sequence at the expense of characterization and a richer narrative is almost justified, however, by the prom sequence. The build-up is careful and measured; Carrie's melting joy and hope that things will be different are almost palpable, thanks to Spacek. The swirling, colored dance concluding with Tommy's kissing Carrie is conventional. The use of slow motion as Carrie and Tommy walk to their rigged (in more ways than one) places of honor is both full of dreamy happiness and powerful tension. The slow motion emphasizes both splendidly.

After the blood spills on Carrie, things are a little confused. Is everyone really laughing at her, or is it all in Carrie's mind? What Carrie does to everyone in the gym — murder — seems less of a tragedy and more like justice if they are really laughing, but it's also unlikely that everyone would do so. The confusion may have been deliberate, to allow both feelings.

The use of split screen in this sequence, and the fine timing in the editing (cause and effect of Carrie's powers) create a scene of destruction that hasn't been equalled since (though some have tried — there was one direct imitation of *Carrie* called *Jennifer*, and several look-alike TV movies). Split screen is one of De Palma's favorite devices, and he's one of the few directors who knows what to do with it.

The finale, in which Carrie screws her house right into the ground, with herself and her dead mother in it, is bizarre and smacks of fantasy rather than the science fiction of the rest of the film. It's the only time when Carrie's powers seem literally limit-less.

Despite its shortcomings, *Carrie* got film adaptations of Stephen King works off to a fine start, and I for one was eagerly awaiting *'Salem's Lot*. In many ways, *'Salem's Lot* is my favorite of King's novels. I love vampires, for one thing, and especially the kind of humor the writer shows here.

The novel has a good deal of flavor of another popular book with a Maine location, *Peyton Place* (also the name of a town), and in fact could be regarded as a blending of Grace Metalious' notorious best-seller with a Hammer Films Dracula picture. Barlow, the vampire in *'Salem's Lot*, is essentially Count Dracula under another name; his description and his ability to grow younger are drawn from Stoker's novel. The town itself is full of its own kind of tensions, though they aren't primarily sex-ual as they were in *Peyton Place*, and also unlike that novel, in-come level is of little importance. Still, the interweaving of lives and the town itself resemble the earlier book, but with less melo-drama. Some of the characters and their relationships, such as Eva and Weasel, are treated by King with much sensitivity.

King's novel is ostensibly about Ben Mears, returned to Jeru-salem's Lot. He's now a fairly well-known author (he meets the heroine by noticing she's reading one of his novels), and has come back to the town because he spent much of his childhood there. But the book is actually about the town itself; Ben Mears is only one of several central characters. He and the boy Mark are more important because they are essentially one protagonist at two ages, and because, of the survivors of the vampire plague, they alone return to cleanse the town by fire, but the town is really the central character. This is one of the book's greatest virtues.

The best parts of King's novel occur after the arrival of Barlow the vampire, and before the death of Mark's parents. In this section, 'Salem's Lot gradually dies, and King is both amus-ing and scary in his detailing the attacks on various people, and what eventually they do when they become vampires them-selves. He makes the old superstition viable again in this section. It's about the death of the town, and King's attitude is a peculiar mixture of sorrow and glee. It is just this aspect, the depiction of a real-seeming community and its dying, that is almost totally absent from the TV movie.

Paul Monash's script blends several of the book's characters with justification and good results. Jimmy the doctor and Bill, the heroine's father, become one character in the film (played by Ed Flanders); a teenaged boy and Larry Crockett (Fred Willard in the film) become the lover of a cuckolded husband's wife. This is perfectly reasonable compression when one is adapting a novel into film. If shot as written, King's novel would have been considerably longer than what is commercially possible for television.

Some character relationships remain, such as Eva and Weasel (Marie Windsor and Elisha Cook Jr., cast because they were a married couple in Kubrick's *The Killing*). But most are dropped, as are virtually all scenes of vampires coming back from the dead. We see young Danny Glick floating outside Mark's window, and Mike (Geoffery Lewis, very good) comes back to haunt teacher Matt (Lew Ayers, likewise good). After that the only vampire we see, other than a few in the background (and in the long version, Ben's girlfriend Susan) is Barlow himself.

Monash's script emphasizes the soap opera elements of the plot. Much more time is spent on Larry Crockett's beddy-bye activities with his married secretary (Clarissa Kaye) than could possibly be justified except that this was made for television, and "smut" sells on TV like mad. At the expense of giving us a sensation of the gradual death of the town, Monash gives us grinning Fred Willard. It's not a fair trade.

The TV movie was directed by Tobe Hooper, who has yet to come near to fulfilling the chilling, extravagant promise of his first horror feature, *The Texas Chainsaw Massacre*. Hooper may simply not be suited to working within the Hollywood system. He was later taken off *The Funhouse* before completion, signed to but did not start *Venom*, and rumors have it that he actually may not have directed his most recent, *Poltergeist*.

In scenes of horror, Hooper is good. He has fun with slow buildups, light and shadow and a moving camera. He manages several effective sudden-shock scenes, including one with Barlow's hand at a cell door that's unlike anything I've seen before. He must have been under considerable strain as the long film had a very short production schedule; considering that the film can be admired in many ways. But Hooper is far less assured in the "straight" scenes, and it is embarrassing to watch David Soul (as Mears) and Kenneth McMillan (as the constable) struggle with their scenes together. Hooper seems to have been unable to give them suggestions, and their acting styles clash; Soul in particular looks helpless.

The best performance, not surprisingly, comes from James Mason as Straker, Barlow's front man. His threatening unctuousness is thoroughly professional and amusing; he even adds a dimension to the character that isn't in the book or the script. At one point, he looks as if he really isn't too happy to be setting up a small town for destruction by a vampire.

There's a clear indication at the end of the novel that Ben and Mark will be able to destroy all the vampires, but this hint is not in the film, neither in the short version called *'Salem's Lot The Movie*, nor in the original 3½-hour production (which will probably never be shown again). King does overlook, almost deliberately, the question that if vampirism can spread so rapidly and readily why aren't we up to our necks in vampires, and why hasn't the whole world gone vampire by now. These thoughts are more likely to occur to viewers of the films than readers of the novel.

Although the connection in the novel between Barlow and Hubie Marsten, the demonic gangster who built the wretched house that Barlow uses as headquarters, seems artificial and forced, I don't regret its inclusion — in the novel. It does make for some creepy flashbacks and a sense that somehow the house called to Barlow. In the film, the references were unnecessary and should have been dropped.

There is one central flaw in *'Salem's Lot* that almost destroys the film. Producer Richard Kobritz insisted that the head vampire, Barlow, be made up to resemble Max Schreck in F. W. Murnau's classic *Nosferatu*. (Kobritz was unaware that the film had just then been remade with Klaus Kinski in almost identical makeup.) In the novel, Barlow is depicted as a traditional Christopher Lee-esque vampire, with dialogue, personality, ego, the works. For the film, Kobritz decided that having the vampire be an inhuman beast resembling Nosferatu six weeks dead was a great idea. He was wrong.

The dialogue left in the film clearly establishes Barlow as a real person, or someone who looks like one. He's given a past and an involvement with Straker going back at least as far as 1943. But in his ghastly blue makeup, Reggie Nalder as Barlow looks artificial and inhuman; hence he isn't a character. He's so patently horrible that he's almost comic, and certainly doesn't seem like a menace except in a few scenes. (This change totally alters the intent of the deaths of Mark's parents, and makes the scene a puzzle.) I might add that to disguise Nalder in the extreme fashion used in the film is really gilding the lily. This talented actor has a scarred, wizened face already, and certainly doesn't need this makeup to look macabre.

In the novel, Mark kills Straker and Barlow seeks revenge. He has it, too, before he's destroyed. The book centers on a battle of wits between the vampire and the men (and boy) out to destroy him. But the film Barlow is just a roaring blue beast; after Straker is out of the way, Barlow is easily eliminated. Having a central vampire that isn't a character, just a thing, undercuts the film so badly it almost collapses.

Because of poor use of locale and a refusal to get into the life of the town, we already do not believe in the movie's 'Salem's Lot as a real living town, as we did in the book. To have a vampire that's such a ghastly monster that he couldn't walk down the street without causing panic only undermines the all-important willing suspension of disbelief. The problem with Barlow in the novel is that he's too traditional a Dracula-type vampire; in the film, he isn't human *or* Dracula-like. Although both King and Kobritz erred, in different directions, Kobritz's failure was greater by far.

'Salem's Lot did not do well in the ratings. It was later cut to less than two hours; the result seems like illustrations for King's novel rather than a full story in itself. This was released theatrically overseas, and plays on U. S. cable TV channels. It's jumpy

and erratic, and I cannot imagine it made much money in foreign theatres. It's the least of the Stephen King films.

When Stanley Kubrick bought the rights to King's novel *The Shining*, the author was quite happy. However, when he saw the film his reaction was different. While agreeing (in *Danse Macabre*) that the film retains Kubrick's brilliance, to King it was "a maddening, perverse and disappointing film."

Each to their own. King thought the ghastly movie of *The Amityville Horror* was "a classic," and regards the disappointing, misconceived *The Stepford Wives* very highly indeed. Myself, instead of considering *The Shining* maddening or perverse, I found it not only a good adaptation of a very good novel, but a challenging, vital horror movie. It is a little disappointing; I'd expected Kubrick to be far more unrelenting, but it's still an outstanding film, ranking above *A Clockwork Orange* but well below *2001* in Kubrick's genre films.

The major difference between King's novel and Kubrick's film has a much to do with budget and difficulty of realization as with a difference in approach. In the novel, some of the best-remembered and most effective scenes involve the hotel's topiary animals: lions, a dog and other beasts sculpted out of living shrubs. They move when you're not looking at them, and the scenes in which, unwatched, they creep up on Jack Torrance and later Danny are powerful. (King goes much too far, however, in having one of them attack Hallorann, the black cook riding to the rescue at the end. The animals are much scarier as shrubs that move when you're not looking; when one does move, it is reduced to a mere lion.) Kubrick did not include these animals; several reasons for this have been proposed, but the main one was probably expense. He would have had to have many poses for each animal, sculpted and fitted into the artificial snow repeatedly. Furthermore, he may have surmised that what works in print would not work on screen. (Example: At the end of the novel, Jack Torrance, now totally possessed by the evil spirit of the Overlook Hotel, uses a roque mallet to smash his own face into an unrecognizable mess. That teeters on the edge of unacceptability in the novel; to have actually seen it would have raised gales of laughter in any audience, no matter how well it was done.)

So Kubrick used a hedge maze instead. One suspects that a major reason he used a maze was to enable himself to indulge in his lust for long tracking shots: the camera backing away from characters walking toward it, or following them as they walk away, generally in corridors. But the maze also functions as a metaphor for Jack's twisting mind, and works well at the end as the howling Jack, armed with a fireaxe, chases little Danny through the angles of the maze.

Most of the changes were matters of compression. King emphasizes a wasp's nest (placid on the outside, horrid on the inside, a metaphor for the Overlook and for Jack) that Torrance finds while repairing the roof of the hotel, but Kubrick doesn't include it. King also pays a great deal of attention to Jack's childhood, and to Wendy's relationship with her mother. The former plays a part in the story, the latter does not, and seems extraneous. In any event, Jack's past is only peripherally treated in the film, but then again, it doesn't need to be dwelled on much in a visual medium. When you see people moving, can hear their voices, can notice their physical responses, you don't need so much background as you do when they exist only as words on a page. Other than awkwardly presented flashbacks, there really isn't a good way to get this material in.

In the book, Tony, Danny's repressed precognitive and telepathic self, is seen by Danny as a real boy, and he finally learns that Tony is himself several years later. In the movie, Tony is "a little boy who lives in my mouth," says Danny, and talks through Danny's finger, which wiggles in time with the words.

In the book, Wendy is blonde, intelligent, a knockout. In the movie, she is plain, average, winsome Shelley Duvall. This change was to make her seem more vulnerable, and she does as soon as you see her. Duvall is an excellent actress, and she makes you feel Wendy's loneliness, isolation and dependence. This makes her battle with Jack at the climax more chancy, hence more effective and frightening.

Kubrick removed the novel's early and frequent references to "redrum," a word Danny is "told" by Tony; he replaces it with an astonishing scene of a flood of blood sluicing down around elevator doors in a hallway at the Overlook, which Danny has yet to see in person. Not only is this more effective visually, but it avoids one awkwardness King created. King establishes clearly that Tony "hears" people when they think, because sometimes he gets the spelling wrong. So why does he see "redrum" spelled that way? It is probably obvious to all but the most dense readers that the word is "murder" spelled in reverse anyway. Kubrick uses the word only briefly, and with it caps the frequent use of mirrors he's employed throughout the film.

The most significant change between the book and the film is the target of the Overlook's evil. In the novel, King makes it very clear, while holding back for suspense, that the hotel's evil spirit is after Danny, to kill him, then retain his spirit and his powers for more mischief in the future. In the film, Jack Torrance (Jack Nicholson) is clearly the target, partly because Danny's powers have been de-emphasized (although they aren't overwhelmingly important in the novel), and perhaps partly to avoid plunging Danny Lloyd into on-screen horrors. Children's agencies prevent using children in horror scenes in movies made in England.

Hallorann, warmly played by Scatman Crothers, is killed by Jack the moment he arrives at the hotel in the snowcat. In the book he survives and, in an epilogue, is shown to have formed a close relationship with Wendy and Danny. (I suspect, based on internal evidence in the novel, that *King* originally planned to kill Hallorann himself; Hallorann has a foreshadowing of his own death, for one thing.) I think Kubrick killed Hallorann to show that all bets are off: Those who read the novel would be surprised by this turn of events. Others would see that Jack is definitely capable of murder, and is quite likely going to kill his wife and child. The tone of the film does not promise an upbeat ending. (In fact, the actual ending was slightly more grim than now shown in the film; originally, there was a final scene in a hospital as Ullman visits with Wendy, who is back to normal, and Danny, who definitely isn't. This was removed after initial screenings.)

King's novel ends satisfactorily but conventionally; he burns the hotel down in a Roger Corman-Poe movie holocaust. In

Kubrick's ending, the hotel is still there, awaiting future caretakers.

In other ways, much of the adaptation is remarkably close. Kubrick and Diane Johnson, his co-writer, must have been very fond of King's dialogue, as they use a great deal of it, particularly in the important scenes in which Jack talks to an imaginary or ghostly bartender (Joe Turkel) and to the ghost of Delbert Grady (Philip Stone). The scenes are shorter in the film, but almost all of the dialogue is lifted directly from the novel.

Many of the incidents are also taken from the novel, although Kubrick adds more visual touches than the book had, such as Torrance banging a ball around the halls of the Overlook. (The ball later rolls up to Danny, and there's no one else around.)

Stanley Kubrick is one of the world's great filmmakers, and *2001* is the best movie I have seen. Since Kubrick is a sardonic man who tends to make cold movies somewhat devoid of emotion, I was afraid that his film of *The Shining* might be *the* most terrifying horror movie, because Kubrick would show his audiences no mercy.

That scary it isn't, and may not frighten some at all, because its best scares are new, and more in the mind than physical. Kubrick's conventional horror scenes have little impact. It's in the tension and implications that Kubrick brings off his best effects. I found it brilliantly frightening and tense, and Jack Nicholson gives one of his best performances; and yes, it is broad. He's totally immersed in the role of a frightened man going completely insane, and Kubrick has brought out the best in a fine and versatile actor. This was done at great pains to both of them; Nicholson told me he gave Kubrick the most he was willing to give. It's the most I've seen him give to any of his directors so far.

When horror movies and plays were first produced, the emphasis was on dangerous people and what they might do. Most of the great silent horror movies are about lunatics, not about undead creatures. (*Nosferatu* is an exception). Eventually, however, this idea slipped away, to be replaced by scary *things* rather than scary *people*. The climax of this trend may have been *Alien*, with its inhuman dreadnaught of a menace.

In *The Shining*, Kubrick puts horror movies back to square

one. King's novel had strong fantasy elements—the title refers to the ESP powers possessed by Danny and by Dick Hallorann, the cook at the Overlook Hotel, which has a lengthy horrible history and is itself possessed by evil. (In the movie version the hotel is located on the site of an Indian burial ground.) Jack Torrance in the film may actually be going crazy, but at the same time the ghosts are absolutely real: they unlock the pantry to free Jack.

The explanation for what's going on comes from a passage in the novel.

> Here in the Overlook all times were one. There was an endless night in August of 1945, with laughter and drinks and a chosen shining few going up and coming down in the elevator, drinking champagne and popping party favors in each other's faces. It was a not-yet-light morning in June some twenty years later, and the organization hitters endlessly pumped shotgun shells into the torn and bleeding bodies of three men who went through their agony endlessly. In a room on the second floor a woman lolled in her tub and waited for visitors.

Later, Jack Torrance realizes that "all the hotel's eras were together now." And, in book and film, Grady tells him that "you've *always* been the caretaker." In Kubrick's picture, the Overlook is not destroyed, and Jack Torrance's spirit is absorbed into the evil past of the hotel. He has always been the caretaker, like Grady always has been a waiter. Apparently the hotel is filling all niches gradually, perhaps even redundantly. Everything exists at once, and the hotel is kind to those it kills: at the film's end, we see a photo on the wall of the hotel. It's dated July, 1921, and shows us a happy, smiling and younger Jack Torrance, now at one with the hotel.

In the movie, the fantasy elements have been diminished by Kubrick and Johnson, but not eliminated. Danny's ESP is basically reduced to his getting clues from Tony about (a) the Overlook and (b) his father. He repeatedly sees Grady's two angelic girls, the daughters he hacked to pieces — and once Danny sees them lying in pools of gore. He also sees that arresting shot of the elevators pouring blood. (At the climax, while in extremes of terror, Wendy is pushed into having "the shining" herself, and she sees scenes from the hotel's past as well as the elevators gushing blood.) And Danny does call Hallorann across the country; no voice is used here, Danny sends the old man hideous images. Danny is terrified of the Overlook, and his powers provide some of the film's most shocking scenes.

After Jack has begun to be possessed by the hotel, Danny knows something evil is happening. He sits on his father's lap uneasily (in another scene featuring a mirror), reading his father's most secret thoughts of death. Not long before, the two girls tell Danny they want him to play with them "for ever and ever and ever." Jack tells Danny he wants to stay at the Overlook "for ever and ever and ever," exactly echoing the girls' phrase. From then on, Danny is always frightened.

As I said, Kubrick and Johnson have placed the film's emphasis on the disintegration of Jack Torrance's mind. In his very first scene, Torrance is already clearly a disturbed and frightened man, clutching at his sanity and this (perhaps last) job offer. The job has come to represent his sanity itself. When the unctuous Ullman (Barry Nelson), a character much like *2001*'s Heywood Floyd in his organization-man bland cheerfulness (and unlike the more stereotyped Ullman in the novel) tells Jack about the previous caretaker's little indiscretion, Jack grins too easily and says it won't happen to him.

Which brings up another point: Never underestimate Stanley Kubrick's proficiency as an intellectual wise-ass. *All* his films are laden with ironic humor. *The Shining* is certainly no exception. The bartender scenes, drawn from the novel, are presented with unique and edgy humor. Jack has gone batty, all right, but he's enjoying himself with byplay with Lloyd the bartender. He tells Lloyd he wouldn't hurt Danny. "I love the little son of a bitch," Jack says. Nicholson's face is lit from below here, and his tension, enjoyment and anger mingle to produce one of the most fascinating scenes in the film.

Near the climax, as Jack hacks his way into the room (a scene borrowed from the novel of *'Salem's Lot*) where his utterly terrified wife Wendy is cowering, he pokes his face into the crack and cries, "Heere's Johnny!" His face is that of a lunatic clown.

Jack Torrance is a failed teacher and would-be writer — in the book, he has been moderately successful — who accepts a job as winter caretaker at the Overlook Hotel in the Colorado mountains. For five months, he and his family will be the only people at the hotel. Partly because of his own paranoia and partly because of the supernatural evil infesting the hotel, Jack slowly begins to go mad. He's quite aware of this — early on he says he felt like he has been at the hotel many times — and for a while, he tries to fight it. But finally, gratefully, he gives in to the seductive powers of the hotel and the madness in his own mind. He was the weakest of the three, and the hotel seizes on this, providing him with imaginary booze — he had been a drunk — a fantasy Jack clutches to allow him to think his drift into madness is simple drunkenness, but he's drunk only in his mind.

In some hands, that story could be awful. Kubrick's handling makes it potent. It's slow getting under way, and is divided rather irritatingly into little chapters ("A Month Later," "Tuesday," "8 AM," etc.), as if Kubrick wants to ease audiences gradually into the icy horror he has prepared. More than most directors, Stanley Kubrick not only respects the intelligence of his audiences, he *demands* intelligence of them. Sometimes, as with *Barry Lyndon*, this may be asking too much. And there are those who have missed what goes on in *The Shining*, who simply cannot understand what happens at the end.

The picture is an elegant, graceful and hypnotic production, not words ordinarily applied to horror films. Part of the elegance lies in the handling of the expensive sets. Hotels are essentially huge volumes of empty space enclosed by high walls, and Kubrick utilizes this fact to the fullest. There are his usual tracking shots as Danny rides his tricycle through the hotel halls (amusingly going thrumm thrumm RUMBLE RUMBLE thrumm thrumm as he rides from carpeting to floor and back again), as Jack lurches about mumbling to himself, as Wendy scampers in terror. This hotel set is gigantic and very impressive (the exterior is, in long shots, Timberline Lodge on Mt. Hood in Oregon, the interior is apparently derived from the Ahwanee Hotel in Yosemite Valley) but it's Kubrick's ability that makes it seem haunted by sardonic ghosts.

The picture is not all it could have been. A terrifying chase through the snowy hedge maze with Jack lurching after Danny builds toward a climax of horror that never comes. The accumulated tension is not resolved. A final shot of Nicholson's frozen corpse is intended as the final crash of horror, but simply does not work.

The movie is probably too long by about twenty minutes, and Jack's conversation with Grady's ghost goes on too long. A key sequence in the novel — the woman in the bath — would seem to have been perfectly designed for filming, and is one of the scariest things I've read, but Kubrick alters the intent and kills the fright completely. It's still interesting, though. The hotel here has become literally seductive, with a beautiful girl replacing the rotting thing that Danny saw. Jack's tiny spark of remaining sanity makes him see the sexual vision as one of suppurating horror. But the scene simply fails to scare. A cackling old lady is still just a cackling old lady, even if she is naked and rotting.

Nicholson's performance bothers many, who think he should have been more restrained, that he shows no discipline. But that's preposterous. His performance *is* disciplined, and he's playing a madman — but he isn't stupid. He is, in fact, more dangerous because he's a smart lunatic; and perhaps the most disquieting thing of all, he hasn't lost his sense of humor. In fact, in his slavering, grinning and capering performance, Nicholson is scary and funny at the same time and for the same reasons, something very daring to try and very difficult to achieve. The only other horror film I can think of that tried it was Rouben Mamoulian's *Dr. Jekyll and Mr. Hyde* with Fredric March's hilarious and horrifying Mr. Hyde.

Nicholson does not pull out all the stops; that would be unrestrained, uncontrolled acting. Nicholson is, in fact, in total control all the time. (Or Kubrick was; on many scenes, he shot over 80 takes.) It is a very carefully judged performance and, I suspect, Kubrick had Nicholson play it broader than the actor would have on his own. Yes, he's clearly nuts from the start —

that's why Kubrick cast him. Nicholson's peculiar eyes make him look a shade crazy all the time, and his intensity of concentration confirms this.

If the film is not a masterpiece — and I don't think it is — it is still one of the most brilliantly concieved and intelligently executed horror movies ever made. There are certainly some sequences of more standard horror within the novelty: Wendy sees a man in an animal suit performing oral sex on someone, a man with a split head toasting her (both scenes come from the novel), and a lobby full of nonchalant skeletons looking at magazines. (The conventionality of that is explained by a casual description of Wendy as a horror movie buff.)

But there are some genuinely scary ideas that are new, and which don't come from the novel. Eventually, when Tony takes over entirely from Danny, there's a chilling moment as, in Tony's gutteral voice, he tells Wendy, "Danny can't wake up, Mrs. Torrance."

But the scariest scene in the film is an intellectual shock. For a month after their arrival at the Overlook, Jack hasn't been able to write anything, and then he begins to type day and night, using old scrapbooks for references, becoming furious when Wendy enters the room, disturbing his concentration. Unknown to the frightened Wendy, Jack is talking to Grady, while she reads his manuscript. To her horror and ours, she discovers that Jack's painfully wrought pages (she flips through at least 40, most of which we don't see) consist of the same phrase repeated endlessly. "All work and no play makes Jack a dull boy." After Jack has a nightmare in which he cuts Danny and Wendy up into little pieces, we have a good idea what Jack's "play" is going to be. And we know that Jack's mind has snapped after the first month.

But the majority of the terror of *The Shining*, which is so tense that my legs were shaking as I stood when the light came up, derives from the basis of real horror: the face of a madman. Kubrick and Nicholson have given us a horror film like no other since *Psycho* (also about a madman). Audiences did not scream at *The Shining* as they did at Hitchcock's film, but respond they did. It is among the ten most profitable films ever released by

Warner Bros., although unaccountably it has gotten a reputation as a flop.

Some critics had great difficulty with the film. One asked: Why does a man who killed himself in 1970 appear in the garb of a butler at a 1921 Fourth of July party? The character says it himself — he has *always been* at the hotel.

The complaints of the critics and much of the audience sounded a great deal like those made about *2001*, when people found themselves helpless in the face of a new approach to telling movie stories. But that film has proved to be the most influential motion picture since *Citizen Kane*. That hasn't happened with *The Shining*, nor is it likely to, but it is an intelligent, richly conceived and hypnotic horror movie.

Stephen King's novels are cinematic partially because the author himself is so fond of movies. Perhaps King's disappointment with *The Shining* lies in that it is not the film he would have made, the movie he saw in his head while writing. Perhaps in time he can readjust his opinion and regard it as another man's variation on his theme. It is the best movie yet made from a Stephen King book, and one of the best horror movies ever made.

From his right, that soft sound again, falling clumps of snow. He looked over and saw the other two lions, clear of snow now down to their forepaws, side by side, about sixty paces away. The green indentations that were their eyes were fixed on him. The dog had turned its head.

(It only happens when you're not looking).

—*from* THE SHINING

Stephen King:
Horror and Humanity
For Our Time

by Deborah L. Notkin

HORROR FANTASY CAN BE PRESUMED to be as old as the first story-telling cultures, but it has never been so prevalent nor so overt as it is today. In a sense, its visibility weakens its powers. Legends once whispered over fires late at night, with extreme care taken to prevent eavesdropping by the wrong spirits, are now the stuff of daytime TV reruns. Today's media-wise audience knows that the werewolf's slavering jaws are a triumph of the make-up artist, that the screaming maiden is being paid Equity scale and that the gore is not blood but catsup. Vampires have become an erotic cliché; ghosts and witches are figures of fun in TV sitcoms and children's comic books. Late night horror movies are practically comic relief from the grim reality of the 11:00 o'clock news. Yet, rather than relaxing in the pleasure of having archetypal fears reduced to the false, the funny and the familiar, our society seems engaged in a desperate search for some sort of horror fantasy at which we cannot laugh.

Such horror in real life is, of course, everywhere. Screaming newspaper headlines and graphic television news films bring every terrorist attack, border skirmish, technological near-disaster or other threat into our living rooms. There are no safe places in which we can ignore the precipice on which we live. In this context, horror *fantasy* takes on an almost comforting aspect:

> When the machines fail. . . . when the technologies fail, when the conventional religious systems fail, people have got to have something. Even a zombie lurching through the night can seem pretty cheerful compared to the existential comedy/horror of the ozone layer dissolving under the combined assault of a million fluorocarbon spray cans of deodorant. (*The Mist*, Chapter 10)

Stephen King has achieved unprecedented popularity as a writer of horror fiction, largely because he understands the attraction of fantastic horror to the denizen of the late 20th century, and because, paradoxical though it may sound, he has reassurance to bring us. For whether he is writing about vampires, about the death of 99 percent of the population, or about innocent little girls with the power to break the earth in half, King never stops emphasizing his essential liking for people. He does not, of course, paint a rosy picture of a loving and flawless human race; he simply focuses, again and again, on people doing the right thing in difficult situations, on people who behave slightly better than we expect. The overwhelming impression to be gained from reading King's books is that the kinks and the sadists are the exception, not the rule. In these novels, the average person is reasonably honest, caring and upright, and can be relied upon in most circumstances — not a fashionable concept, these days, but one which has obvious attractions for contemporary audiences.

Although King's six novels discussed here reflect the author's essential respect for his characters, they otherwise fall neatly into two groups. To use a distinction that King himself has articulated three are about evil and three are about EVIL. This concept is formulated in the musings of Father Callahan, an aging Catholic priest:

> He wanted issues and battle lines and never mind about standing in the cold outside supermarkets hand-

> ing out leaflets about the lettuce boycott or the grape
> strike. . . . But there were no battles. There were only
> skirmishes of vague resolution. And EVIL did not
> wear one face but many, and all of them were
> vacuous and more often than not the chin was slicked
> with drool. (*'Salem's Lot*, Chapter 6, section 9)

Father Callahan is granted his desire for battle lines, and eventually succumbs because the strength of his faith and his Christian symbols are not equal to the sheer evil power of the vampire he confronts. He can be found in *'Salem's Lot*, which, along with *The Shining* and *The Stand*, describes clear-cut contests in which the representatives of good are human, mortal and vincible while EVIL (or at least its leadership) is supernatural, well-protected and very easy to identify. *Carrie*, *The Dead Zone* and *Firestarter*, on the other hand, are books focusing on humans with supernatural talents (not clearly labeled as either "good" or "evil"), fighting the "skirmishes of vague resolution" which are much more familiar to contemporary folk than the battles in the other three books, and hence somewhat less romantic. Interestingly enough, King began with one of the "wild talent" books, followed it with the three books where the villains are clearly nonhuman, and then returned, with sharpened skills and a greatly increased audience, to the examination of cloudier issues. King's later books demand far more judgement and ethical analysis from his readers than his earlier books do — a trend that I earnestly hope will continue.

'*Salem's Lot*, the only one of King's novels which pits his characters against a traditional evil, is particularly rich in the author's affection for his characters. No human characters in the book can be described as worse than unpleasant — and even the unpleasant few are minor, and generally necessary pivots for the plot. The heroine's mother is hyper-conventional and unsympathetic (and forms the background for the romance); the cuckolded husband is almost comically over-jealous (and the tensions he creates draw the reader's attention away from the mounting threat of the vampire); and the realtor has his eye too much on the main chance (and without him the vampire could not have bought the Marsten house). Hubert Marsten, long since dead at the beginning of the story, is painted as thoroughly rotten, but we have reason to believe he may have been corrupted by the same vampire who is now bringing evil to the town. Additionally, Marsten's house has a miasma of its own, of a sort which King examined much more thoroughly in *The Shining*, which could easily be responsible for the misery of those who dwell therein.

King's love for his characters, however, is not demonstrated merely in the negative sense of not hating them. *'Salem's Lot* is, in fact, more of an unconventional love story than it is a horror story, and this fact about the book's nature is more clearly revealed by its structure. The book begins with a flashforward sequence which partakes of the character of a love poem, an abstract and precisely written fragment of the tale of a young boy and a man who is not his father. The bond between these two is unexplained and indisputable. Such non-familial, non-sexual love relationships are rare in literature and rarer still in genre fiction. When the prologue is over and the main plot develops in the more familiar boy-meets-girl fashion, the reader *already knows* that this relationship is not the focus of the author's attention. By beginning (and ending) the book with Ben and Mark, King reinforces the importance of their relationship and their common humanity. Their bond becomes more important than the vampires, more important than the typical romantic love story. By the flashforward technique of showing us that bond after the battle is over, King emphasizes the often-overlooked benefits of living through the very worst of situations. Terror becomes a force which forges bonds though its purpose is to break them, which teaches love even while it loosens bowels. King holds out the hope that, if fear doesn't kill you, it leaves you with something invaluable which you could not otherwise attain.

Where *'Salem's Lot* is a more-or-less traditional vampire novel (at least the villains are familiar), *The Shining* is a maverick haunted-house story. It may well be the only ghost story ever written where the ghosts could be entirely excised and the story not significantly changed. Like *'Salem's Lot, The Shining* is short on less-than-admirable human characters—the worst of them is Ullman, the manager, a petty bureaucrat who has nothing to do with the main action. There is a great deal that is likeable about the main character, Jack Torrance, despite his alcoholism, his uncontrollable temper (which at one point leads him to break his two-year-old son's arm), and his inability to retain a job or make a success of his writing career. Once Jack and his family are isolated for the winter in the snowbound Overlook Hotel, the pressures that come to bear upon them are far from completely supernatural. Jack may glibly declare that he and his family are too sophisticated to fall prey to "cabin fever," but King wants us to realize that Jack could easily be fooling himself. If the hotel were not malevolent, if the boy were not telepathic, Jack's deterioration, loss of self-control and eventual destruction could still take place. This, of course, is why it takes Wendy Torrance so long to perceive that more than just her husband's weakness is at work. The hotel merely provides enticement and color for Jack's descent into hell; the descent itself has been prefigured throughout his life. King's involvement with his characters is never so evident as in his portrayal of Jack — a weak man, striving to be better than he is, forgivable despite everything. By making Jack a writer, King gives himself a chance to express this directly: ". . . he liked all of his characters, the good and the bad. He was glad he did. It allowed him to try and see all of their sides and understand their motivations more clearly." (Chapter 32.) In fact, one of the manifestations of Jack's loss of humanity is that he *stops* sympathizing with some of the characters in his own writing.

The relationship between Danny Torrance and Dick Hallorann, the black cook, contains an interesting echo of the relationship between Ben and Mark which unifies *'Salem's Lot.* Once again, King departs from the normal fictional portrayal of parent/child interactions to make the point that affinity and understanding are neither an innate property of parenthood nor antithetical to family situations. Both Danny and Mark love their parents, yet both have whole sides of their nature that their nature that their parents are completely incapable of comprehending. When an author portrays children as human beings in their own right, it is not at all surprising when they form bonds with people who are not their parents, nor even their parents' friends. These bonds, throughout King's work, are formed out of human responses rather than artificial age divisions, and help to make both the child characters and the books themselves more plausible and more interesting. *The Shining*, once again, ends with the bonds formed by such human responses, after affirming (through the self-sacrifice of Dick Hallorann) King's belief that people *will* risk their lives for one another.

In *The Stand*, King's longest and most ambitious novel, all of the ghost and vampire trappings are discarded to reveal the plain, ungarnished EVIL. *The Stand* is really two books: It begins with a short "novel" in which the author disposes of 99 percent of the world's population by means of a rapidly mutating flu virus accidentally released by the U. S. armed forces. This section is written in familiar disaster-novel, bestseller style and focuses in graphic detail on the experiences of several individual flu victims. By the time the epidemic is over, the reader feels as though she personally witnessed all the deaths. Having cleared the world of extraneous population and thus of interfering societal problems, King is now free to set the stage for his second part: a Tolkienesque battle between good and evil. Good is personified by Mother Abagail, who is quintessentially human. She is old but not immortal, wise but not infallible, kind, loving and closer to God than most of us, but suffering from the pains of false teeth and acid indigestion. Evil, in contrast, is Randall Flagg — the Dark Man, the Walkin' Dude. Flagg, though he appears human, has supernatural powers. He can inhabit the body of an animal, can travel large distances apparently instantaneously, and, before the plague "never spoke at rallies because the microphones would scream with hysterical feedback and circuits would blow." (Chapter 17.) Flagg controls his followers, as a rule, with inducements to power and incitements to greed, but he has more deadly ammunition available, should his troops get out of hand. Mother Abagail cannot (and would not) control her flock, but instead offers suggestions which carry no more strength than that of her conviction and her persuasiveness. Good thus becomes a human attribute and evil one dominated from elsewhere. To defect from good to evil is a simple act of will; to leave evil for good is at best extremely dangerous and at worst literally impossible. By setting up the dichotomy in this fashion, King guarantees that all the followers of evil will be forgivable, and all the followers of good admirable. For evidence of this, we need only look at Flagg's army: Trashcan Man is lonely, retarded and crazed by persecution in his childhood; Lloyd Henreid is a man whose loyalty was bought in the most extreme circumstances (while he was literally starving to death in an abandoned jail cell); and Harold Lauder has all of the limitations and constraints of the hyper-bright adolescent, compounded by misinformation and intense stress. Harold is, in fact, the prime example of King's tenderness towards his characters. Even while Harold is writing acid hatred into his diary, plotting to kill his colleagues while hypocritically working with them, and planning his glorious entrace into Flagg's camp, King continues to treat him with not only indulgence, but respect and comprehension. Finally, it is King's unwillingness to place blame anywhere but on Flagg or to leave Flagg with any trace of humanity which makes *The Stand*, though engrossing, too simplistically structured for a successful novel. It is, however, this same simplicity which makes this book the most obvious example of King's faith in humanity and in the eventual triumph of love over its apparently stronger opponent.

King's first published novel was *Carrie*, the only novel in which he experiments with a fragmented, journalistic style (though most of his books use more than one viewpoint). *Carrie* lacks a unifying narrative thread; in fact, more than half of the book is "excerpts" from fictitious books or newspapers dealing with the incidents in question. It is a wild talent novel, the story of an outcast adolescent who discovers her own telekinetic ability. As in his other wild talent books, King rests the responsibility for violence in human beings rather than in outside forces, but not in an obvious fashion. He makes the possessor of the talent sympathetic, likable and threatened by the realities of the world — and therefore makes the use of that talent protective rather than arbitrary. Carrie White strikes a responsive chord in any reader who ever considered himself a misfit (and which of us did not?). Carrie's situation is, of course, extreme. She is burdened by her mother's extraordinary religious fundamentalism, which prevents the young girl from sharing any of her schoolmates' activities or interests. When she discovers her power, she uses it for nothing more reprehensible than finessing her mother into granting permission for her to attend the school dance. Her mother's actions are close to unforgivable, but they result from enslavement to a belief system which she cannot escape, a religion which has trapped her even more conclusively than it has victimized her daughter. Eventually, of course, Carrie does go to the prom, and the focus of villainy shifts from her mother to her schoolmates. Chris Hargensen and Billy Nolan, instigators of the practical joke which sets off the tragedy, are small minded and cruel, but Billy can be partially excused on the grounds of terminal stupidity and Chris is merely young and spoiled. We might be more inclined to blame Chris if we weren't shown a short (and otherwise gratuitous) scene with her father — a difficult man to live with. King seems to have been striving very hard in this book for the sense that everyone in it was caught in a trap not of her own making. Unfortunately, King chose to focus his story around the behavior of adolescent girls (perhaps because most poltergeist activity is attributed to that group), and he didn't adequately convey an understanding of his subject. He lsoes his grip fairly early in the book with lines like "Maybe there's some kind of instinct about menstruation that makes women want to snarl" (a line spoken by a woman) (Part One). Also, he never quite succeeds in convincing the reader of the book's essential plot pivot: we *must* accept Sue Snell's sacrifice of her prom date to Carrie's happiness, and we don't. This isn't essentially implausible, as teenagers are especially prone to grand gestures and high moral impulses, but King just doesn't provide enough background and motivation about Sue to make it work. Probably he would do so more successfully now. This early work, however, is notable mainly for its sense of kindness to the outcast and its stress on the durability of love. The scene in which Carrie and her mother face each other in ultimate torment, still loving each other very powerfully, forecasts the sort of strong emotional writing that King has since produced.

The Dead Zone is the book where King's wild talent format

comes into its own. For this article, it provides the exception that proves the rule: it contains the only thoroughly evil, totally unexcused human character in any of King's novels. Greg Stillson is sadistic, power hungry, randomly cruel, and inescapably terrifying. The protagonist, however, is John Smith (a name that conjures up Everyman as assuredly as Nick Andros' name does in *The Stand*) and he is everything that Stillson is not: gentle, caring, nonviolent and thoughtful. He recovers mentally as well as physically from four years in a coma, from losing a woman who didn't wait and from his mother's descent into religious fanaticism. He does not find it impossible to forgive Sarah or to understand his mother, but he does find it difficult enough to demonstrate that he is a human being and not a saint. He struggles with learning to handle the supernatural talent which has developed during his four-year sleep — the (unpredictable and uncontrollable) ability to read intimate details of a person's life and future from touching them or articles they have handled. Johnny has not love for his talent, although he accepts its existence. King draws Johnny as a loving, lonely man, a gifted teacher, and Stillson as the only sort of character who could lead Johnny into destructive obsession. The indisputable iniquity of Stillson is the only possible lever for the action of the book. Johnny, we are shown, is the sort of man who can feel guilty about revealing the identity of a policeman who rapes and murders young children; yet he must grow to hate Stillson enough to be willing to assassinate him, or there would be no book. Where Carrie views her talent with an adolescent's self-interest, and Charlie McGee with a child's directness, Johnny Smith approaches his with an adult's judgment and thus an adult's torment. With this novel, King reached indisputable maturity as a writer who tackles complex human questions and refuses to oversimplify issues.

Firestarter continues this trend admirably. The possessor of the talent is Charlie McGee, the young daughter of two experimental subjects who were given an extremely dangerous drug. If we can overlook the scientific improbability of such a drug having genetic effects, the premise is terrifying. Charlie's parents had bad trips and were left with minor psychic powers; Charlie was born with an astonishingly strong pyrokinetic talent. (King is quite convincing describing the problems of raising a child whose subconscious sets things on fire as soon as she is crossed.) Charlie's antagonist in the book is John Rainbird, American Indian Vietnam veteran and complete, certifiable maniac. Despite his homicidal tendencies, his shoe-collecting fetish and his total amorality, Rainbird is somehow almost likeable (or perhaps just understandable), even if he does put quite a strain on the reader's credibility. His characterization carries with it none of the opprobrium of Stillson's. We are given some insight into the forces that shaped him and some sympathy for his pressures and problems. It is much easier to dislike Cap Hollister, the intelligence bureaucrat who masterminds the persecution of Charlie and her father, but then we aren't given much background on Cap, so we don't know what brought him to where he is. Andy McGee, Charlie's father, is an ordinary, rather weak man who does a little better than he otherwise might because of his love for his daughter. King cares for all the characters in Fire-*starter*, treating even the subconscious neuroses of the government agents with affection tempering the ridicule. Nowhere, however, is his caring more apparent than in his treatment of Irv Manders, a character who might well be only a spear-carrier in a different book but who is yet another Everyman. Irv is a farmer who picks Andy and Charlie up hitch-hiking and whose behavior becomes a model for all that is good and strong in humanity. He has compassion for people he cannot understand, he is able to withstand his own fears in the face of holocaust, he never loses perspective, nor kindness or independence. He is a character more familiar from the fiction of an earlier age: a man of deeds rather than words who can still find the words when they are truly needed. Irv seems to personify King's faith, for he can take people on their own recognizance despite contrary evidence, can stand up for their rights as if his own were in jeopardy, and can shelter them without regard for his own danger. In describing Irv's reactions, King makes the assumption that people's behavior can be affected by threats to unknown relatives half a world away, simply because they care about what happens to others. Irv (and to a lesser extent his wife Norma) are good and warm people, and King conveys his belief in their commonality with the rest of us by never remarking on their behavior as abnormal or particularly laudable. Very few writers of contemporary fiction would even create such a simply good character as Irv Manders, let alone imply that he might be the rule rather than the exception.

Firestarter also continues King's trend of treating children as full-fledged humans. In fact, one of the qualities of Rainbird that makes him forgivable is his understanding of Charlie's determination and toughness. Where everyone else assumes that she is "only a child" and can be easily broken, Rainbird realizes that the quality of her resolution is as strong or stronger than that of most adults. There is hardly a novel of King's that does not make room for the ignored characters of literature — children, non-caucasians, the disabled. In *The Stand*, one of the heroes is deaf, not because it is necessary to the plot, but simply because some people are deaf and King is attempting to write about a cross-section of humanity. In an increasingly homogenized culture, any attempt to remind us that we leave a lot of people out of our picture of "people" can only be a good thing.

Stephen King has achieved a wider range of popularity than any other writer of horror fiction. While most horror writers either develop an avid genre following (H. P. Lovecraft), a good reception in literary and critical circles (Shirley Jackson) or huge sales and little staying power (William Peter Blatty), King has crossed all lines. While collectors sift patiently through musty stacks for old issues of *Cavalier*, sales figures and bestseller list records pile up and academic essays and teachers' guides are rushed into production. Prestigious directors convert his novels into movies, and the books sell well even before the movie tie-in editions are released. A certain amount of this popularity can be attributed to the "superstar" phenomenon which currently dominates our entertainment industry. Having reached superstar status, King is guaranteed huge advertising and promotion budgets for his books, which accounts for a portion of their sales. Nonetheless, it seems obvious that anyone who has achieved such an encompassing spectrum of popularity (and engendered so little dissent) must be saying something that people want (or perhaps need?) to hear.

We live in a time when the most natural response to all but our most immediate associates seems to be hate and distrust. There is little confidence in our future as a civilization or even as a race. King, who belittles none of our fears, sounds a note of hope to counter them. If we can trust each other, hope is never lost. Stephen King is one of the few writers today, in any field, whose primary theme is one of hope and survival, despite the odds. In this light, his popularity is predictable, and perhaps his large audience is in itself a small portent of hope for the future.

That night he dreamed of the man with no face standing on the high roof, his hands stretched out to the east, and then of the corn — corn higher than his head — and the sound of the music. Only this time he knew *it was music and this time he* knew *it was a guitar. He awoke near dawn with a painfully full bladder and her words ringing in his ears:* Mother Abagail is what they call me . . . you come see me anytime.

— from THE STAND

The Grey Arena

by Charles L. Grant

To ASCRIBE TO AN AUTHOR personal beliefs after sifting through volumes and pages of his work is at best a precarious undertaking. Many critics tend to forget in their moments of revelatory zeal that an author will assume postures which best suit the story at hand, even espouse causes he may find personally unrealistic or offensive but which are necessary to the continuing development of plot structure and character evolution.

It is not surprising that writers of Dark Fantasy are continuously bombarded with the same questions: Do you really believe in vampires? werewolves? ghosts? ghouls? Do you really think houses can be haunted? possessed? intrinsically evil? Do you really believe in a Devil? a God? a multitude of netherworld demons? The assumption is that the writer will say yes. The disappointment comes when the writer says no, he doesn't really believe in all that business, but using it makes for a hell of a good story, doesn't it?

Aside from the usual pop-psych assignments to this genre — it helps us face death by showing us vicariously what's on "the other side"; it enables us to handle fear without the attendant real dangers; it unsettles us by proving Poe's admonition that all is not what we see or seem — it also provokes for a brief moment during the unraveling of the story the belief that there is something else coexistent on this planet which may either preserve or threaten us, depending on the writer's penchant. The story does not have to deal specifically with gods or devils. But it assumes the reality of Forces which may be actively imbued with intelligence, which permit the denizens of the supernatural their existence.

The problem with this assumption is twofold: It presumes knowledge of an author's personal beliefs, and it directs critics and readers on a search for obvious symbolism, rather than taking the trouble to peel away outer layers to the core (and that core generally has little to do with the supernatural per se).

Thus, Stephen King receives reviews from people like Meyer Levin who, in taking on *The Stand* for *The New York Times* "Sunday Book Review," dismisses the 823-page novel as a pseudo-sf/fantasy duel between God and the Devil, and not very well done at that. The book's artistic success (and excesses) is debatable, but not the God/Devil aspect. Had Levin bothered to read *The Stand* more closely, or had he bothered to acquaint himself with others of King's works, he would have known with what thematic threads he was dealing — for the simple reason that King has spelled it out rather clearly so there would be no mistakes from haphazard reviewers.

In Stephen King's literary world, God and the Devil are only small parts of a far larger and more pervasive whole. A Force, which is divided into the White and the Dark, although the division is not always even or clear. God belongs in the ranks of the former, the Devil in the latter, and their occasional head-to-head confrontations are a result only of the clashes between the two greater universals. Thus, in *The Stand*, Fran Goldsmith, Stu Redman, and Nick Andros are clearly not agents of the Lord, but of the White; while Whitney Horgan, Lloyd Henreid, and Trashcan Man belong to the Dark. Randall Flagg is not the Devil, nor is Abagail Freemantle a symbol for God — assigning these two such simplistic roles ignores the broader canvas upon which King is working.

It is a canvas which, despite the explosive ending of *The Stand*, does not include within its borders the finality of Armageddon.

What King prefers to deal with are the skirmishes which result in very real casualties on both sides. What may appear to be a happy (good triumphs and we are all saved) ending for the White (as in *Firestarter*, *'Salem's Lot*, and *The Shining*) is, in fact, an ending laced with melancholy when you consider the "after" of each novel — the ever-so faint implication that while the Dark Force has been thwarted, the apparent White victory is at best a temporary one.

Many other writers have seized upon the White/Dark conflict (though not as obviously as has King), and any number of them have stacked the deck in favor of one side or the other. So much so, however, and with so little skill, that the outcome becomes monotonously predictable, and it's rather easy to leap ahead and go straight to the end without stumbling.

One way of stacking the deck is by employing children in the forefront, the front lines, the lines of demarcation between good and evil.

This is what is known as commercial viability.

It's also known as going for the reader's gut; and going for the sure thing.

With few exceptions, those who constitute the American book-buying public (and most of these are women) have a special affection for children. I suspect it's either because they've forgotten what it's like to be a child, or because the Romantic within them insists that children are innately White (good, innocent, unstained) and should be saved at all costs — if for no other reason than that they represent the future.

To cast them in roles which we do not ordinarily ascribe to them is a calculated marketing/writing device. Because they are (from the popular Romantic viewpoint) the innocents, they become all the more terrifying when they are discovered to be prime agents of the Dark. After all, who would suspect a helpless blind girlchild of wanting to return from the dead (after being shoved off a cliff) to destroy a family and a seacoast town (*Comes the Blind Fury*), or a rosy-cheeked little shaver who has an ambassador for a father and a curious black dog for a guardian (*The Omen*)?

Stephen King is not unaware of these marketing/stylistic/calculating devices. But he is a Romantic. He does believe in the innate goodness of children. He abhors vehemently that very calculation which creates children as evil antagonists, and children as helpless-but-guaranteed-to-produce-sympathy victims. For writers of lesser skills, to give a short character the proper age and cute (or common) dimunitive name is all that's needed to goad plot into movement. For King, there is far more to it. In his view, children are in their way as complex as adults, and should be treated with just as much dignity. The struggle toward adolescence and adulthood is as meaningful as anything a grown-up has to contend with.

King, however, deliberately exploited the nasty children gimmick only at the beginning of his career. "Suffer the Children" and "Children of the Corn" deal with the sort of preadoloescents and teenagers which have become so popular. But because he does not believe (or perhaps does not want to believe) in children of this ilk, these two stories fail on the most important, Dark Fantasy level — the creation of real people to fear and to cause fear. His children in these stories are not real, not three-dimensional, *because they do not exist in King's own world.*

For King, children belong in the vanguard of the White. And his use of them is effective not only because they are not throwaway characters who can be popped in and out of dire situations, but also because they touch upon emotions easily tapped in the reader's actual life, emotions not gerrymandered to produce predictable results but which are unashamedly honest.

By the same token, because children (and many of his adults) are out there in front, they are sometimes lured into a rather broad grey area which blends and separates the main sectors of White and Dark. And it is here that they are most effective. They are neither absolute victims nor pure Innocents; they hate as well as love, they can rightly survive the travails as well as seek revenge, and they claim the reader's special attention because their fates are not always as clear-cut as they might appear.

Carrie White. Her name is no accident. Of all the King children she is the most obviously placed in the grey arena. Her special gift could very easily have been used gratuitously in lesser hands less sensitive, but here it becomes an effective symbol of all the frustrations and setbacks an adolescent must experience before reaching adulthood. Nor is it an accident that her foes are also part of that arena, shifting from good to bad as teenagers do when admonished to act their age while, at the same time, they're ordered to grow up and act like adults. When Carrie is finally driven beyond endurance, and Chamberlain High — seat of everything which attracts and terrifies her — is virtually annihilated, she is using the only weapon she knows will work. It is not White versus Dark, nor hate versus love — it is the continuous battleground of the grey, where White and Dark intrude but seldom overwhelm.

Charlie McGee is not quite so complex. Her pyrokinetic ability, and her youth, seem less effective because *Firestarter*'s plot has her continually on the run. She, unlike Carrie, has no place to settle down, no ordinary life to struggle through, experience, and grow from. Her weapon is a chemically induced accident, not a genetic quirk; she reacts as a child does, by striking out blindly, without Carrie's intellectual and emotional curiousity and despair at the type of person/freak she may be. She is, in fact, so much deeper in the White Force than Carrie that she is less threatened than is her father, who has had too much time to think about his own "skill." Despite the dangerous situations in which she is placed, and from which she escapes, Charlie is as solidly entrenched in her rank as are the classmates of "Suffer the Children" in theirs.

In *'Salem's Lot*, however, the reader is faced with virtually the entire field of battle — Dark, White, and the grey arena between. And while King does use children here as White (Mark Petrie) and Dark, the Dark victims are given a sardonic twist to save them from complete, and unsettling, exploitation.

Dud Rogers is not (to put it mildly) adverse to the opportunities Straker and Barlow offer him (". . . [he] understood everything and welcomed it, and when the pain came it was as sweet as silver . . ."). The other adults are not quite so willing. Some of the children, on the other hand (once the village has been swept under by Barlow's relentless campaign) do manage to turn their vampiric affliction to some "good" turn: Charlie Rhodes, the school bus driver, receives his comeuppance, not from any of the adult vampires, but from a busload of those children he had tormented for years; it is a moment of marvelous horror, and at the same time somewhat sweetened by the knowledge that the kids have found the perfect revenge. Note too, though, that while these children are victims of the Dark, the holocaust finale purifies them, saves them, so that they are not condemned to eternal damnation.

As with Carrie White, this is no accident. King uses the evil/victim device (which Dark Fantasy provides him) for terror and at the same time snatches the children away from their Dark fates through the cleansing fire — the Romantic is at peace with the fictional ploy.

The grey arena too is the perfect setting for Straker's activities as he prepares the town and the Marston House for Barlow's coming. While Ben Mears and Mark Petrie are vivid slashes of White in the grey, Straker is the Dark. And much more so than the vampire, Barlow, because Straker has his loyalties to the Dark while at the same time moving through the human world. He worries. He plans. He completes the necessary sacrifices of body (Ralph Glick) and soul (Larry Crockett), then falls into an all-too-human (and therefore an underscoring of his real nature) fretting about whether he's done everything he's supposed to. These moments do not last long, but they last just long enough to turn bits of him grey. Even the evil ranks are not absolutely evil.

And with few exceptions, this is where King's strength lies. Not with Barlow, or with the fourth graders, or with Maggie White, or the Dark Man, but with those skirmishes in the mid-arena, with Carrie and Andy and Susan and Straker. Unlike the absolutes presented to readers of John Saul and Graham Masterson and those less popular, King with his White/Dark Force permits the creation of that grey arena, that place where nothing is absolute and no one is safe, where victories and defeats are, at his best, unpredictable.

It is like the real world, and Dark Fantasy is a way of casting some illumination there.

Darkness.

Fading.

Until all that was left seemed to be a giant red-and-black wheel revolving in such emptiness as there may be between the stars, try your luck, first time fluky, second time lucky, hey-hey-hey. The wheel revolved up and down, red and black, the marker ticking past the pins, and he strained to see if it was going to come up double zero, house number, house spin, everybody loses but the house. He strained to see but the wheel was gone. There was only blackness and that universal emptiness, negatory, good buddy, el zilcho. Cold limbo.

Johnny Smith stayed there a long, long time.

—from THE DEAD ZONE

King and the Literary Tradition of Horror and the Supernatural

by Ben P. Indick

I.

As ONE OF THE MOST SUCCESSFUL writers in the history of the horror tale, Stephen King has constructed his work on a sure knowledge of the fiction of his predecessors. References to authors and titles abound in the pages of his novels. Even more important, he has absorbed and utilized those qualities which characterize the different types of stories in the horror genre. In his own distinctive style are mirrored the major traditions he has inherited.

The ghost in fiction is at least as old as the Graeco-Roman era, but Pliny the Younger's chained ghost is merely a plaintive creature seeking proper interment. Chaucer's "Nun's Priest's Tale" tells of a traveler who dreams of seeing his companion's wounded and bleeding body, but the purpose is to help him discover that murdered friend. With the Witches of *Macbeth* and the ghosts within *Hamlet* and *Macbeth*, Shakespeare added a sense of fright to Elizabethan theatre, in which the ghosts' purpose was largely the furthering of the mechanics of the play.

It was the dawning era of Romanticism which gave birth to the supernatural story as we know it: an anti-rationalism accepting essentially unknowable and hidden aspects of nature. A very real world was busy exploring, geographically and industrially; in response, poets and story-tellers looked for mystery, and found it in strange islands and weird creatures of imagination. For Horace Walpole, a devotee of Medievalism, what better period could there be than that era called the Gothic?

Others obviously agreed. The novel Walpole wrote in 1764, *The Castle of Otranto*, precisely caught the mood. He populated his decaying castle with an array of noble lords, helpless females, scheming villains and a battery of supernatural forces, all of whom were manipulated through real as well as fantastic dangers directly menacing the heroes. The story itself was frequently absurd and the plot melodramatic. The narrative style was ponderous and the dialogue, which would influence a century of stage melodramas to come, was formal and stilted. (A friar speaks: "The will of heaven be done! I am but its worthless instrument. It makes use of my tongue to tell thee, prince, of thy unwarrantable designs. The injuries of the virtuous Hippolita have mounted to the throne of pity.") The style did not bother the reading public. The book became a best-seller. Its weaknesses are excusable, for it was, after all, the *first* Gothic novel. Issued under a nom-de-plume, the novel's enormous success quickly persuaded the author to have his true name appended.

Walpole's ingenuity resulted in an endless flow of similarly inspired Gothic novels, which offered better characterizations as well as more sensational fears. Moral tone was usually present, to justify the excesses. Thus, Clara Reeve concludes in *The Old English Baron* (1777): "All these . . . furnish a striking lesson to posterity, of the overruling hand of Providence and the certainty of RETRIBUTION." Sometimes, as in the very popular *The Mysteries of Udolpho* (1794) by Ann Radcliffe, weak explanations for the supernatural events were offered; fortunately for her readers, these rationalizations came too late to dilute the action.

Sensationalism reached early heights in Mathew Gregory "Monk" Lewis' work, particularly his lurid *Ambrosio or the*

Monk (1795). To the mysterious knights and swooning maidens of his predecessors, he added explicitly personal terms of fear with strong sexual overtones and violence. Lust, matricide, incest and murder are ladled up with many fantastic elements, upon none of which he wastes a word of rationalization.

The style and manner of the Gothic would begin to appear in fiction distinguished by grace and honesty in writing. Charles Dickens used ghosts effectively if sentimentally in *A Christmas Carol* (1843) and quite unsentimentally in such stories as "The Trial for Murder" (1865). Charlotte Brontë employed the essence of the Gothic form powerfully in her non-fantastic novel *Jane Eyre* (1847) with the castle, the mysterious owner and his dark secret, and a suffering but courageous heroine. Her sister Emily eschewed the trappings but retained the potency of ghostly images with her ill-starred lovers of *Wuthering Heights* (1847).

While the broad outlines of the original Gothic style withered, the supernatural elements, particularly the ghost story, prospered. The 19th and 20th centuries have been rich with lastingly effective examples of the genre. The external ghost as limned by Montague Rhodes James (1862–1936) in "Oh, Whistle, and I'll Come to You, My Lad," wherein a figure composed of the crumpled linens of a bed suddenly rises, remains potent. Algernon Blackwood (1869–1951) made equally feasible the presence of a Satanic mystery and willing human followers in "Ancient Sorceries." The tradition of the ghostly tale is well exemplified in the stories of such writers as Henry James, Edith Wharton, Mary E. Wilkens Freeman, J. S. Le Fanu, E. F. Benson and H. R. Wakefield. Their prose is characterized by subtlety and avoidance of the sensational.

The castle of the Gothic novel, with its ghostly accoutrements, would survive in humbler form as The Haunted House, beloved alike to fictioneers and spiritualists. Perhaps the most distinguished modern example is Henry James' *The Turn of the Screw* (1898), a subtle work with ghosts so tenuous that the reader must decide whether or not they truly exist. A half century and many haunted houses later, the form still retained its potency in *The Haunting of Hill House* (1959) by Shirley Jackson. Ira Levin's *Rosemary's Baby* (1967) utilizes a huge apartment house, gothic in its architectural details, as a fine counterpoint to his lively New York scene. Peter Straub fills a mansion with a ghost's vindictive terror in *Ghost Story* (1979). Stephen King himself displays a splendidly classic haunted house in *'Salem's Lot* (1975) and the haunted house to end all haunted houses, the craggy Overlook Hotel of *The Shining* (1977).

But the Gothic held little validity for serious writers of the 19th century. In the hands of Edgar Allan Poe (1809–1849) for the first time the point of view was significantly altered. The weird tale would not merely provide fear for the characters of the story, but would provide *the reader* the greater fear of self-identification. "The Tell-Tale Heart," "The Cask of Amontillado," "The Fall of the House of Usher" have no Satan, no externally influential force, no abstract presence of Evil to direct the characters. The vengeance that is so much a part of Poe's fiction always stems directly from the actions of his actors, and they must later bear full responsibility for their acts. Their own decisions will finally destory them.

In this sense, Poe's writing is of true psychological content; the grotesque behavior actually represents the normal distorted by emotion to the extreme. Even his allegorical tales follow a line of inevitability and deterministic logic. His weird stories are as rational as his detective stories, and his use of the fantastic must be understood as the ultimate extension of this logic. As a poet, his language was both natural and important to him; his favored themes of murder, retribution and dissolution are couched in a florid and gorgeous tapestry of words so evocative of mood and place that in themselves they heighten the tension. The characters are intense, humorless, compulsive and expressive.

This vein of psychological insight which Poe added to the supernatural tale was exploited by others. Fitz-James O'Brien (1828–1862) wrote what was basically science fiction to create terror in "What Was It?": an invisible, inimical creature is discovered in a hotel room and is finally beaten to death. Guy de Maupassant (1850–1893) offered a more subtle approach in "The Horla." His narrator is threatened also by something unseen; it may be of extra-terrestrial origin, or it may indicate his own growing madness. Ambrose Bierce (1842–?) had insight as sharp as Poe, tempered by cynicism. The psychological power of his stories derives from the eternal hope of his characters, who eventually discover it to be a futile snare. Fate, to Bierce, is not only blind but cruel.

The inner psychiatric maze Poe opened lies at the heart of the Victorian world of Wilde's *Dorian Gray* (1891) and Stevenson's schizophrenic *Dr. Jekyll and Mr. Hyde* (1888), each a study of internal evil. May Sinclair, Walter de la Mare, Oliver Onions and numerous others continued the tradition. With one notable exception, the Vampire Tale, the course of the weird tale would not change again until the advent of H. P. Lovecraft.

In 1816 at Lake Leman, Switzerland, three travelers had a ghost-story writing contest. They were Lord Byron, John William Polidori, his traveling companion, and Mary Wollstonecraft Shelley, wife of the poet. Mrs. Shelley's *Frankenstein* would become immortal; Byron's "Fragment" would be completed by Polidori as "The Vampyre, A Tale," the first popularization of the vampire theme. Byron later disowned any part of it, professing to dislike "Vampires," but no doubt the attribution to him helped the work, as it achieved great popularity in print as well as in a stage adaptation.

The first modern treatment of the vampire theme, in plot, writing and characterization, is "Carmilla" (1872), a novella by Joseph Sheridan Le Fanu. Its turns, plot surprises, and sexual undertones hint at the potentials of the vampire novel. Yet none of his successors surpassed the sensitivity of Le Fanu, as expressed in his concluding lir es: "To this hour, the image of Carmilla returns to memory with ambiguous alterations — sometimes the playful, languid, beautiful girl; sometimes the writhing fiend I saw in the ruined church; and often from reverie I have started, fancying I heard the light step of Carmilla at the drawing-room door."

Bram Stoker's *Dracula* (1897), a novel written entirely in the form of letters and journals, scarcely had a "light step." The trappings of the Gothic novel are notable here: the sepulchral castle, the brave heroes, the weak, helpless women, and a frightful, nearly insuperable villain. Yet the book soars beyond the limitations of the Gothic and its own self-imposed style of narrative. The action is continuous, and the book is packed with excitement and sexual allure (satisfying a Victorian preoccupation, yet remaining within the bounds of propriety). Stoker combined genuine pathos with a satisfactory psychological development in the characters. Innocent at the outset, they suffer deepening fear and a sense of guilt because of their increasing, if involuntary, complicity and debasement. The combination of these elements renders *Dracula* truly the first "Neo-Gothic" novel, indebted to the romantic past, yet contemporary in its characterizations and mores. It is interesting that Count Dracula himself has very few actual lines to speak in the book (he can only be quoted by others) yet emerges unforgettably.

In the Twentieth century H. P. Lovecraft reached into space and Time to give horror new dimensions. If Poe was the Newton of the weird tale, Lovecraft was its Einstein, bringing it into the Atomic Age. Horror in his writings arises from the helplessness of his protagonists before the awesome forces they have called up or else inadvertently encountered. These mysterious entities antedate Man, are extraterrestrial in origin, and survive, hidden and dormant, yet possessing limitless power. The pantheon of "gods" associated with Lovecraft represent more, however, than a "mythos" of squirming, tentacled creatures: they are inimical forces which taint man and his earth. This taint is an irreparable demeaning of the self and the ego, and the initial horror is in the realization of it. This leads to the final horror, which is death or capitulation, *the surrender of one's humanity.*

II.

THAT KING IS AWARE OF HIS GENRE and its beginnings is clear from the numerous references to writers and titles in so much of his writing. In *Carrie*, an interviewer on the west coast is described as having "an odd, pinched look that is more like Lovecraft than Kerouac out of Southern Cal." The first paragraph of Shirley Jackson's *The Haunting of Hill House* is utilized to hint at the horror of the Marsten House in *'Salem's Lot*. A passage from Poe illuminates the living-dead nature of the final state of the doomed Lot, while Poe's "Masque of the Red Death" is inspiration for and encapsulation of *The Shining*, and is subliminally referred to in its climactic pages.

H. G. Wells, Washington Irving, Algernon Blackwood, J. R. R. Tolkien, Bram Stoker and others roam his pages. Even King himself is present, when, in *The Dead Zone*, a hysterical woman accuses his hero of having started a fire "by his mind, just like in that book *Carrie!*"

The Dead Zone is, significantly, a tribute to one of King's most important inspirations, Ray Bradbury. Bradbury's early weird fiction had initiated the use of a natural vernacular and ordinary individuals in their own homes and small towns. The knowledge that horror could be local and the victim a common man produced a more personal fear in the reader. King's novel not only owes much of its carnival ambience to Bradbury's *Something Wicked This Way Comes*, but it acknowledges the debt in mentioning the title and author, and, in another reference, yet another Bradbury title, *Dark Carnival*. (It even features a character who sells lightning rods, an occupation much discussed in Bradbury's first chapter!)

The heroes of *The Shining* and Lovecraft's "The Shadow Over Innsmouth" bear valid comparison. Each carries within him the seeds of his fate. For Lovecraft, it is the taint of the decadent subhuman followers of the fish-god Dagon; in King, it is Torrance's connection with the evil essence of the hotel: "It laid its Jack Torrance hands on the valve . . . 'I WIN!' it cried." The "it" is Torrance, lost forever to the hotel.

King's references to other writers in the field are not strictly in emulation. He has succeeded because he has forged his own style. Nevertheless, there are influences upon his thinking and his writing, and these may be examined, as follows:

1. The Poesque

KING IS NOT ABOUT TO BECOME a poet, however much he enjoys quoting poets and lyricists. The feverish prose of Poe is antithetic to King's terse and rapid narration, although he is capable of expressive imagery: " The womb of his young wife had borne a single dark and malignant child" (a metaphor for cancer in *The Stand*); "The skeletal fingers danced and clicked on the dark air like marionettes" (the convulsive, final gesture of the vampire in *'Salem's Lot*); "Overhead, the moon rode the sky, a cold sailor of the night" (a moment of foreboding mood from *The Dead Zone*). Such passages are uncommon. Action, not metaphor, moves King's stories. Even in *The Shining*, which is so directly affected by atmosphere adapted from Poe, the writing is devoid of any self-conscious attempt at beautiful prose.

Poe's influence lies in the psychological honesty of his writing, which discarded worthless labels of Virtue and Villainy, and in the subsequent burden of introspection which Poe gave his heroes. King, always a story-teller first, is not above having villains to spice the action; however, with the exception of a fantasy villain such as Barlow, the vampire of *'Salem's Lot*, there is a measure of explanation for such destructive individuals as Greg Stillson and Frank Dodd of *The Dead Zone*, in early maternal acts of harshness and even cruelty. (In a sense King offers us the opportunity of seeing Dodd, the compulsive rapist, from another view, in his short story "Strawberry Spring." Here the narrator is a compulsive murderer much like Dodd, but is sensitive and aware of his acts — too late. It is pure Poe.) King's more normal characters such as Larry Underwood (*The Stand*) and Charlie McGee (*Firestarter*) tend to deliberate their future courses of action carefully, rueing past actions which resulted in grievance to others. The heroine of *Carrie*, no more mature than most of her fellow teenagers, nevertheless tries to understand herself and particularly her mother. Her destructive acts come only because she has no way to respond emotionally and intellectually.

The psychic powers of Carrie, Johnny Smith (*The Dead Zone*), Danny Torrance (*The Shining*) and Charlie McGee are thus in no way employed for *deus ex machina* pyrotechnics. To some degree they are a curse to the characters, who must try to control the powers, and to understand that they can never be a magic carpet of escape. It is the Fantastic made Real, instead of being accepted as simply fantastic. This is the triumph of Poe.

2. The Vampire Tale

STOKER'S DRACULA OPENS IN THE ROMANTIC, Gothic-inspired setting of the hills of Transylvania. King's *'Salem's Lot*, his major contribution to the vampire genre, is set, characteristically for the author, in a typically small New England town. Its inhabitants are stereotypical; major character receive individual chapters, titled for themselves, the others are covered broadly by chapters titled "The Lot." In a sense this repeats the individual epistolary and journal-entry division of *Dracula*.

Stoker wastes little time establishing his fantasy; Jonathan Harker quickly realizes he is a prisoner of the Count and then almost at once encounters three female vampires. When Dracula deprives them of feasting on the hapless Harker, he gives them instead a bag "which moved as though there were some living thing within it." They vanish with the bag, and "Then," writes Harker, "the horror overcame me, and I sank down unconscious."

King likewise moves quickly into the horror of his story, although not revealing at once the presence of vampirism. Hints of terrifying acts mount in the brief sub-chapters, usually commencing prosaically and concluding ominously. Only pages after a child has vanished, a "dark figure" appears at the cemetery, bearing the body of a child. An obscene prayer to a "Lord of Flies" is offered, along with the body. The subsequent lone line, "It became unspeakable," is the commencement of a crescendo of horror, which quickly becomes very explicit.

Once the presence of a vampire is suspected, the balance of Stoker's baggage is brought out, the garlic, the crucifix, the heroine who has been despoiled by the vampire and must be given the ritual absolution, the great Vampire himself. King actually attempts to avoid linking the fate of the vampire to the counter-power of Christianity; to a priest of insufficient faith, the vampire Barlow says "The Catholic Church is not the oldest of my opponents . . . I was old when it was young . . . My rites were old when the rites of your church were unconceived." Nevertheless, the crucifix remains a potent weapon for young Mark against a vampire, who hisses "as if scalded" when confronted with it.

At the climax, King's monstrous Barlow must die as did Stoker's Count, each still helpless at sunset, with the strength of immortality moments away, each in his coffin. King, however, is true to his own emotional style. Whereas Stoker's hero, Jonathan, sweeps a knife across the helpless but vindictively staring body, and causes it to "crumble into dust"; King's Ben Mears is far more physical. Barlow, conscious, screams: "Let me GO!" Mears must climb into the coffin, knees planted on the vampire's chest for a solid perch to hammer in a stake. "Here it comes, you bastard . . . here it is, leech" and he "brings down the hammer again and again," while the dying Barlow, blood gushing wildly, screams through a graphically described dissolution into dust.

King's villain manages more mayhem than Stoker's, and furthermore leaves his flock of Un-Dead behind him in the Lot, where fire may finally destroy them. (Perhaps not. In a related short story, "One for the Road," from King's collection, *Night Shift* (1978), a family traveling through the Lot during a blinding snowstorm experiences vampirism in a terrifying and poignant way.)

The credibility of so fantastic a tale in a setting so mundane is remarkable.

Nevertheless, *'Salem's Lot* must remain a footnote to its inspiration, *Dracula*. By choosing to portray a town's entire population, described individually to a great extent, King is forced to utilize readily recognizable types; the result is predictability in hero, heroine, villain. Without the fully rounded individuality which creates memorable characterizations, the danger of overkill and eventual ennui in the reader's mind is strong. Only King's most powerful allies, relentless pace and devastating shock, prevent this.

Finally, King cannot escape the sense of pastiche. Aware of this, he has his hero muse: "One was taught that such things could not be; that things like Coleridge's 'Cristabel' or Bram Stoker's evil fairy tale were only the warp and woof of fantasy. Of course monsters existed . . . hijackers . . . mass murderers. . . ." It is true enough, but still cannot disguise the essential imitation. *'Salem's Lot* becomes one more of the Un-Dead in the train of the evil Master.

3. H. P. Lovecraft

EXCEPT IN DELIBERATE PASTICHE of Lovecraft's style and thematic material,* King seldom emulates a writer he obviously knows. The influence of Lovecraft is in his creation of horror wherein the fantastic element has a basis in scientific reality. The intrusion in such fiction of purely imaginative elements (ghosts, elves, demons and the like) would destroy the fabric of truth which sustains it.

Lovecraft's book of formulae, "The Necronomicon," is no mere medieval rune-book, nor are the powers it is capable of summoning such fantasies as Asmodeus or Beelzebub. The powers are "like some monstrous intrusion from outer space — some damnable, utterly accursed focus of unknown and malign forces." In his "The Colour Out of Space" such a force appears on a New England farm, no more tangible than an eerie color, but leaving desolation and death in its wake, "a frightful messenger from unformed realms of infinity beyond all Nature as we know it." These forces are real, and the horror which results from their intrusion into mundane life is real.

King employs no extra-terrestrials and no arcane books. Novels such as *Carrie, The Shining, The Dead Zone* and *Firestarter*, however, are dependent on reader acceptance of various extra-sensory abilities, a theme as unproven as any of

---

*King's "Jerusalem's Lot" in *Night Shift*, 1978, ably recaptures the style and ambience of a Lovecraft story. His "Crouch End," in *New Tales of the Cthulhu Mythos*, 1980, adds an original tone to an addition to Lovecraft's "Mythos" cycle.

Lovecraft's imaginings. Like the latter, King must establish a scientific basis for credibility. It is entirely the opposite of such outright fantasy as "The Turn of the Screw" and *Ghost Story*, which need offer no such basis in reality.

King asks no indulgence from his readers; he offers "evidence" to make the remarkable powers acceptable. By setting Carrie a few years into the future, King is able to refer to articles, books and the work of governmental commissions of inquiry which have already acknowledged Carrie's telekinetic powers. One such book, *The Shadow Exploded*, states "It is now generally agreed that the TK phenomenon is a genetic-recessive occurrence." By comparing it to the genetically transmitted disease of hemophilia, King makes it an apparent fact.

Johnny Smith of *The Dead Zone* has precognitive powers. We learn that he suffered an injury as a child which gave him "a very new human ability, or a very old one." A "tiny part" had "awakened." In an epilogue, a physician states that Smith "had an extremely well-developed brain tumor," and then, in a letter written to his father, Smith writes that this tumor was probably part of the accident which was coincident with the beginnings of his "flashes."

In *The Shining*, the boy Danny Torrance possesses telepathic/precognitive powers. No scientific basis is offered other than the cook Hallorann's explanation that it is shared by him and others. "I call it shinin' on, the Bible calls it having visions, and there's scientists that call it precognition." In this instance, the strength of Danny's visions is so intense that the reader accepts the explanation. (Inasmuch as this novel is actually a ghost-tale, it operates within emotional rather than rational parameters.)

With *Firestarter*, King develops his strongest scientific basis for a psychic power. The terrifying ability of Charlie McGee to create fires is the result of chemicals administered to the young man and woman who would become her parents. The altering of their germ-plasms results in a unique child. If it is a stage beyond drugs such as Thalidomide, which affects an embryo, it is nonetheless credible.

4. The Ghost Story

THE SHINING, INSPIRED BY EDGAR ALLAN POE's allegorical "The Masque of the Red Death," is Stephen King's consummate ghostly tale. The palace of Poe's Prince Prospero becomes the Overlook Hotel, and his "assembly of phantasms" is played by the vast number of shades who have occupied its many rooms and left behind their evil essence. In time they will hold their "gay and magnificent revel," but they are peripheral to the heart of the novel. This is the conflict of a man bent on self-destruction and his son, a telepath, who sense the horror of the hotel and the evils which will come upon them.

The story is contructed with extreme care, inexorably moving toward the terrible climax which it continually foreshadows. Almost at once the boy's apprehensions create a foreboding fear, which is enhanced by his mother's distrust of her unstable husband. With the episode of the wasps, badly stinging the boy when, by all rights, the wasps should have been dead, the family further disintegrates with fears and doubts. The abrupt fantasy is in the tradition of M. R. James, as Reality is unhinged and disbelief is challenged.

Torrance's encounter with the hedge animals of the topiary, apparently alive and threatening, is subtle in its psychological significance ("*NO NO I WILL NOT BELIEVE THIS NOT AT ALL!*") It is, after all, a delusion which might happen to anyone. An hallucination, thinks Torrance, "a bad scare but it was over now." It is, in its implications, quite in the spirit of that other James, Henry.

It is the beginning of Torrance's breakdown, his absorption into the Hotel, and the Supernatural will now complement the final playing out of the family conflict. A rotting corpse of a woman in a bathtub appears not only to the sensitive child but to his father, who refuses to acknowledge it. Torrance is now able to discover the deceased caretaker and bartender as well as the many revelers of the Hotel's past.

The horrors mount swiftly, ghostly as well as human, as the man deteriorates, until the *Walpurgisnacht* of the climax. For an instant the blood-red presence of Poe's Red Death, in the *persona* of the Hotel itself, promises to "hold illimitable dominion over all," but it dies of its own weakness and evil. "The party was over."

The Shining is a tour de force, dependent like any good ghost story and supernatural tale upon neither science nor explanation, but only on its own inner logic and compelling narrative voice.

5.   The Gothic

THE ANCIENT GREEK PHILOSOPHERS preached the virtues of moderation. Their playwrights knew better. Scandal, murder, hair-rending and railing against the gods sold tickets.

King is not a philosopher. He knows how to sell tickets. He manages in his novels to encompass the desolation of a school, most of its students and much of the town as well by one distraught girl. He turns a village into a nest of vampires. He unleashes an army of ghosts, then utterly destroys their huge home. He polishes off New York City's teeming millions as well as 90% of the world's population. He uncovers a nuclear bomb and explodes it, but tops that by finding a child who has the ability of "creating a nuclear explosion simply by the force of her will."

King revels in excess on more private levels as well: the public menstruation of Carrie, followed by its reflection in her drenching with pig's blood; Frank Dodd as raincoated rapist, killing and dying with frightening violence; bodies literally torn to pieces by the monsters of *The Mist*.

Nevertheless, excess is only one element King inherited from the Gothicists. There is another, far more important. For Stephen King, who remembers shuddering through monster films as a child and claims he still cannot sleep without at least one light glowing in the house, the indispensable mainspring in his stories is Fear. Its origins may be psychological, physical, or even supernatural, but the fear itself is real, and his horror stories succeed because his readers share it.

Walpole's school had foundered when fear lost its rationality.

Drs. Van Helsing and Freud rediscovered it beneath Prince Albert coats. King has put it into the shopping basket, next to the tomato sauce, the Sanka and the Tab. Fear has become a commonplace, no longer the evil dispensation of noble or supernatural villains. No one can be trusted, not teenaged school kids, not a cop or a prosaic motel-keeper, not even a small baby. It is a world with neither security nor stability.

We all live in Otranto.

Before drifting away entirely, he found himself re-flecting — not for the first time — on the peculiarity of adults. They took laxatives, liquor, or sleeping pills to drive away their terrors so that sleep would come, and their terrors were so tame and domestic: the job, the money, what the teacher will think if I can't get Jennie nicer clothes, does my wife still love me, who are my friends. They were pallid compared to the fears every child lies cheek and jowl with in his dark bed, with no one to confess to in hope of perfect understanding but another child. There is no group therapy or psychiatry or community social services for the child who must cope with the thing under the bed or in the cellar every night, the thing which leers and capers and threatens just beyond the point where vision will reach. The same lonely battle must be fought night after night and the only cure is the eventual ossification of the imaginary faculties, and this is called adulthood.

— from 'Salem's Lot

The Marsten House
in 'Salem's Lot

by Alan Ryan

CHILDREN ARE BEST AT LISTENING to stories and being affected by them. And we, as readers, are at our best when we are most like children. Tell a child fairy tales often enough and he or she will inevitably adopt one as a particular favorite, demanding that it be told again and again. Whether the tale is read aloud from a book at bedtime, or simply made up, perhaps unique to the family, and told by the fireside on rainy days, again and again the child will listen happily to the same story told over and over in the same way. In most other regards, children are easily bored by anything repetitive or overly familiar, yet they will demand the repetition of a favorite story. Why? The most basic, most universal, appeal of storytelling — the satisfaction of finding out what will happen in the end — is supplied in the first telling. And yet they listen. And listen again.

The answer lies in the protests raised when the teller alters the story. If details are changed or omitted, the child immediately complains: Tell the part about such-and-such! More significantly, if the teller alters the *manner* of the telling, the child complains: That's not the way you told it before!

Certainly there are other factors at work here—the easiness, the comfort and safety, of something already familiar—but clearly the central element in the appeal is the telling itself, specifically the *manner* of the telling: the way in which the story is shaped, the careful ordering of its details, the pacing of the events, the structure of the effects. When the teller wantonly or carelessly changes the mood of the language or dares to omit a significant episode or detail, the child instantly knows that something of value is being lost and that the story is in danger of being robbed of its essence, the very thing that makes it what it is. This unconscious awareness in the child is much more sophisticated than the simple desire to find out how the story ends.

Were this not the case, parents could get off pretty easily at story time. There was this little girl, see, and she was heading for Grandmother's house and a wolf saw her and ran ahead and dressed up like Grandmother and almost got the little girl but she escaped. The End. But you can't get away with that. The story needs the details, all of them: the woods, the basket, the teeth, Grandmother's bonnet. It needs the buildup of sympathy for the girl, the delineation of the danger that threatens her, the gradual tightening of suspense. Indeed, it is only when we see that wicked wolf in Grandmother's bed and *actually wearing her bonnet* that we truly see the immediacy of the danger, feel the tension, sense the confrontation of Good and Evil, witness the frightening distortion of reality that is at the heart of any good horror tale. The story *needs* Grandmother's bonnet in order to create the right effect at the right moment. It needs the proper telling.

As experienced, adult readers, we still respond first and foremost to simple curiosity about what will happen to the characters from the beginning of the book to the end. Will the butler be revealed as the murderer? Will the cavalry arrive in time? Will the monster eat the scientist's beautiful daughter? Will Odysseus survive and bring his men safely back to Ithaca? We respond especially well to tales that offer an interesting weave of subplots, because there are that many more interesting questions to be answered, that many more sources of tension.

But we really do require more than that. We require the same things the child responds to so strongly, so possessively. We require skill in the telling. The most wonderfully fascinating plot premise or story device ever invented by a writer will crumble, dry and dusty and boring, if the story is not related with skill, with a craft subtle enough and sophisticated enough to make us care for the characters, to make us feel what they feel, to transport us to their world, to make the ending of the story something that *matters* as much to us as it does to them.

Horror tales require this high level of craft and care even more than other forms of storytelling because they so often deal in things beyond the ordinary, things at the very edges of credibility, and because they rely so heavily on atmosphere. Plot is still essential, of course. Plot is always essential. But the telling counts for more here than elsewhere because here the reader seeks — and needs, if his disbelief is to be suspended — more than simply a revelation of how things turn out. To be honest about it, we know (more often than not) perfectly well how things will turn out from the minute the story begins. The hideous beast will not mangle the scientist's beautiful daughter because she will manage to escape just in the proverbial nick of time. The monster will be kept from devouring Cleveland by the quick thinking (after two hundred pages or two reels of film) of the hero of the story. We knew that all along. By the time we open a book or take a seat in a movie theatre, we have already agreed to suspend disbelief. But, because of the nature of horror literature, we need more than the usual help to accomplish that. Try stating in plain language the plot or premise of a favorite horror story. Chances are good that, stripped down that way, it sounds pretty silly. No, it's all in the telling, and that carefully timed view of Grandmother's bonnet on the head of the wolf is essential to our enjoyment.

❦ ❦

Stephen King knows the importance of that bonnet, and his best work is filled with carefully chosen and fully imagined details, with places that seem real and tangible, with characters who seem to have been alive even before the time of the story, who move in a human context we can recognize as our own. Then, into this very real world, among these very believable characters, he introduces an element of horror, something nominally *un*real and *un*believable. And yet the reader believes it. And is, like the characters, frightened by it.

How do the stories get that way? How are the effects created? They must, in fact, be constructed, and a thousand words of manuscript require many times that number of minute and careful decisions.

Although the level of King's writing is generally very high, not all of it is uniformly well-crafted. Some of his work (*Firestarter*, *The Mist*, "The Jaunt") — perhaps showing the haste brought on by commercial pressures — lacks much of the tight control we expect from his best work. But at its best (*'Salem's Lot, Cujo*, "Do the Dead Sing?"), his writing offers a rare immediacy, a recognizable reality, a sense of feelings shared by writer, character, reader. His people notice the kinds of things we notice; they feel the kinds of things we feel. Beyond that, there are the plots: stories of characters we can like and care about (because they are so much like us) who find themselves in highly threatening situations and who must (like all of us, finally) find a way to deal with the Dark and the Unknown. And beyond the characterizations and the plots, there is the manner of the telling.

'Salem's Lot offers a particularly good opportunity to examine the text closely and see how the effects — emotions, atmosphere, tension — are constructed. First, however, we should note that the devices — vocabulary choices, phrasing, pacing — work (i.e., have their effect on the reader) whether or not the reader is aware of them. Indeed, they work *best* when the reader is unconscious of them and is simply carried away by the story. At the same time, we can only profit by a clearer view of how writing actually works.

✳ ✷

At the beginning of *'Salem's Lot*, after the Prologue (which sets up the very important sense of unease that marks all good horror literature), King immediately introduces the Marsten House, the source of evil that will figure centrally in everything that happens later in the story. It is essential that the Marsten House, from the first moment we lay eyes on it, be scary. King predisposes the reader to see it that way by quoting, just before the actual story begins, the first paragraph of Shirley Jackson's *The Haunting of Hill House*. This is, especially with that memorable phrase, "not sane," and its eerie last line, an outstanding bit of evocative writing. But King is doing more here than paying tribute to a distinguished predecessor. Always the pragmatist, he gets full value from the epigraph by the inevitable carryover of those associations to his own Marsten House.

Now, with the reader in the right frame of mind, the story itself can begin.

We see Ben Mears driving through a very realistically detailed Maine. King carefully outlines his route for us, with road numbers, exits, turns, landmarks along the way, a view of little boys with fishing poles on their shoulders at the side of the road. We are drawn along with Ben's movement and his growing excitement as he nears the end of a journey, a natural and easy enough reaction for the reader to share. Ben seems like a nice enough man, we think. Where is he going? Why is he so excited about getting there? What does it mean to him? Then we get a sudden view of the sign indicating his goal, the same view Ben gets as the sign comes "twinkling up out of the landscape." JERUSALEM'S LOT. And instantly Ben suffers a "sudden blackness" that hits him with "savage power."

That "sudden blackness" is related to the vague bits of memory we are getting about a violent and disturbing incident in Ben's past — something about a motorcycle, a van, his wife Miranda's scream — but in the reader's mind the reaction is firmly linked to that first view of the sign bearing the name of the town.

As he draws closer and closer, we follow each turn of the road, getting actual street names now, the information filtered to us in the same order and perspective with which Ben perceives it. Then he sees something that causes him to jam on the brakes. Even the car, as if joining in the spirit of the moment, enhances the drama by shuddering to a stop and stalling. But King has not told us yet what caused Ben's startled reaction. It is caused only by "what he saw," and King withholds the specific sight, building further tension, for the length of one more paragraph.

Now we get a sweeping view of trees and sloping hills as we scan the horizon along with Ben. Unlike Ben, however, we still don't know the principal object in the scene, and the waiting raises the level of anticipation. Stretching it further, making us wait still longer, King gives us an almost elegiac repetition: "Only the trees, and in the distance, where those trees rose against the sky. . . ." Finally, following the long buildup, and saved for the strongest position at the end of both sentence and paragraph, we at last get to see "the peaked, gabled roof of the Marsten House."

To intensify the moment and guide us toward the response he wants, King shows us Ben gazing at it, "fascinated," his mind filled with "warring emotions" — not merely mixed or confused, but "warring." At the same time, we realize that this house, and not merely the town of Jerusalem's Lot, has been the object of his journey.

As he looks at the house, Ben murmurs a few words and his arms break out in gooseflesh. Many writers are too reticent, too sophisticated, to speak of homely things like gooseflesh. But King is not shy about it at all and knows very well that the bold stroke works best every time. It may not be elegant, but it works. And gooseflesh is like a yawn; it's contagious. King knows that, and uses it, and only a reader with a heart of stone could avoid staring at that house with the same creepy fascination that Ben feels himself.

That brief glimpse of the Marsten House is all we are going to get for a moment. As if savoring the eerie sensations, like a child making the chill last as long as possible, Ben resumes his journey by skirting the town and approaching it again from the other side. The paragraph describing the route he takes is filled with cozy and comforting images of childhood and life in the country, the warmth of the details contrasting sharply with the chilly memory of the house. And finally, unavoidably, Ben's route brings him back to Marsten's Hill, the name again saved for the end of another paragraph.

Now, at last, as Ben and the reader actually come abreast of the house, a curious thing happens. The grammar of the narrative starts coming apart, reflecting Ben's "warring emotions," and, probably with his conscious awareness, jarring the reader further into the necessary state of unease. Watch. "At the top, the trees fell away on both sides of the road." There is nothing unusual here yet, although it is worth noting the strength of "fell away," a usage that imparts an active life of its own to the landscape, a practice common in King's writing. But here is the next sentence: "On the right, you could look right down into the town proper — Ben's first view of it." This is still very simple and straightforward description, but the reactions are built into the language itself. In that sentence, Ben's gaze is turned away from the house as he looks down toward the town from the road. But it is an awkward and nervous sentence — try reading it out loud — and there is no easy grammatical parallel between the two parts of it. And then the next sentence: "On the left, the Marsten House." The single item of information, standing there stark and alone, rather like the house it refers to — and not even graced by a verb — takes on a special import. It actually provokes Ben to a very specific action, narrated almost as quickly as it happens, with not a word to spare: "He pulled over and got out of the car."

The next paragraph consists of only three brief sentences, almost breathless in their pacing, coming with the quickness of thought that is automatic and unconsidered. The second sentence of the three again contains an ungrammatical quirk (the use of "not" where we would expect the more usual "none") and the effect again is jarring. "It was just the same. There was no difference, not at all. He might have last seen it yesterday."

We still have not had a good look at the house itself. We know something of its situation, we know something of its effects, but we still don't know *it*. And we'll have to wait longer still, because now King drops our gaze to the ground as he describes in detail the approaches to the house, like a camera eye taunting us and making us wait. He shows us the witch grass (conveniently named), the flagstones of the path, the front yard, a hint of the porch. The visual focus here is tight, close, and we are almost compelled to keep our eyes down, away from the house. We see even the crickets and grasshoppers that inhabit and animate this tiny bit of landscape. The details here are not casually chosen. The witch grass grows "wild and tall," the grasshoppers jump in "erratic parabolas" (a fine description for any number of reasons), and even the flagstones leading up to the porch are "frost-heaved," a much stronger, more picturesque, and more psychologically disturbing description than, say, *irregular* or *uneven* or *broken*.

Now, finally, after the long wait, after the endless taunting, we see the house itself. Tension has been built, curiosity aroused, uneasiness intensified, each of these factors helping to color what we actually see. And what we actually see, after all this, is not merely a house, but a monster, a living beast. It is, he tells us, "huge," "rambling," "sagging," "sinister," "gray," "slumped," "hunched." That's no house; that's the monster of our darkest dreams.

From the first sentence of that paragraph, the thing is alive. "The house itself looked toward town." The word "looked" establishes the house as active, almost conscious, rather than static as the word *faced* would have suggested. King doesn't lose the strength of that otherwise simple word, "looked," by burying it in a lengthy, complex sentence; the fact is stated, bare and complete and very effective. Adjectives like "rambling" and "slumped" and "hunched" add further to our perception of the house as something alive. And the things that have happened to it there on the hill — windstorms have "ripped" away the shingles and a storm has "punched in" part of the roof — are things that happen not to inanimate objects but to living creatures.

Ben, reacting in a manner we can understand all too readily, is drawn toward the house, tempted almost to go inside, like a casual passerby who can't help looking at the scene of an auto accident and perversely hoping to see the bodies. Staring at the house and swallowing nervously, he is "almost hypnotized." Small wonder. And the house, monster that it is, stares right back at him "with idiot indifference."

Then we follow Ben's thoughts through a long paragraph of reminiscence about the interior of the house. King almost literally takes us by the hand and leads us inside. It is natural enough here to use an indefinite form, and the impersonal "one" would certainly be correct. Instead, King characteristically uses the more natural, more controversial, "you," which has the advantage of immediacy as well as the power to disarm the reader by its very casualness, to get him to go along willingly. We get a number of very realistic, yet atmospheric, details here—mice skittering in the walls, gritty plaster dust underfoot, the precise count of steps up to the next floor—details that enhance the reader's sense of unease. There are fourteen steps, for example, "exactly fourteen," and our attention is drawn to the fact, not only because the bit of information sounds so right, the sort of thing we might remember ourselves about a house we had once known, but because of the emphasis placed on it. "But the top one was smaller," King tells us, "out of proportion, as if it had been added to avoid the evil number." King, who deals so often and so easily in large gestures, can also be reticent when reticence is most effective. Here the simple statement, made and as quickly dropped, would have been cheapened by actually saying the number.

By now we are at the top of the stairs (almost before we know it, and lost in the illusion as much as Ben is lost in the memory), walking down a hall toward a closed door. But this is not an ordinary house, remember; this is a house that we are already pretty well convinced is alive and somehow threatening. So as you walk down that corridor, you don't move gradually closer to that mysterious and ominous closed door. "You walk down the hall toward it, watching as if from outside yourself as the door gets closer and larger." In fact, that *door* moves closer to *you*. And finally, as hand touches doorknob and we are about to see what lies behind that door, something that obviously fascinates and frightens Ben, he draws back, turns away, at the peak of curiosity and tension.

Suddenly we are in another paragraph. Ben has physically turned away from the house, pulled himself and us back out of memory (memories that have now been firmly planted in our minds as our own) and brought us back to the reality of the moment. Ben acknowledges his fascination with the house and his memories of it. "Not yet," he thinks. "Later, perhaps, but not yet." We are, at this point, as convinced as Ben himself that the house has "waited for him." And will continue to wait.

Now Ben looks away, his gaze sweeping "out over the town." We learn that he is considering leasing the house. We are not certain the thought was in his mind before this encounter, but it is there now, testimony to his fascination with the house. But there is more, another and almost simultaneous part of the same thought. Even if the house comes into his hands, "he wouldn't allow himself to go upstairs." And the memory, now our own, of that closed door coming closer and larger, snaps back to us. Without ever actually saying so, King lets us know that there is something thoroughly awful and terrifying up there, something that is waiting only for the right moment to show itself. And will that happen? Will that moment come? It might, indeed, because Ben thinks here that he wouldn't go upstairs "unless it had to be done." Both the structure of that thought and the thought itself admit the compulsive power of memory and terror to make us do what reason forbids, to put ourselves in the way of danger. We will, we are certain, see the Marsten House again. And we will see that closed door. And we will open it.

The thought of future possibilities like that is now suddenly too much, too unsettling, and Ben precipitously flees the house and the thoughts and memories it conjures. "He got in his car, started it, and drove down the hill to Jerusalem's Lot." That sentence doesn't waste a word, and that car positively zooms away to safety.

✳ ✳

Between Ben's first view of it on that first day and the later revelation of its dark history, the Marsten House is mentioned only once. Brief though that mention is, King uses it to good effect.

We have seen Ben meet Susan Norton in the park. Like him, we have been attracted to her, and we have shared the warm and friendly and somehow comforting reminiscences they indulge in over ice-cream sodas. The scene and the conversation are long, casual, downright heartwarming, *nice*, and the sudden warmth of their new relationship holds the promise of greater warmth to come. When they part outside the shop, knowing they will see each other again, they both marvel over the "easy, natural, coincidental impingement of their lives." Everybody — Ben, Susan, the reader — is lulled into a sense of comfortable peace.

Ben, alone now, strolls to the corner and "casually" looks up toward the hill and the Marsten House. Instantly the whole mood changes, turns threatening. A memory, unpleasant and unsettling, snaps suddenly into his mind, erasing the warmth of his meeting with Susan. "The great forest fire of 1951 had burned almost to its very yard before the wind had changed." The unvoiced implication is that the house had somehow controlled the elements, controlled the wind and the fire, and refused to burn, its time not yet having come. "Maybe it should have burned," Ben thinks. "Maybe that would have been better." The reader, after sharing Ben's first frightening view of the house, sharing his nervous reaction and his memory of fear inside it, and sharing this jolting new memory of a fire that couldn't burn it, can only agree.

The next time we hear of the house, in a conversation between Ben and Susan as they drive home from their first date, we finally learn the history of "scandal and violence" associated with it. It is a tale of "horrors," the kind of story that small towns pass down "ceremonially from generation to generation." By that point, having felt the effects of the story through its working on Ben, we hardly feel that we are learning the details for the first time. Rather, we seem to be virtually remembering them ourselves.

❋ ❋

We see much more of the Marsten House in *'Salem's Lot*, of course, since it serves throughout the book as the focal point of evil. Each mention of it is fraught with similar nervousness and fear, which constantly enlarges and enriches our perception of the house as a source of Darkness. And since the evil at the center of the story is entwined with the evil of the house, the reinforcement of the house as something terrible and powerful and frightening is essential to the very center of the novel. That conviction is embedded in the reader's mind from the first pages of the story, from the moment we first become aware of the house, and, because of the specific language employed, is the product equally of the details themselves and the careful structure of the telling.

❋ ❋ ❋

One of those terrible visions came to me — I think they are reserved exclusively for husbands and fathers — of the picture window blowing in with a low hard coughing sound and sending jagged arrows of glass into my wife's bare stomach, into my boy's face and neck. The horrors of the Inquisition are nothing compared to the fates your mind can imagine for your loved ones.

—from THE MIST

The Night Journeys
of Stephen King

by Douglas E. Winter

I.

"To the three Ds — death, destruction and destiny.
Where would we be without them?"

— Stephen King

"THE REACH WAS WIDER IN THOSE DAYS," says Stella Flanders, the oldest resident of Goat Island, Maine. Ninety-five years old and dying of cancer, Stella Flanders has decided to take a walk. It is winter, the Reach is frozen over for the first time in forty years, and Stella Flanders has begun to see ghosts. Having never before left Goat Island, she has decided it is time for a walk across the Reach. The coast of Maine is a mile and a half distant, and so far as we know, neither the coast nor Goat Island has had occasion to move. But Stella Flanders is right — the Reach *was* wider in those days.

The storyteller's name is Stephen King, and although he asks

"Do the Dead Sing?",* his story is about a journey. Stella Flanders, having left her home behind, sets forth on a voyage of discovery that looks homeward with every step. The lonely crossing of the dark waters of the Reach means death for Stella Flanders, and the question "Do the Dead Sing?" refers to what really lies on the far side of the Reach.

That question, in different guises, resounds throughout the fiction of Stephen King. Not very far from Goat Island, but in another version of reality called *The Stand*, Fran Goldsmith stands on the mainland coast at Ogunquit, Maine. She is pregnant, alone, and one of the few people left alive in a world decimated by a deadly flu. Fran Goldsmith has also decided to take a walk, and though the distance she must travel is considerable, her journey crosses a Reach no different than that facing Stella Flanders.

That Stella Flanders' journey is westward may be a fluke of geography; but the westward direction taken by Fran Goldsmith and the other travellers in *The Stand* is purposeful. Both stories enact the recurring American nightmare experienced by Poe's Arthur Gordon Pym, Melville's Ishmael and a host of fellow journeymen — a search for a meaningful utopia while glancing backward in idyllic reverie to lost innocence. It is a journey taken by Jack Torrance in *The Shining*, driving west toward the promise of a new life at the Overlook Hotel; by Johnny Smith in *The Dead Zone*, who crosses time itself; by character after character in King's fiction, caught between fear of the past's embrace and fear of progress in a world that placidly accepts the possibility of total war. It is a night journey, both literally and symbolically, and Stephen King is its foremost practitioner in contemporary fiction.

Stella Flanders' crossing of the Reach provides an appropriate introduction to the night journeys of Stephen King. As an archetype of American nightmare, "Do the Dead Sing?" suggests the major reasons for the importance and popularity of horror fiction, and the writings of Stephen King in particular. It will

---

*"Do the Dead Sing?" was first published in *Yankee*, Nov. 1981.

serve as a roadmap of context, by which we will travel through King's recent novels, beginning with his epic novel of journey, *The Stand*, and concluding with the dark stasis of *Cujo*. And the question "Do the Dead Sing?"—like the night journey—will haunt us throughout these novels in literal and symbolic manifestations that may prove more frightening than the face of fear itself.

Asking whether the dead sing is much like asking where we would be without "death, destruction and destiny." These questions have been asked since the first horror story was told by firelight, yet are as unanswerable as the inevitable question of why we tell and listen to horror stories. The tale of terror is an inextricable element of the human condition—a guilty fascination with darkness and irrationality, with the potential for expanding human consciousness and perception, and with the understanding of our mortality and our universe. Western society is obsessed with horror fiction—the past fifteen years have seen an eruption in the reading and writing (and filming) of horror fiction rivalled only by the halcyon days of the ghost story at the close of the nineteenth century. Since 1974, over forty million copies of the books of Stephen King alone have been printed.

To ask why we read horror fiction is to ask why Stella Flanders took that walk on that cold winter's day of the storyteller's imagination. Death stalks Stella Flanders, and her faltering steps onto the Reach are an adventure, an escape from a mundane life and death. At a minimum, horror fiction is a means of escape, sublimating the very real and often overpowering horrors of everyday life in favor of surreal, exotic and visionary realms. Of course, escapism is not necessarily a rewarding experience. Horror fiction's focus upon morbidity and mortality suggests a masochistic or exploitative experience, often conjuring subjective fantasies in which our worst fears or darkest desires are brought into tangible existence. "It was the way things worked," suggests Officer Hunton in King's story "The Mangler" (*Night Shift*), "—the human animal had a built-in urge to view the remains." But conscientious fiction of escape can provide something more —an art of mimesis, a counterfeiting of reality whose inducement to imagination gives the reader access to truths beyond the scope of reason. So D. H. Lawrence would write of Poe's fiction: "It is lurid and melodramatic, but it is true."

The tensions between fantasy and reality, wanderlust and nostalgia, produce an intriguing paradox. Stella Flanders' escape across the Reach in search of the ghosts of her past can only lead to her death, reflecting the alternately seductive and repulsive nature of horror fiction. In the words of critic Jack Sullivan: "What is sought after — the otherworldly — makes us realize how much we need the worldly; but the more we know of the world, the more we need to be rid of it."*

The six o'clock news is sufficient to show our need to be rid of the world: assassination, rampant crime, political wrongdoing, social upheaval and war are as much a part of our daily lives as the very air we breathe. And we can no longer trust that air — or the water that we drink, the food that we eat, our machines or our neighbors. Just ask Harold Parkette, who employed "The Lawnmower Man" (*Night Shift*); or the young woman who met "The Man Who Loved Flowers" (*Night Shift*); or the characters of *Cujo*, whose reality is, in the final trumps, as inescapable as our own. And we live in the shadow of the atomic bomb, harbinger of our total destruction and the ultimate proof that we can no longer trust even ourselves.

Pyschoanalyst and sleep researcher Charles Fisher once observed that "Dreaming permits each and every one of us to be quietly and safely insane every night of our lives."** His words apply as well to the waking dreams of horror fiction. We can breach our foremost taboos, allow ourselves to lose control, experience the same emotions — terror, revulsion, helplessness — that besiege us daily. Yet the confinement of the action to the printed page or the screen renders the irrationality safe, lending our fears the appearance of being controllable. Our sensibilities are offered a simple escape from escapism: wanderlust fulfilled, we can leave horror's pages and shadowed theatres with the

---

*Jack Sullivan, *Elegant Nightmares: The English Ghost Story from Le Fanu to Blackwood* (Ohio University, 1978), p. 18.

**"Sleep: Perchance to Dream . . .", *Newsweek* (Nov. 30, 1959) p. 104

conviction that the horror was not true and cannot be true. Every horror novel, like every nightmare, has a happy ending, just so long as we can wake up, and we can say, like Herman Melville's *Pierre*, that "It is all a dream — we dreamed that we dream we dream."

But horror fiction is not simply an unquiet place that we may visit in moments of need. Along with its obvious cathartic value, horror fiction has a cognitive value which helps us to understand ourselves and our existential situation. In its pages, prosaic everyday life clashes with a mysterious, irrational and potentially supernatural universe. The mundane existence of Stella Flanders is never the same after she sees the ghost of her long-dead husband. Her haunting is traditional, and Stephen King conjures an atmosphere of suspended disbelief by his very reliance upon the trappings of supernatural traditions. Like settling into a comfortable chair, King's conscientious reliance upon supernatural traditions — both thematic (as in the vampire lore of *'Salem's Lot* and the Gothic castle/hotel of *The Shining*) and in terms of narrative technique (as the Lovecraftian epistolary tale of "Jerusalem's Lot" and the Kiplingesque smoking room reminiscence of "The Man Who Would Not Shake Hands") — lends credibility to the otherwise unbelievable. The supernatural need not creep across the floorboards of each and every story, however; reality itself often is sufficiently frightening — and certainly credible — as short stories like King's "The Last Rung on the Ladder" and "Strawberry Spring" prove through themes of psychological distress and aberration.

The early Gothic novel observed a rigid dichotomy between fiction based in supernaturalism and in a rational explanation. The latter form, rekindled briefly in the "shudder pulps" of the 1930s and certain of the "Baby Jane" maniac films of the 1960s, proposed apparently supernatural events that were explained rationally at the story's end. As the modern horror story emerged in the late 1800s, however, neither a rational nor a supernatural explanation of events needed ultimately to be endorsed. Even formalist ghost story author M. R. James would write: "It is not amiss sometimes to leave a loophole for a natural explanation, but I would say, let the loophole be so narrow as not to be quite

practicable." Indeed, the archetypal ghost story, Joseph Sheridan Le Fanu's "Green Tea" (1869), posed a mystifying dual
explanation of its events, using the inevitable tension between
the rational and the irrational to exacerbate its horror — a tension replicated nearly one hundred years later in the wholly
inadequate interpretation of the psychiatrist at the conclusion
of Hitchcock's *Psycho* (1960) and the recommendation for
exorcism by the physicians in *The Exorcist* (1973).

Stephen King's most pervasive short story, "The Boogeyman"
(*Night Shift*), suggests that explanation, whether supernatural
or rational, may simply *not* be the business of horror fiction —
that the very fact that "Do the Dead Sing?" is unanswerable
draws us inexorably to his night journeys. "I came to you
because I want to tell my story," says Lester Billings, comforta-
bly enthroned on the psychiatric couch of Dr. Harper. "All I did
was kill my kids. One at a time. Killed them all." Billings then
explains that he did not actually kill his three children; but he is
"responsible" for their deaths, because he has left certain closet
doors open at night, and "the boogeyman" has come out. A
rational mind must reject such a confessional; and Billings is an
abrasive personality — cold, insensitive, filled with hatred for
the human condition. Immediately, we doubt his credibility
and his sanity. By the story's close, Billings has made clear that it
is he who fears "the boogeyman"; and the reader can only conclude that he has murdered his children. Dr. Harper states that
therapy will be necessary; but when Billings returns to the psychiatrist's office, he notices that the closet door is open — first, by
just a crack, but it quickly swings wide: "'So nice,' the boogeyman said as it shambled out. It still held its Dr. Harper mask in
one rotted spade-claw hand."

On a metaphorical level, the boogeyman's appearance may
be an affirmation of Billings' psychosis — this is the loophole for a
natural explanation. Symbolically, we see psychiatry, the sup-
posedly rational science of the mind, succumb to the slavering
irrationality of a "boogeyman." The retrogression to childhood,
so intrinsic to the Freudian solution, ironically affirms the cor-
rectness of childhood fears. And this very image is revisited
again and again in King's fiction. When Father Callahan con-

fronts "Mr. Barlow," the king vampire of *'Salem's Lot*, he recognizes the face: it is that of "Mr. Flip," the boogeyman who haunted the closets of his childhood. The thing that haunts Tad Trenton's closet in *Cujo* prefigures that rabid nightmare unleashed in daylight. And the Overlook Hotel of *The Shining* is revealed in the end as the penultimate haunted closet, from which the boogeyman shambles:

> A long and nightmarish masquerade party went on here, and had gone on for years. Little by little a force had accrued, as secret and silent as interest in a bank account. Force, presence, shape, they were all only words and none of them mattered. It wore many masks, but it was all one. Now, somewhere, it was coming for him. It was hiding behind Daddy's face, it was imitating Daddy's voice, it was wearing Daddy's clothes.
>
> But it was not his Daddy. (Chapter 54)

On both the literal and symbolic levels, "The Boogeyman" shattered the distinction between the supernatural and the empirical, offering the chilling possibility that there is no difference. In its wake, King put forward a theme of "rational supernaturalism" in his novels — first seeded in *Carrie*, but brought to fruition in the genre-transcending *The Stand, The Dead Zone* and *Firestarter* — granting credence to unnatural phenomena through elaborate rationalizations not unlike those of science fiction, and simultaneously suggesting a dark truth that we all suspect: that rationality and order are façades, mere illusions of control imposed upon a reality of chaos.

Like the mask worn by the boogeyman, what Stella Flanders left behind in the small Goat Island community is deceptive. The apparent serenity and pastoral simplicity of Goat Island is stripped away through Stella Flanders' memories of the town's complicity in the deaths of a mongoloid baby and a child molester. Artifice and masquerade are recurring themes in Stephen King's novels, reminding us that evil works from within as well as from without — that we are clothed with the thin veneer of civilization, beneath which waits the beast, eager to emerge.

Horror fiction is thus an intrinsically subversive art, which seeks the face of reality by striking through the pasteboard masks of appearance. That the lifting of the mask may reveal the face of the boogeyman is our existential dilemma: the eternal tension between doubt and belief that will haunt us to our grave.

Stella Flanders does not read horror fiction in "Do the Dead Sing?", but she does the next best thing — attend a funeral. The ritual is not unlike a horror story, organizing and packaging fears, giving meaning to death (and thus, to life). And Stella Flanders helps us see something more: her attendance is compelled as much by mere inquisitiveness, sublimation, catharsis and the demands of society as by memory of the past. Things were better then — certainly for the deceased, but also for the attendees; after all, the Reach was wider in those days. Thus, when Stella Flanders embarks upon her journey, she understands what she is leaving behind in the "small world" on this side of the Reach: "a way of being and a way of living; a feeling."

This is a powerful motif; it may cause the reader to look to his or her own life as well. In King's works, we reexperience those occasions in our lives when it seemed important to understand and honestly express ourselves, to perceive a genuine identity beneath the social exteriors of manners, habits, clothes and job. Such moments are most common in childhood, when no one's identity is certain and when any exterior is likely to be impermanent or false. Uncertainty in our own sense of self renders the process of knowing and communicating with others difficult and emotionally intense. For most of us the business of life is the process of social relation and social judgment; we constantly attempt to fix our views of others, to justify our emotions and judgments. Yet language seems always inadequate to express completely what we *know*. We leave that world behind us as we grow older; as King wryly notes in *'Salem's Lot*: "the only cure is the eventual ossification of the imaginary faculties, and this is called adulthood." We lose our sense of mysticism — of fear and fantasy, of unhindered and yet inexplicable vision, of unscalable heights and limitless possibilities. It is the world that Stella Flanders finds on the far side of the Reach. It is the same world that we recapture in the fiction of horror.

Our haunted childhood offers one truth that is often obscured by the countless rationalizations, psychological interpretations and critical insights offered to explain the reading and writing of horror fiction. We knew that truth on those nights when we feared the dark, or the slightly open closet door, or the abyss beneath our bed, yet we were drawn to the darkness and dread. It is a truth that anyone who steps upon a roller coaster must recognize.

The truth is that it was fun — frightening ourselves, having nightmares, realizing that there is something that we do not and may not ever understand. The Reach was wider in those days, and the question "Do the Dead Sing?" did not need to be asked. Now that we are older, we may ask that question and offer explanations, but that one truth prevails throughout the night journeys of Stephen King: "We had some fun tonight," says comedian Steve Martin, "considering that we're all gonna die."

II.

"Underneath this reality in which we live and have our being, another and altogether different reality lies concealed."
— Friedrich Nietzsche

STEPHEN KING'S NOVEL OF JOURNEY, *The Stand* (1978), signalled a definite turning point in his fiction. Prior to this work, his novels and short stories were structured within fairly conventional horror traditions. *The Stand* would be the first of several highly successful novels that transcended specific literary formulas.

If one must pigeonhole *The Stand* (which was packaged both in hardcover and paperback as a horror novel), it is best described as epic fantasy. Such a description refers not simply to its length — over 800 printed pages — but to its affinity with the fantasies of J. R. R. Tolkien and E. R. Eddison, as well as classical epics from Homer to Milton's *Paradise Lost* to Thomas Mann's *The Magic Mountain* and *Doctor Faustus*.

Like Tolkien's famous *The Lord of the Rings*, *The Stand* takes the form of a noble quest and employs a host of characters, some heroic, some darker and monstrous. Like Mann, however, King does not set his epic in an imaginary Elfland, but — with chilling impact — in the world we know. *The Stand* creates a modern myth, portraying the timeless struggle between good and evil in terms and geography distinctly American: evil haunts not dark, clammy caverns or mist-laden mountains, but the cornfields of Nebraska, the backroads of Montana, the oil refineries of Indiana; its seat of power is not Mordor but Las Vegas. Evil does not strike with sorcerous spells, bat-winged nightriders or flame-breathing dragons, but with .45 caliber pistols, radio-controlled explosives, Phantom jets, and nuclear warheads — its victims lie in the crowded corridors of overworked hospitals, in the vomit of drug overdose, in pools of bullet-rendered blood, and even in a bowl of Campbell's Chunky Beef Soup.

In the brief introductory note to his American epic poem "Paterson," William Carlos Williams described the essential quality of the modern epic: "A taking up of slack; a dispersal and a metamorphosis." So too are these essential qualities of *The Stand*. The novel's first third is a creation myth involving the "taking up of slack": the birth of a new world through the destruction of our modern world. The motive force is a "superflu" that escapes from a secret military installation. Called "Captain Trips" (ironically the nickname of Jerry Garcia of The Grateful Dead), the superflu is 99.4% pure, not unlike Ivory Soap, and its infection is always fatal. Only six-tenths of one percent of the population, who are inexplicably immune to the superflu, survive its onslaught.

Their new world is a haunted one. King's short story "Night Surf" (*Night Shift*), which was the genesis of *The Stand*, vividly distills the horror of the reign of Captain Trips. Its focus is on a group of teenagers who grimly frolic along the resort beaches of southern Maine in a brief holiday, waiting for seemingly inevitable death from the disease. A first person narrative, "Night Surf" is concerned with subjectivity, inviting the reader to interpret the narrator not simply by what he says, but by what he chooses to say. What we see is bitterness, alienation and defeat.

King exposes the tragi-comedy of regret: a childhood — and a world — that the narrator cannot regain, buried beneath the ironic epitaph: "Just the flu." And omnipresent is the sea — traditionally a symbol of journey and death — its night surf creeping toward shore.

Much of the power of King's epic draws upon the juxtaposition of the world that was with a post-apocalypse wasteland. The Gothic tradition has always played a major, but unspoken role in apocalyptic fiction, and *The Stand*, much like Mary Shelley's *The Last Man* (1826) and Shirley Jackson's *The Sundial* (1958), brings that tradition to the foreground. In particular, apocalyptic fiction implicitly invokes the "dual life" or "dual landscape" theme present in most Gothic fiction and used as a touchstone for much criticism of all nineteenth century literature. This portrayal of duality attempts to burrow beneath surface illusions to reach the inevitable dark reality below. Thus, in Bram Stoker's *Dracula* (1897), the king vampire's castle is schizoid: its upper levels include a Victorian library and well-furnished apartments, while underneath lie labyrinthine vaults; likewise, Dr. Seward's mansion encloses an insane asylum. Similar landscapes are presented in *The Stand* — for example, the Disease Center in Vermont is a bright, sterile environment that exudes order and authority but is transmuted to a maze-like chaos, filled with death and dread. In *Heart of Darkness* (1902), Joseph Conrad described a similar duality as the "whited sepulcher";* and perhaps no better description exists for Las Vegas, where King's evil forces congregate.

This duality of life and landscape is the central metaphor of *The Stand*. Superimposing the illusions of our modern world upon the ravished landscape of catastrophe, King explores the strange mixture of myth and reality that comprises our perception of America, recently catalogued in James O. Robertson's *American Myth, American Reality* (1980):

From the colonial years, Americans have seen themselves as a

---

*Conrad's source was *The Gospel According to Matthew* 23:27, which itself aptly describes the Gothic duality: "Woe unto you, scribes and Pharisees, hypocrites! For ye are like whited sepulchers, which indeed appear beautiful outward, but are within full of dead man's bones, and of all uncleanliness."

people of great mission — of destiny. The westward urge of this "manifest destiny" saw the conquest of a continent and the creation of the very imperialism that we sought to escape. We see ourselves as independent and democratic, even though two political machines control the electoral process, many of us never vote, and the spirit of independence is likeliest to be shown by dissent. Our heroes typically have been cowboys and rugged individualists — only recently have we embraced our martyrs. We think of ourselves as non-violent and peace-loving, but we cannot successfully regulate, let alone ban, the sale of handguns. We have conquered ruthlessly when our destiny has been challenged, and we have found war to be a cleansing experience. Our science created the atomic bomb to end a great war, and we must live in its shadow evermore. We romanticize small towns, yet flock to our crowded cities. "All men are created equal," but this may not include women, gays, blacks, chicanos. . . . "In God We Trust," but missile silos and germ warfare hedge our bets.

We pursue happiness, believe in progress, materialism and the infallibility of science, but we doubt our success, our power, ourselves. As we watch the evening news, if we reflect even momentarily upon our social fabric, we begin to question the validity of the engine of progress. Our position as a society is a precarious one — and principally because of our misguided belief in the divinity of civilization and technology. When crime and inflation run rampant, when our nuclear reactors threaten meltdown, when our diplomats are held hostage in foreign lands, our doubts intensify. These are the precise fears that King explores in *The Stand*.

This dual landscape, psychic and geographic, provides the setting for the remainder of the novel, which takes the form of the quest so common in epic literature. The "dispersal" and "metamorphosis" quickly focus on the traditional epic struggle of man against monster, Odysseus confronting Scylla and Polyphemus, Beowulf squaring off with the Dragon. By the Fourth of July, less than three weeks after the epidemic begins, only the immune remain, and a new America rises purposefully from the human rubble. The survivors are visited with strange and often highly personalized dreams involving two recurring images: a dark, faceless man offering enticement and threat, and an ancient black woman who exudes peace and sanctuary. These images form the parameters of a choice between good and evil in which each individual's intrinsic predisposition plays an important role; and that choice divides the survivors into opposing camps, the evil forces at Las Vegas, the forces of good at Boulder, Colorado.

The embodiment of good is Abagail Freemantle, a one hundred and eight-year-old black woman from Nebraska, affectionately called Mother Abagail. Her image is that of an earth mother, spawned from the fertile cornfields and imbued with a frontier Christianity; she is less an active force than a vessel through which courses of action are revealed. About her gather an incongruous collection of folk heroes, not unconsciously paralleling the multi-racial band of adventurers of Tolkienesque epic fantasy: a Texas blue collar worker; a mute, self-educated orphan; a pregnant Maine college student; an emerging rock star; a retarded Oklahoma man; a New Hampshire sociology professor; and what may be the last surviving dog.

The protagonist of *The Stand* is Stu Redman, the factory worker from Arnette, Texas. His soft-spoken, stoic reliability evokes Gary Cooper, Clint Eastwood and other archetypal American heroes. He is the character to whom we are first introduced, and he is one of the few lead characters to survive the novel; as his last name suggests, he is the new native American. Yet despite his traditional heroic and American qualities, his role is one of continuum — he does not change through the course of the novel. The critical character is burnt-out rock musician Larry Underwood, whose internal strife places him on the knife-edge between good and evil, hinted at by his very name. As his mother ironically realizes before dying of the superflu that Underwood may have communicated to her: "[T]here was good in Larry, great good. It was there, but this late on it would take a catastrophe to bring it out." (Chapter 5) Underwood is particularly interesting because he lacks traditional heroic qualities; he is self-destructive and avoids taking personal responsibility.

The entwined fates of Redman and Underwood culminate in

the novel's final third, when "the stand" — the confrontation between good and evil — occurs. Foreshadowed in the novel's early
pages, the destiny of these characters seems clear. As Captain
Trips ravages the nation, Redman is locked in isolation, confined by government authorities desperate to understand his
immunity; Underwood meanwhile experiences the mass graveyard of New York City. When Redman, Underwood and two
others go to take "the stand," Redman's leg is broken *en route*; he
must be left alone in the desert while the others proceed to Las
Vegas. His "stand" takes place in isolation, as if it were a reaffir-
mation of his individualism. Underwood, the rock performer,
must take the center stage, this time to die before the masses.

An effective counterpoint to Underwood is Harold Lauder,
who also wrestles with impossible self-demands but makes a
conscious decision to reject good in favor of evil. Lauder is never
a truly sympathetic character. Initially obese, neurotic and self-
pitying, he matures outwardly, repressing his repulsiveness and
lack of understanding to the breaking point, when he is used and
and cruelly cast aside by the forces of evil. Lauder's fate is dictated not only by selfishness, but by the American dream; he is
unwilling or unable to exist within the post-apocalypse society.
Lauder shows us that the choice for evil is never freely taken;
and the moment of self-recognition at his death suggests that
this choice is never irreversible.

The focal point of the wrong — west — side of the Rocky
Mountains is Randall Flagg, the Dark Man, the "Walkin Dude."
His earliest memory is of attending school with Charles Stark-
weather; but he also recalls meeting Lee Harvey Oswald in 1962,
riding with the Ku Klux Klan, cop-killing with black men in
New York City and whispering plans to Donald DeFreeze about
Patty Hearst. One almost expects him to cry out, like the narrator of The Rolling Stones' "Sympathy for the Devil": "Pleased to
meet you, hope you guess my name."

Yet Randall Flagg is neither Satan nor his demonic spawn. He
is an atavistic embodiment of evil, the "last magician of rational
thought." Flagg is the epitome of the Gothic villain: his appearance is indistinct, malleable, a collection of masks. Phantom-

like, he wanders the corridors of the haunted castle of the American landscape, symbolizing the inexplicable fear of the return of bygone powers — both technological and, as his last name intimates, sociopolitical. He is a Miltonic superman whose strength originates in dark mystery. At his right hand is Donald Merwin Elbert, the "Trashcan Man," whose pyromania is matched only by his instinctive technical wizardry at finding and operating the machinery of death — symbolic of blind science. At his left hand is Lloyd Henreid, street wise and stir crazy, the two-bit criminal gone big time — symbolic of the moral weakness at the heart of Flagg's empire. Like many Gothic villains, Flagg is curiously inept, helplessly watching his well-laid plans go awry at every turn. He is a rhetorician of self, seemingly obsessed with convincing himself and others of his importance and destiny. And as the novel's climax discloses, Flagg, like Tolkien's Sauron, is a straw man who literally collapses when confronted.

There is almost a compulsion to view *The Stand* as a sustained allegory; but its climax produces instead a sense of brooding mystery. The quest to Las Vegas does not simply seek the safety to rebuild what is lost; the survivors are searching for redemption for the desolation of the world. In counterpoint to typical post-apocalypse fiction, whose journeys are structured by the acquisition of material things, King's quest is marked by the stripping away of possessions. It is a heroic show of faith, a sacrifice of the flesh toward an uncertain end. When Larry Underwood is brought before the city's populace for execution, it is with lightning rod effect. Out of the desert emerges the Trashcan Man, an atomic bomb in tow. His countenance reflects the horror:

> He was in the last stages of radiation sickness. His hair was gone. His arms, poking out of the tatters of his shirt, were covered with open running sores. His face was a cratered red soup from which one desert-faded blue eye peered with pitiful intelligence. His teeth were gone. His nails were gone. His eyelids were frayed flaps. . . .

> Flagg watched him come, frozen. His smile was
> gone. His high, rich color was gone. His face was sud-
> denly a window made of pale clear glass. (Chapter 63)

The "last magician of rational thought" has exceeded the
bounds of his pentacle; the powers that he invoked have escaped
his control, and the face of evil has passed to another. Flagg's
clothes suddenly are empty:

> . . . Flagg was no longer there. He had a bare impres-
> sion of something monstrous standing *in front* of
> where Flagg had been. Something slumped and
> hunched and almost without shape — something with
> enormous yellow eyes slit by dark cat's pupils.
>
> Then it was gone. (Chapter 63)

Above Las Vegas stands a vision of the "Hand of God." Then the
bomb explodes: "And the righteous and unrighteous alike were
consumed in that holy fire." (Chapter 63) We are reminded of
the last appearance of the great seabeast in *Moby Dick*, or of the
primitive, unexplained world of Grendel's lake — the source of
poetry. This Biblical imagery heightens the sense of destiny and
mysticism. King refuses to accede to the typical demand that
horror fiction tie and knot all loose ends together. Beyond the
novel's conclusion, mystery and horror remain — the mystery of
the human condition, of life and death in a universe of good and
evil, of destiny and chance — and of hope.

The climactic destruction of Las Vegas also re-echoes the
Gothic themes present in *The Stand*, harkening to the exploding
walls and collapsing turrets at the climax of Walpole's *The Castle
of Otranto* (1764). Ruins, the central metaphor and repetitive
prop of Gothic fiction, express a triumph, a movement toward
freedom and away from control and discipline, much as the
Gothic movement was itself, at least in origin. *The Stand* glories
in these ruins, as King admits in *Danse Macabre*: "Yes, folks, in
The Stand I got a chance to scrub the whole human race, and *it
was fun!*"

Although the most mystical of King's novels, *The Stand* is also
his most explicitly didactic work. The paradoxes of myth and
reality that seemingly riddle the fabric of American society are a
Gordian Knot, split and unwinding in the ruins. This socio-

political subtext poses difficult questions about order and authority. Humans need companionship, but companionship produces society, which in turn seems to require order. To have order, someone must have authority, but someone must be subject to this authority. Order and authority benefit us by providing a stable society and technological development; but they also mean oppression, the atomic bomb and the spectre of Captain Trips. . . .

The problems of order and authority recur throughout Stephen King's novels, and provide one explanation for his consistent concentration on children and the dynamics of growing up. King depicts children with a sympathetic aura of recapitulation: the child literally "as father to the man," a miniature rehearsal of the development of the adult race unrestrained by the illusions and realities of order and authority. Perception is heightened; passionate feelings and animistic thoughts abound. In King's words:

> None of us adults remember childhood. We think we remember it, which is even more dangerous. Colors are brighter. The sky looks bigger. It's impossible to remember exactly how it was. Kids live in a constant state of shock. The input is so fresh and so strong that it's bound to be frightening. (*College Papers* interview, winter 1980)

King's fiction accordingly characterizes children with a more open attitude to the supernatural and a wider range of responses to their environment than the "rational" adult.

King similarly attributes such heightened powers of perception to the alcoholic, the feeble-minded and the insane. A drunk in *Carrie* is the first to "know" who is responsible for the town's destruction. And Tom Cullen in *The Stand*, forever simple-mindedly assuring us that M-O-O-N spells something, displays precognitive fugues under hypnosis and ultimately receives guidance through visions of the dead.

In *The Stand*, King's message is clear. Freed from the yoke of civilization, the survivors of the superflu epidemic begin to experience heightened perception:

> As the gigantic quiet of the nearly empty country

accumulated on you day by day, imprinting its truth
on you by its very weight, the sun — the moon, too, for
that matter — began to seem bigger and more important. More personal. These bright skyships began to
look to you as they had when you were a child.
(Chapter 37)

Indeed, the narrative structure of the novel emphasizes this
theme, beginning with a disjointed multiple-viewpoint technique that subtly collapses inward until even the consciousness
of characters is interwoven at the conclusion.

King holds in an interview in *High Times* that "the curse of
civilization is its chumminess." One senses a gleeful sarcasm as
he recounts the antics of the Free Zone citizenry in developing a
reconstruction democracy. The organizers stress the need to re-
affirm the Constitution and the Declaration of Independence,
while at the same time conspiring to assure that hand-picked individuals assume leadership positions. Committees, town meetings, census-taking and jails spring weed-like into existence as if
a natural function of togetherness. The Free Zone, so focused on
ordering its lives, literally fiddles with matches, while the totali-
tarian reign of Randall Flagg readies napalm for its Phantom
jets; and only a final visionary experience by Mother Abagail
rouses the Free Zone from the comfortable sleep of socialization,
provoking "the stand."

The problem may be insoluble: the malignancy of order seems
to balance the social benefits of the lack of chaos. At the conclusion of *The Stand*, it is clear that the destruction of Flagg provides but a respite. Redman returns to the Free Zone to find that
its police have been given authority to bear arms — and the possibility remains that other societies will hold interests adverse to
the Free Zone. King's characters ask and answer the novel's ultimate question: "(D)o you think people ever learn anything? . . .
I don't know" (Chapter 68). That question is posed continually
in post-apocalypse fiction, as in the classic *A Canticle for Leibo-
witz* (1960) of Walter M. Miller, Jr.: "Are we doomed to do it
again and again and again? Have we no choice but to play the
Phoenix in an unending sequence of rise and fall? . . . *Are we*

doomed to it, Lord, chained to the pendulum of our own mad clockwork, helpless to halt its swing?"

Stephen King offers no pat answer: "My own lesson in writing *The Stand* was that cutting the Gordian Knot simply destroys the riddle instead of solving it, and the book's last line is an admission that the riddle still remains" (*Danse Macabre*). King shares Miller's existential dread, but *The Stand* does not present a dystopian vision. Although anti-scientific, *The Stand* disavows scientific ignorance as the answer; instead, King is assured by a faith in faith — he does not despair of man. As in all of King's novels, *The Stand* tells us that the need for action is on an individual level. Its conclusion finds Stu Redman and Fran Goldsmith, mother of the first post-apocalypse baby, retreating to Maine from the renascent civilization of the Free Zone, an Adam and Eve cast out of the wilderness and into a temporary Eden. Hope remains, even if the worst is expected or indeed has occurred; as King has written, "*The Stand* . . . echoes Albert Camus's remark 'happiness, too, is inevitable.'" (*Danse Macabre*).

III.

". . . but that would be wrong."
— Richard Milhous Nixon

THE WHEEL OF FORTUNE is the central symbol of *The Dead Zone* (1979). It is blind chance, whirling hypnotically, the bright colors and numbers blurring. All bets have been laid, and we wait, breathless, for our number to come up. At the wheel's side, the carnival barker patiently smiles — the odds are with him, and perhaps a small lever assures his take. Yet if we look closely at the spinning wheel, the colors and numbers alter for an instant, revealing a second disc. At its heart is an eagle, but its edges are slotted as if, like the wheel of fortune, it awaits the silvered ball. It is the Presidential Seal — a symbol of the paradoxes of our politics: of martyrdom and tyranny; of idealism and peacefulness, corruption and warmongering; of truth and lies; and of peanut farmers and B-movie actors. Thus are fate and politics intermingled in modern America.

American literature has produced countless political horror novels, Sinclair Lewis's *The Iron Heel* (1908) and Robert Penn Warren's *All the King's Men* (1946) eminent among them; but few of these novels have dealt with the supernatural. Since the 1950s, novels from authors such as Allen Drury and Fletcher Knebel have echoed recurring fears that politics and power have vanquished our democratic system of government in favor of a somewhat benign, conspiratorial totalitarianism. Such novels probe the individual's feeling of helplessness in face of the machinations of our political system — one in which races for even our highest office are decided not so much by the exercise of choice, but by factors as diverse as video images and rampaging policemen, media access and dirty tricks, untimely remarks and assassin's bullets. In such a system, the power of the individual seems nil; he or she becomes an observer, and choice seems a meaningless myth.

The Dead Zone explores the nature of choice, political and personal, in modern society. It is the story of Johnny Smith, whose intended resemblance to Everyman is signalled in the prosaic simplicity of his name. At age 22, Smith seems primed to live a full, happy, productive life. He is successfully employed as a high school teacher and he is in love with Sarah Bracknell. In October, 1970, Johnny and Sarah visit a carnival; as they prepare to depart, Smith is drawn to a sideshow wheel of fortune game. With unerring and uncanny accuracy — and despite heavily biased odds — he defeats the wheel and its brassy sideshow barker; while Sarah becomes alarmed and ultimately ill at this sudden obsessive change in his character.

As he returns home by taxicab from Sarah's apartment, the wheel of fortune spins, and Smith's number comes up: a dragracing automobile crashes head-on with the taxi, instantly killing the driver. Smith is rendered comatose for five years. The world drifts swiftly past: people die, the named few (Jimi Hendrix and Harry Truman) and the nameless millions; the war in

Vietnam ends; a Vice-President and President resign; and Sarah Bracknell marries and bears a child, while Smith's mother develops a religious fanaticism to the point of insanity.

And then, one day in May, 1975, Johnny Smith regains consciousness. But he wakes up with something more — a "secret strangeness" that is a staggeringly powerful cognitive ability. With a mere touch of the hand, Smith can *see* into people or objects, glimpsing their past, present or future. Ultimately, he will shake the hand of Greg Stillson, an unlikely congressional candidate, at a New Hampshire political rally. Smith perceives a strangely clouded vision of Stillson as the President of the United States, in which Stillson, riddled with madness, provokes a nuclear holocaust. That perception demands that he choose whether or not to act to stop Stillson, even if assassination must be the result.

Stephen King perceives two kinds of evil at work within the realm of horror fiction. The first is an internal evil; its classic depiction is in Robert Louis Stevenson's *Dr. Jekyll and Mr. Hyde* (1886), where unknown drugs released an evil being repressed within the self of Dr. Jekyll. The evil within is a traditional horror theme, often expressed in the form of a logical insistence that unpleasant consequences await those who meddle in matters best left undisturbed. Its archetypes include the myth of Pandora, the "true life fairy tale" of Bluebeard, and the powerful allegory of Faust.

In *The Dead Zone*, the symbolic device of the masquerade is used to depict the internal element of evil. Ahab cries in *Moby Dick* (1851): "All visible objects, man, are but as pasteboard masks. But in each event — in the living act, the undoubted deed — there, some unknown but still reasoning thing puts forth the moulding of its features from behind the unreasoning mask." Or in the words of Robert Bloch, author of *Psycho* (1959): "Horror is the removal of masks."

We are introduced to the masquerade on the night of Johnny Smith's fateful trip to the carnival, when he dons a bizarre mask as a Halloween prank to frighten Sarah:

> (T)he face appeared before her, floating in the darkness, a horrible face out of a nightmare. It glowed a

spectral, rotting green. One eye was wide open, seeming to stare at her in wounded fear. The other was squeezed shut in a sinister leer. The left half of the face, the half with the open eye, appeared to be normal. But the right half was the face of a monster, drawn and inhuman. . . . (Part I, Chapter 1, section 1)

This one-eyed, bifurcated visage is recurrent in King's novels. It was worn by the Trashcan Man of *The Stand*, dying of radiation sickness as he wheels his atomic bomb through the streets of Las Vegas; it is also the face of Rainbird, the haunting assassin of *Firestarter*. The visage is highly symbolic: Sarah identifies it as a Jekyll-Hyde appearance, invoking the duality of good and evil competing within each of us. In the case of Trashcan Man and Rainbird, the monstrous face is the explicit externalization of their surrender to evil. But in the case of Johnny Smith, the face is but a mask that may be removed with the flick of a wrist: it is an externalization of Everyman's *possible* evil — one that Smith, who still has a choice, may wear or discard.

The masquerade also pervades the novel's subplot of the "Castle Rock Rapist," whose identity is withheld until the moment of Smith's psychic revelation. When Smith is asked to undertake a Peter Hurkos role in attempting to determine the identity of the rapist, he succeeds — it is an evil that has hidden for years behind the mask of one of the town's trusted police deputies.

But the prominent focus of *The Dead Zone* is the masquerade of politics. Greg Stillson has taken the Vietnamese masquerade-game of the "Laughing Tiger" one step further: ". . . inside the beast-skin, a man. . . . But inside the man-skin, a beast" (Part II, Chapter 20, section 1). King's political commentary is unmistakably clear — the many faces of Stillson are no less real than those demonstrated by the politicians of Watergate, Koreagate and Abscam infamy. That an actor should become President in 1980 is an affirmation of what the 1970s have taught us (or failed to teach us) about the nature of politics, and a disturbing warning of the power of the mask.

Ironically, when Stillson is confronted with his masquerade by Smith's assassination attempt, it is Stillson's effort to mask himself — to hide behind a small child — that discloses his true nature to the public and brings about his downfall.

The second form of evil addressed here by King is symbolized by the wheel of fortune: chance or predestination. It is the child whose mother was prescribed thalidomide; it is the stand-by passenger whose flight went belly-up on takeoff. It is an evil we cannot — and indeed, do not — dwell upon because of its frightening implications; it awaits us at every turn of the spinning wheel of fortune, every toss of the dice, without apparent logic or motivation. It cannot be changed and it cannot be avoided. As King wrote in his compelling short story "The Monkey":

> It might be . . . that some evil — maybe even most evil — isn't even sentient and aware of what it is. It might be that most evil is very much like a monkey full of clockwork that you wind up; the clockwork turns, the cymbals begin to beat, the stupid glass eyes laugh . . . or appear to laugh. . . .

From *The Stand* through *Cujo* — and most dramatically in *The Dead Zone* — Stephen King's protagonists face "the monkey" involuntarily and accidentally, victims of the spinning wheel of fortune. These characters are extraordinarily ordinary people, lacking hubris or even the innocent curiosity of Bluebeard's wife, let alone the Faustian hunger for forbidden knowledge that possesses the likes of Victor Frankenstein. They have such prosaic names as Johnny Smith.

These King protagonists have much in common with the lamented Reverend Jennings of Joseph Sheridan Le Fanu's "Green Tea" (1869), whose sole offense is the consumption of green tea. Jack Sullivan describes the world view so expressed by Le Fanu:

> The very title of the tale registers the fundamental irony: the awful disjuncture between cause and effect, crime and punishment. What emerges is an irrational, almost Kafkaesque feeling of guilt and persecution . . . Jennings never experiences even a flash of tragic recognition; on the contrary, he never knows why this horrible thing is happening. There is no insight, no justice and therefore no tragedy. There is only absurd

cruelty, a grim world view which endures in the reader's mind long after the hairs have settled on the back of the neck.*

Although this horrifying aesthetic is principal in King's later novels, he does not embrace entirely the grim world view espoused by Le Fanu. An enigmatic element is present, lurking in the twilight intersection of rationality and supernaturality — a hint of insight and of justice in the workings of the wheel of fortune that does not sacrifice the horror and foreboding sense of doom inherent in its spin. It is the element of *destiny*.

When one of *The Dead Zone's* characters describes Stillson as a "cynical carnival pitchman," the import is not simply literal. Destiny links the internal and external elements of evil. In *The Stand*, the imagery of destiny is focused principally in religious terms; four leading characters — Stu Redman, Larry Underwood, Fran Goldsmith and Nick Andros — are said by Mother Abagail to be touched by the "finger" of God. Later, when retarded Tom Cullen flees from his espionage mission in Las Vegas, he is instructed by a vision of Andros to seek "God's Finger," a geographical landmark on a trail that leads ultimately to Cullen's discovery of the injured Redman in the desert. In the lonely jail cell where Glen Bateman will meet his death, fearing no evil, he writes: "I am not the potter nor the potter's wheel, but the potter's clay . . ." (Chapter 63). And at the climactic confrontation in Las Vegas, when "the stand" finally is taken, it is all of the fingers — the "Hand of God" — that descends to obliterate the city.

In *The Dead Zone*, this image of the touch of destiny is also explicit, principally through the raving religious mania of Smith's mother, who can rationalize her version of God with the tragic accident that has befallen her son only by the notion of predestination: "Not the potter but the potter's clay. . . . You'll know the voice when it comes. It'll tell you what to do. . . . And when it does, Johnny . . . *do your duty*" (Part I, Chapter 12, section 1). Again we see the image of the hand of God, its touch molding the clay of humanity to the service of destiny.

---

*Sullivan, *Elegant Nightmares* (1978), p. 18

Touch is, of course, the means by which Smith's awesome power is exercised. The implications of his touch are highlighted in the first moments after Smith awakens from the coma. In a strikingly disturbing scene, Smith touches his doctor's hand:

> When Smith had grabbed his hand, he had felt a sudden onrush of bad feelings, childlike in their intensity; crude images of revulsion had assaulted him. He had found himself remembering a picnic in the country when he had been seven or eight, sitting down and putting his hand in something warm and slippery. He had looked around and had seen that he had put his hand into the maggoty remains of a woodchuck that had lain under a laurel bush all that hot August. He had screamed then, and he felt a little bit like screaming now. . . . (Part I, Chapter 6, section 4)

This touch serves as the opening parenthesis to the "life between death" of Johnny Smith, and it signals the horrors that will be visited upon him because of his strange powers.

The Dead Zone explicitly raises two interpretations of its title. When Smith emerges from his marathon coma, intensive medical testing discloses a modicum of brain damage. Smith occasionally is unable to visualize certain common items, and he describes such items as being "in the dead zone." It is the landscape of the forgotten: the memories — and symbolically, the life — that Smith cannot retrieve. From this perspective, it is Smith's coma — Latin for "sleep of death" — that is the "dead zone." Smith is a Rip Van Winkle who awakens not to the thunder of 1970, but to the silent yawn of 1975. His five years of sleep have brought him to an alien world:

> . . . there are still times when it's hard for me to believe that there ever was such a year as 1970 and upheaval on the campuses and Nixon was president, no pocket calculators, no home video tape recorders, no Bruce Springsteen or punk-rock bands either. And at other times it seems like that time is only a handsbreadth away. . . ." (Part III, section 12)

The Dead Zone is a novel about the 1970s, and the isolation and alienation experienced by Smith find ready equation to that of people maturing in the early 1970s. Smith is besieged with an elusive sense of loss, an ennui beyond the simple explanation of his missing five years. He has lost more than just time; he has lost his youth, and with it, his idealism. That the woman he loved has married another man and that his mother has died are but elements of that loss.

The closing portion of the book provides a brief glimpse into the aftermath of Smith's death, in the macrocosm of a Congressional investigation and the microcosm of letters from Smith to his father and Sarah. It is entitled "Notes from the Dead Zone," suggesting that the "dead zone" holds a literal meaning, referring to the death and the "dead zone" of human memory to which Smith has been committed. Yet Johnny Smith is not really "in the dead zone"; he is remembered within the alternate history of the novel, and the epilogue juxtaposes those memories. In both *Carrie* and *The Dead Zone*, King provides apt commentary on American myth-making. Both Carrie White and Johnny Smith are subjected to the *post hoc* rationalizations of a disbelieving civilization, whose single-minded obsession with a "suitable explanation" of events obscures reality in favor of a palatable myth. One cannot help but draw comparisons with our national obsession with the death of John F. Kennedy, and with the Congressional committees organized fifteen years after that assassination in an attempt to apply a salve to this wound in the American psyche.

King also uses these examples of American myth-making further to increase the thematic tensions of his exploration of the powers of heightened perception. The selective perception of events is vividly portrayed as an inevitable attribute of civilization and its tenants, be they investigative committees, news media or less institutionalized rumormongers. Susan Snell, whose instant of heightened perception at the fading moments of Carrie White's death renders her the only person fully to understand—to *see*—the tragedy of Carrie White, becomes the scapegoat of the selective perception of civilization. Likewise Johnny Smith, the only person who has glimpsed completely behind the mask of Greg Stillson, ironically fits the profile of the mad lone assassin, as if packaged for comfortable consumption by the six o'clock news.

The parentheses opened by Smith's touch of his doctor's hand are closed in the book's final scene with imagery so similar as not to be coincidental. Many readers find Sarah's visit to Smith's grave quite disturbing; there is considerable *frisson* as an unexpected hand descends to touch her, and she turns to find no one. The scene is not simply theatrics (or an homage to Brian De Palma's film of *Carrie*). This closing touch signals both release and reassurance. Sarah's emotions spin from horror to an uplifting understanding and affirmation; she *knows*, despite all the tragedy: "Same old Johnny."

IV.

"In the Country of the Blind, the One-eyed Man is King."

—H. G. Wells

STEPHEN KING INTRODUCES *Firestarter* (1980) with a quotation from Ray Bradbury's *Fahrenheit 451* (1953): "It was a pleasure to burn." The reference is two-sided: it is a recognition of *Firestarter*'s affinity with *Fahrenheit 451* in its concern with individual freedom; but it also is a wryly succinct expression of the moral dilemma at the heart of King's sixth novel. *Firestarter* is not a horror novel, but a further breeding of the science fiction, suspense and supernatural forms first explored by King in *The Stand* and realized in his finest novel, *The Dead Zone*. With nearly perfect conception and delivery, *Firestarter* follows a pursuit and confrontation pattern native to espionage novels; the important difference is the nature of the quarry.

Firestarter is a seven year old girl named Charlie McGee. Her parents had once needed two hundred dollars. It was 1969 and they were newly-acquainted college students; marriage and a child were as yet uncontemplated. The money was obtained by participating in an experiment with a low-grade hallucinogenic called Lot Six. Two days were required, under the auspices of one Dr. Wanless, who conducted research for the Department of Scientific Intelligence (otherwise known as "The Shop"), an ephemeral CIA-style agency dedicated to scientific developments "bearing on national security." That the unwitting subjects of Lot Six might develop extraordinary psychic talents from the experiment was known to The Shop. That its long-term effects could be lethal to the subjects was a risk that could be anticipated. But that two of the participants should subsequently marry and procreate was a possibility so inconceivable as to escape safeguards. Yet a child is born—of a mother who had residual telekinesis, and of a father who had developed an awesome power of suggestion that he calls "pushing." The child inherits not her parents' abilities, but a mutated effect of Lot Six that produces pyrokinesis: mentally-controlled combustion. And when this firestarter is aged seven, The Shop wants Charlie McGee; they kill her mother and drive Charlie and her father underground—penniless, paranoid outlaws who have nowhere left to hide.

Many of King's novels have featured principal characters who are societal aberrations, typically because of their psychic abilities. King's genius as a prose stylist is his portrayal of these characters in strikingly real, *human* terms. His works repeatedly dramatize the compelling human consequences of the possession of strange talents, by developing a sympathetic reader identification with the protagonist and then producing an intense conflict on both physical and emotional levels that culminates in confrontation. In both *The Dead Zone* and *Firestarter*, this confrontation plays a climactic role, but is secondary to a moral choice that precedes it: a choice that offers an interesting reflction on the nature of "good" and "evil" in King's fiction.

In this King tradition, Charlie McGee is very much an ordinary little girl despite her extraordinary talent. She is neither the robot-like simpleton nor the precocious miniature adult that most horror fictioneers attempt to pass off as children. Starkly conscious that she is the subject of pursuit because she possesses a power that she cannot understand or fully control, she is a vulnerable creature of reaction, maneuvered by circumstances that intensify her inner conflicts. She is tormented by the need to use her power to save her father and herself from capture and death; by the guilt instilled by her parents' careful training that use of the power is a "bad thing"; and by the realization of a growing pleasure in the power's use. Yet despite the book's title, its principal character is Charlie's father, Andy McGee. Lacking Charlie's childhood state of grace, it is Andy who must confront the moral consequences of their collective talents — including the grim knowledge that Charlie's power is growing, while continued use of his own "push" will likely cause his death.

The forces of evil are depicted with an intriguing cyclopean imagery. Dr. Wanless, the chief proponent of the experimental drug program, has a mien said to be reminiscent of the "Dr. Cyclops" of motion picture infamy. The Shop is a monolithic bureaucracy conceived in cold war perspectives; it has grown ruthlessly immoral, conspiratorially pervasive and nightmarishly inept. Both The Shop and its leader, Cap Hollister, are creatures whose time has passed, much as the mythical cyclopes were the stranded remnants of an earlier time. And then there is Rainbird — "a troll, an orc, a balrog of a man." He "stood two inches shy of seven feet tall, and he wore his glossy black hair drawn back and tied in a curt ponytail. Ten years before, a Claymore had blown up in his face during his second tour of Vietnam, and now his countenance was a horror show of scar tissue and runneled flesh. His left eye was gone." ("Longmont, Va: The Shop," section 7)

Rainbird is the Polyphemus who entraps the McGees in the underground chambers of The Shop's Virginia headquarters. He is obsessed with death, an assassin whose motive is neither greed nor revenge, but a patient quest for understanding of his own inevitable death. King tends to identify "evil" with moral weakness — such characters as Greg Stillson of *The Dead Zone*, Lloyd Henreid of *The Stand*, and the townspeople victims of *'Salem's Lot* are ready examples. Rainbird is no exception; but his tendency to moral ambivalence adds a subtle twist, creating a frighteningly real yet curiously opaque character.

The conflict between Rainbird and the McGees evokes the

highly symbolic fairy tale "Beauty and the Beast." Beauty's father is menaced by the Beast in a plan to capture Beauty—to obtain her love and so release the Beast from the spell that makes him gruesome. The parallels follow clearly until the ending: when Charlie is rejoined with her father at the climax of *Firestarter*, she realizes that she has been deceived by Rainbird. The "marriage" he seeks is a joining in death; and the ending is anything but a happy one. In the fairy tale, Beauty resolves the conflict between her love for her father and the Beast's needs in a beautiful manner. In *Firestarter*, the world is not a fairy tale where the good live in happiness. The good are subjected to death, to all forms of evil, for no apparent reason—other than that they are human. King has noted:

> Horror . . . deals inevitably with a conflict between good and evil; both sides must be well represented. The monster doesn't always have to die (take *Rosemary's Baby*, for example), but when a horror novel has no moment of reintegration, there is often no real emotional satisfaction. . . . On the other hand, a happy ending can't be Boy Scout stuff. There needs to be a pay-out as well as a pay-off. Good isn't free.*

In considering the role of good and evil in King's fiction, a critical perspective borrowed from anthropology provides significant insights. The "night journey" is an archetypal myth dramatised in much great literature, from the Old Testament's *Book of Jonah* to Joseph Conrad's symbolist masterpiece *Heart of Darkness* (1902), with its most memorable portrayal in James Joyce's *Ulysses* (1922). It is a solitary passage through darkness involving profound spiritual change in the voyager. In its classical form, the night journey is a descent into the underworld, followed by a return to light. A familiar use in Gothic fiction concerns passage through a tunnel or other dark, enclosed space, such as the crossing of the Lincoln Tunnel in *The Stand*: a claustrophobic groping through a dream-like landscape from the

---

*"Stephen King's Reign of Terror," an interview by Bill Ott, *Openers*, fall, 1981.

teeming island of humanity's past to the bright freedom of an uncertain future — a stunning, microcosmic enactment of the novel's principal theme.

The night journey need not represent more than literal adventure, particularly in horror fiction, whose essence is the experiencing of mystery and evil, most often depicted by darkness. Rarely does horror fiction relate the archetypal myth in a symbolic manner — the night journey into one's own unconscious, confronting an entity *within the self*. Yet such symbolic use of the night journey is apparent in the works of Stephen King.

For Russell Kirk, whose supernatural tales bear a very Christian intent, the night journey is an effective allegory of Christian redemption that "penetrates to spiritual depths and spiritual heights."* For H. P. Lovecraft, whose mechanistic materialism tended to transcend ultimate notions of "good" and "evil," the night journey had no end; it was a downward, irreversible spiral into the abyss of oblivion. In King's works, however, there is an element of choice: men and women are moral beings capable of right or wrong, good or evil, and the existence of that choice is both the source and the solution of the night journey. Yet King also embraces the notion of an inherent predisposition for good or for evil, most obviously depicted in *The Stand*, where the final remnants of humanity are divided by some non-conscious obsession into two rival groups, good and evil. Although this view, similar to that of Kirk, suggests spiritual depths and heights, it lacks any explicit religious underpinning.

In both *The Dead Zone* and *Firestarter*, the element of choice is paramount; and it is echoed in haunting depictions of the night journey. Johnny Smith's decision to assassinate Greg Stillson is presaged by the obvious night journey of Smith's coma: "It was a dream, he guessed. He was in a dark, gloomy place — a hallway of some kind. . . . Something else crept in: a feeling that he had *changed*. . . . He had gone into the darkness with everything, and now it felt to him that he was coming out of it with nothing

---

*Russell Kirk, "A Cautionary Note on the Ghostly Tale," *The Surly Sullen Bell* (Fleet, 1962), p. 239.

at all — except for some secret strangeness." (Part I, Chapter 6, section 2) This "strangeness" is Smith's second sight, which will reveal Stillson's possible destiny and confront Smith with the moral question of whether to commit murder.

A similar choice is presented to Andy McGee. Confined in the underground Shop installation, forcibly addicted to Thorazine, apparently bereft of his "push," Andy undergoes the night journey in a claustrophobe's ultimate nightmare. Storms disable The Shop's electrical systems, leaving McGee's small chamber locked and in absolute darkness. He reels into the depths of his unconscious, to face the decision whether to concede his impotency against The Shop or to resist despite the likelihood of death and the chance that Charlie's powers will be unleashed. He dreams of a journey through dark labyrinthine corridors "until there was no light . . . a living dark," ("The Blackout," section 10) in which he subconsciously overcomes the addiction, restoring his power, and he faces for the final time the image of a riderless black horse and its beating hoofs — the inescapable aftereffect of a strenuous "push." The image is profound — intensely evocative of Andy's pain and ironically suggestive of the final confrontation between Andy, Charlie and Rainbird, which occurs in The Shop's stables. Like Johnny Smith, Andy McGee must face himself before he will face the antagonist; he must recognize that the ultimate "evil" is within himself. And as Johnny Smith's choice saved others from a likely holocaust, Andy's choice saved Charlie to face herself and to make her moral choices in the novel's closing pages.

The climax of *Firestarter* confirms the power that King attributes to knowledge and moral choice. That Rainbird should fail in the face of Andy's sacrifice — and in the wake of Charlie's awesome power — is previewed in the defeats of Randall Flagg and Greg Stillson. Likewise, that The Shop proves to be inept should not surprise the devoted King reader:

> The thing about The Shop is that you see it first as
> monolithic authority and when you get down to the
> bottom you just see a bunch of [harried] bureaucrats
> doing their job. The thing that worries me more than
> monolithic authority is that there may be no such

thing, and that if you could meet Hitler, at the end
you would find this [harried] little bureaucrat saying,
"Where are my maps? Where are my armies? Gee
whiz, gang, what happened?"*

For King, the strength of evil often lies in secrecy and masquerade. In *Firestarter*, and in *The Stand* and *The Dead Zone*, the
night journey forces evil from the shadows into the daylight of
confrontation and open conflict, where it cannot survive.

Firestarter has the hallmarks of a transitional work; King's
revisiting of concepts and themes explored in *Carrie*, *The Stand*
and *The Dead Zone* suggests a tying up of loose ends — most
striking is the manner in which the lingering pessimism of the
apocalyptic, self-destructive use of strange talents in *Carrie* and
The Dead Zone is again invoked in *Firestarter*'s climax, and
then resolved in the clear optimism of its conclusion.

That optimism fulfills the traditional night journey — it is th
"return to light," overcoming the dark night of the soul and
ascending to redemption or salvation. That outcome is not inevitable, however, as the classical myth of Orpheus makes clear:
his descent to the underworld in search of his dead wife Eurydice
failed when, at the very instant of success, he looked backwards.
In the words of Nietzsche in *Beyond Good and Evil* (1886): "If
you gaze long into an abyss, the abyss will gaze back into you."
Such a night journey would form the basis of King's chilling
"back to basics" horror novella, *The Mist*.

V.

"Where there are no gods, demons will hold sway."
— Novalis

IN THE MIST, KING CONJURES a faceless horror: a white opaque
mist that enshrouds the northeastern United States (if not the

---

*"Interview: Stephen King," by Martha Thomases and John Robert Tebbel,
High Times (Jan. 1981), p. 96.

world), the apparent result of a secret government experiment. This short novel is a paradigm of the complicated metaphors of experimentation and technological horror consistently woven into his fiction. Readers will not likely forget the haunting inability of its characters to understand, let alone explain, what is happening to them.

The halcyon years of "technohorror" were the 1950s, when fear of the possibilities of technology, omened by the nuclear devastation of Hiroshima and Nagasaki, was exposed at the visceral but readily dismissed level of grade B science fiction movies. In the 1960s and 1970s, celluloid unrealities called *Them* (1954) and *The Beginning of the End* (1957) were hauntingly evoked in grim realities under equally colorful names like Agent Orange, Three Mile Island and Love Canal. Our fear of lethal technology, and growing doubts about the ability of technology to solve the complex problems of modern society, make "technohorror" a theme of undeniable currency. The horror author has to take but a simple step beyond the front-page news.

Stephen King's concern with "technohorror" can be found in early short stories depicting technology run amok, such as "The Mangler" and "Trucks." Although *Carrie* included a suggestion of genetic mutation, *The Stand* first probed in depth the fears generated by technological testing. Both *The Stand* and *Firestarter* linked science and government in an amoral tryst, yet concluded with hope for new beginnings. In *The Mist*, King sees only the End.

David Drayton, the narrator of *The Mist*, is a commercial artist — a person whose career is devoted to creating artificial representations of human life. With his wife Stephanie and five-year-old son Billy, Drayton leads an almost idyllic existence at a lakefront home in Bridgton, Maine. Their life is shattered by a freakish summer storm that sends the Draytons to their cellar, where David has a remarkable precognitive dream:

> I had a dream that I saw God walking across Harrison
> on the far side of the lake, a God so gigantic that above
> the waist He was lost in a clear blue sky. In the dream
> I could hear the rending crack and splinter of breaking
> trees as God stamped the woods into the shape of His

footsteps. He was circling the lake, coming toward the Bridgton side, toward us, and behind Him everything that had been green turned a bad gray and all the houses and cottages and summer places were bursting into purple-white flame like lightning, and soon the smoke covered everything. The smoke covered everything like a mist. (Chapter 1)

In the morning, a peculiar mist brews over the lake. It is moving across the water toward Bridgton — moving against the wind. When Drayton's wife asks what it is, Drayton thinks: ". . . the word that nearly jumped first from my mouth was *God*." (Chapter 2)

Drayton, his son and a neighbor drive into town to report downed electrical lines and to obtain groceries. They find Federal Foods Supermarket jammed with people. Speculation is rampant that something has gone wrong at the government's secret "Arrowhead Project" across the lake. As Drayton waits in the checkout line, he is distracted by an intangible concern. His son interrupts his reverie, and Drayton observes: ". . . suddenly, briefly, the mist of disquiet that had settled over me rifted, and something terrible peered through from the other side — the bright and metallic face of pure terror." (Chapter 3)

The mist settles over the supermarket; many people rush out to observe the peculiar phenomenon but none return. Gradually, the monstrous inhabitants of the mist are divulged. Tentacles writhe out of the mist to snatch a bag-boy; bug-things stretching four feet in length flop along the store windows, only to be gobbled up by pterodactyl-like monstrosities that plummet out of the mist. Huge spidery creepy-crawlers spin corrosive webs, and segmented parodies of lobsters crawl across the parking lot. The spawn of the mist seem endless in horrifying variety; but the mist, and what it signifies, is more important than its monsters: "It wasn't so much the monstrous creatures that lurked in the mist. . . . It was the mist itself that sapped the strength and robbed the will." (Chapter 10) The mist takes on symbolic significance — it is the unknown product of experimentation.

Conspicuous by its absence from *The Mist* is a stock character of the "technohorror" nightmare: the scientist. We are offered

only straw men: two young soldiers trapped within the supermarket, who commit gruesome suicide, confirming the feared
source of the disaster. The culprits of the Arrowhead Project
remain as faceless and opaque as the mist itself. And this increases our unease: there is no patent lunatic or misguided zealot
on which to foist responsibility.

The elements are those of a nightmarish, surreal disaster film.
The besieged occupants of the supermarket are a representative
sample of humanity, put to the test of the external threat of the
mist and the internal claustrophobia — and madness — of the
supermarket. They undergo hysteria and fragmentation, performing acts of courage and stupidity as inevitable leadership
struggles to take place.

King deftly creates the tension between illogic, religion and
materialism that is his forte. Drayton's neighbor, a vacationing
New York City attorney, proves not to be a pillar of objectivity
or calm; rather, he heads a group of people — wryly described as
the "Flat Earth Society" — which simply refuses to believe in the
disaster despite quite tangible evidence; they walk into the mist,
to their deaths. Another group, which grows in number as time
passes, believes perhaps too strongly in the disaster, interpreting
it as God's punishment. They are headed by Mrs. Carmody, an
otherwise innocuous old lady given to folk tales and remedies,
who seemingly thrives on the disaster. This group soon demands
a human sacrifice in appeasement of the mist. A third group, including Drayton, attempts a rational, practical solution to the
horror. They construct defenses, fight off the intrusions of monsters and ultimately undertake an ill-fated expedition to a neighboring pharmacy. Their failure gives credence to Mrs. Carmody;
and leads Drayton to organize an escape effort.

Readily apparent in *The Mist* is the influence of George A.
Romero, virtuoso low-budget filmmaker of the classic *Night of
the Living Dead* (1968) and its sequel, *Dawn of the Dead* (1979).
Romero's films plunder our dire unease with death and decay,
hypothesizing that the dead will return to life with a singular
hunger for human flesh. On another level, however, these films
address, in an intelligent and ironic sense, the horrific siege of
reality. Romero terms his masterwork "an allegory meant to

draw a parallel between what people are becoming and the idea that people are operating on many levels of insanity that are only clear to themselves."*

In *Night of the Living Dead*, zombies besiege a group of people in a deserted farmhouse. Romero supplants melodrama with nihilistic abandon: the young attractive couple is killed in an escape attempt; the older businessman is a raving coward rather than a calm, take-charge leader; the little girl turns on her mother, butchering her with a garden tool and devouring her; the "token" black becomes the leader — and only survivor — of the defense, only to emerge the next morning so shattered by the experience that he is mistakenly shot as a zombie. The theme is replayed to an almost absurdist premise in *Dawn of the Dead* as a similar band of survivors barricades itself within a monstrous suburban shopping mall.

The thematic parallels between *The Mist* and Romero's *Living Dead* films are numerous; perhaps more striking is the manner in which the imagery of *The Mist* evokes the intensely visual and visceral quality of film. "You're supposed to visualize the story in grainy black and white,"** notes King. Unlike any of King's other novels to date, it is written entirely in first person singular and structured on a scene-by-scene basis. Its narrator consistently repeats, as if in self-assurance, that the creatures of the mist are the stuff of grade B horror movies. Not only does King thereby reinforce the several levels of perspective; he presents an irony equal to that of the "Just the Flu" epitaph of his story "Night Surf"—that the end of the world should indeed evoke a grade B horror movie.

The defense of the supermarket takes on surreal aspects that intermingle shock and sardonic humor, reminiscent of the shopping mall confrontations of *Dawn of the Dead*. One of the pterodactyl-like creatures breaches the defenses, savaging a defender before being set aflame. King recounts the incident

---

Filmmakers Newsletter, quoted in Danny Peary, *Cult Movies* (Delta, 1981), p. 227.

**Paul R. Gagne, "Stephen King," *Cinefantastique* (spring 1981) p. 9.

with delightful imagery and an obvious send-up of the gravely serious Gothic narrator:

> I think that nothing in the entire business stands in my memory so strongly as that bird-thing from hell blazing a zigzagging course above the aisles of the Federal Supermarket, dropping charred and smoking bits of itself here and there. It finally crashed into the spaghetti sauces, splattering Ragu and Prince and Prima Salsa everywhere like gouts of blood. (Chapter 7)

A bug-thing immediately clambers through the broken window; but before the male defenders can act, Mrs. Reppler, a sixty-year-old grade school teacher, charges with a can of Raid in each hand and sprays it to death.

Although clearly self-conscious, *The Mist* is not parody. Like George Romero, King attempts — and succeeds — in balancing a pandemonium seesaw whose ends are occupied by pure horror and outrageous black humor. We are disturbed by *The Mist* because, like its narrator, we do not know exactly what to do when confronted by its horrors. "I was making some sound. Laughing. Crying. Screaming. I don't know." (Chapter 9)

The typical disaster movie produces a fascist answer — strong leadership will persevere, while the weak are dispensible. In *The Mist*, King, again like George Romero, holds differently: horror produces not the best but the worst in people, and when it does produce the best, the best is usually unrecognizable to the world outside. Drayton is less than a heroic figure: he feels compelled to have sex with another of the survivors, and he is drawn into the ill-fated expedition to the neighboring drug store. Finally, under the twin compulsion of the growing religious mania of Mrs. Carmody's group and of the simple urge to see the sun again, Drayton leads a tiny group to his Land Rover — suffering the loss of two companions. By the novel's close, Drayton and his comrades are barricaded within a Howard Johnson's; only then does he ponder the difficulty of refueling — and only then does he face the reality that the mist may go on forever.

The flight from the supermarket is King's most literal and most Lovecraftian night journey. Drayton's narrative has no ending in the traditional sense. His group is heading south, hoping for escape from the dark and seemingly endless tunnel of the mist; but they find only a surreal landscape of desolation and monstrosity. The ultimate horror is nearly unseen; and it is all the more horrible given Drayton's dream preceding the mist:

> Something came; again, that is all I can say for sure. It may have been the fact that the mist only allowed us to glimpse things briefly, but I think it just as likely that there are certain things that your brain simply disallows. There are things of such darkness and horror — just, I suppose, as there are things of such great beauty — that they will not fit through the puny doors of human perception.
>
> . . . I don't know how big it actually was, but it passed directly over us. . . . Mrs. Reppler said later she could not see the underside of its body, although she craned her neck up to look. She saw only two Cyclopean legs going up and up into the mist like living towers until they were lost to sight. (Chapter 11)

This numinous vision, a nonrational confrontation with the apparently divine, omens the impossibility of escape. The growing sense of a mysterious profanity, latent in the religious hysteria of Mrs. Carmody, is manifest in this dark mirror-image of the God of Drayton's dream. Like *The Stand*, *The Mist* explicitly evokes Biblical stories of plagues embodying the wrath of God and, of course, the archetypal story of the great flood. Although *The Stand* confirms the power of faith, *The Mist* offers a universe without salvation, imbued with the feeling of one's own submergence — of being ant-like, trivial, before the footsteps of an unseeable God-thing.

For many readers, horror fiction is meaningful because its focus upon the existence of evil implies the existence of good. *The Mist* is particularly terrifying because it proposes a transcendence of notions of good and evil, right and wrong; King moves his characters and readers through an ever-darkening universe of chaos and hostility. The line separating civilization from chaos — and, indeed, life from extinction — has parted like the mist; and only "pure terror" remains.

Writing about the horror story, King has noted:

The best tales in the genre make one point over and over again — that the rational world both within us and without us is small, that our understanding is smaller yet, and that much of the universe in which we exist is, so far as we are able to tell, chaotic. So the horror story makes us appreciate our own well-lighted corner of that chaotic universe, and perhaps allows a moment of warm and grateful wonder that we should be allowed to exist in that fragile space of light at all.*

Although the dark, apocalyptic quality of *The Mist* suggests that our "fragile space of light" may be dwindling, the night journey has not yet reached its end. The novel's final word is "hope," even if this hope is clouded by ambiguity and despair. And unlike Drayton, the reader has the protection of perspective. The setting, so reminiscent of the grade B horror film, is one of total security: we can leave at any moment, the lights will flicker on, and we can step into a more familiar world.

Or can we? That is the question posed by King's most pessimistic and most horrifying novel, *Cujo*.

VI.

"Nope, nothing wrong here."
— The Sharp Cereal Professor

CUJO WAS A GOOD DOG: a two hundred pound Saint Bernard with sad eyes and an intrinsic love for a life that demanded little more than playing with children and chasing an occasional rabbit. But one day, he followed a rabbit down a hole, and what he found was most definitely not Alice's Wonderland.

"Once upon a time" begins *Cujo* (1981), Stephen King's sev-

---

*Stephen King, "Introduction," Bill Pronzini, Barry Malzberg and Martin H. Greenberg, comps., *The Arbor House Treasury of Horror and the Supernatural* (Arbor House, 1981).

enth published novel; but it is not the sort of fairy tale to which we are accustomed. There is no ogre, dragon or evil witch, no thinly-veiled childhood lesson, no happy ending. *Cujo* is steeped instead in a reality that is as inescapable as it is frightening, emphasizing not only the role of horror fiction as the modern fairy tale but the importance of realism in creating effective horror fiction.

Cujo is set in the spring of 1980 in the fictitious town of Castle Rock, Maine, the stalking ground of the "Castle Rock Rapist" in *The Dead Zone*. Its storyline evolves about two marriages: Donna and Vic Trenton, whose son Tad is racked with night fears concerning a monster that he swears is haunting his closet; and Joe and Charity Camber, whose son Brett has a dog named Cujo — inexplicably the *nom de guerre* used by William Wolfe of Symbionese Liberation Army infamy. For the two children, dreams echo with nightmarish reality; for the adults, reality itself has become the stuff of bad dreams. The two marriages are in jeopardy: Donna Trenton, bored and conscious of aging, has succumbed to an extramarital affair that disgusts her, while Vic must grapple with the impending loss of his small advertising agency's major client; and Charity Camber, hoping to better her son, strives belatedly to assert her independence from Joe, who sinks deeper and deeper into indolence and alcoholism. Through this slice of everyday life in modern America walks a dog who has fallen into a dark hole, succumbing to the bites of rabid bats.

The horror of *Cujo* is not supernatural. It is woven from the dark strands of the American social fabric: decaying marriages, economic woes, malfunctioning automobiles and junk food. *Cujo* affirms the irony of King's popular success: we are obsessed with fear, running scared of our daily lives, where we can no longer trust the food we eat, the neighbor's dog, or even ourselves. Money, love and death are the framework of our fear, and King reminds us of their everyday presence with incisive, relentless effect. Fear strikes at the supermarket:

> They went to the Agway Market and Donna bought
> forty dollars' worth of groceries. . . . It was a busy trip,
> but she still had time for bitter reflection as she waited

in the checkout lane . . . on how much three lousy bags
of groceries went for these days. It wasn't just depressing; it was scary.

And at our jobs:

Since the Zingers fiasco, two clients . . . had cancelled
their arrangements with I-E, and if Ad Worx lost the
Sharp account, Rob would lose other accounts in addition to Sharp. It left him feeling angry and scared. . . .

It invades our personal relationships:

Now things could be admitted. How he had wanted
to kill her when she called him a son of a bitch, her
spittle spraying on his face. How he had wanted to
kill her for making him feel old and scared and not
able to keep on top of the situation anymore.

And it is with us always, if only in the passage of time:

There was no personal mail for her; these days there
rarely was. Most of the people she knew who had
been able to write were now dead. She would follow
soon enough, she suspected. The oncoming summer
gave her a bad feeling, a scary feeling.

These are the big leagues of fear, the actualities behind the
masks of the ghoulies and ghosties that normally inhabit horror
fiction. They cannot be laughed away — they won't ever meet
Abbott and Costello — and in *Cujo*'s pages, we find that even
horror fiction provides no respite.

The function of realism in horror fiction has always been
paradoxical. We have noted that horror fiction serves as a means
of escape for its readers, suppressing the very real and often
overpowering horrors of everyday life in favor of surreal, exotic
and visionary realms. In *The Mist*, King described this escapist
function in explicit terms:

When the machines fail . . . , when the technologies
fail, when the conventional religious systems fail,
people have got to have something. Even a zombie
lurching into the night can seem pretty cheerful compared to the existential comedy/horror of the ozone
layer dissolving under the combined assault of a mil-

lion fluorocarbon spray cans of deodorant. (Chapter 10)

Yet horror fiction is not simply a place to which we seek to escape; it is also a place to which we are drawn seductively by a hidden need. As Joseph Conrad wrote in *Lord Jim* (1900), "to the destructive element submit yourself. . . . In the destructive element immerse." Or in Stephen King's colloquial rendition, we must "keep the gators fed."* Horror fiction does not only vent emotions that run counter to "civilized" society, allowing us to air our innermost fears and to breach our foremost taboos. At its most extreme, it acts as a surrogate "night journey" for its reader, which King consciously fulfills:

> I think that all horror fiction (all of the good stuff, anyway) is an attempt to carry the reader from the land of the living to the land of the dead, and that this journey becomes a kind of easily graspable, but nevertheless surreal mythic allegory for our own life passage toward death. Seen in this light, the writer of horror fiction is a little like the boatman ferrying people across the river Styx. . . .**

And as for Cujo, the novel speaks clearly: "Wasn't there a dog in the front of the boat in that story about the boatman . . . ? The boatman's dog. Just call me Cujo."

Horror fiction is indeed alternately repulsive and seductive; the closer our familiarity with reality, the greater our need for escape. King's horror fiction is conscious of this paradox, operating with one foot firmly within waking reality. If anything, his horror fiction draws the reader *closer* to reality, as King acknowledges:

> [T]he tale of horror and the supernatural *is* an escape, but the reader must never believe that it is only an escape outward, into a kind of never-never land . . . ;

---

*Stephen King, "Why We Crave Horror Movies," *Playboy* (Jan. 1981), p. 246.

**Letter from Stephen King to Douglas E. Winter, Dec. 24, 1980. Copyright 1982 by Stephen King the tale of terror and the supernatural is also an escape *inward*, toward the very center of our perceived humanity.*

In this light, the intrinsically subversive art of King's horror fiction proposes what H. P. Lovecraft called "an absolute and stupendous invasion of the natural order," while forcing the reader to consider whether there is order and, indeed, whether anything is natural.

In *Danse Macabre*, King used the term "subtext" to describe how the best horror fiction is a dark analog of reality, its authors consciously or unconsciously expounding fantasy fears that are a reflection of actual fears. King's own novels seem to demonstrate several evolving subtexts for which *Cujo* provides a climax. His early books were inward-looking, claustrophobic expositions of the fears and guilt of interpersonal relationships. *Carrie* concerned the problems of maturation in contemporary society, effectively juxtaposing the dark side of adolescence with the consequences of attempting to ignore or to suppress the dark side of the psyche. In *'Salem's Lot* King subverted — or the cynic might suggest, modernized — Thornton Wilder's *Our Town*, depicting a small town whose moral disintegration is distilled in a clutch of vampires. In *The Shining*, the real terrors of alcoholism, child abuse and family breakdown were translated into a surreal Gothic atmosphere.

With *The Stand* and *The Dead Zone*, King's novels began a more outward-looking perspective, bringing sociopolitical fears — the curses of civilization — to the forefront. King's concern with this theme seems rooted both in lessons about our social and political processes taught in the 1960s and 1970s, and in the failure of technology and dangers of government experimentation. His first six published novels disclose a pattern of increasingly monolithic evil, culminating in the cyclopean imagery of *Firestarter* and climaxing in *The Mist*, whose penultimate faceless evil spews forth a flurry of creepy-crawling monsters like an

---

*King, "Introduction," *The Arbor House Treasury of Horror and the Supernatural*.

endless, insane Creature Feature. What could be worse? Only one thing, responds King in *Cujo*: reality.

Written in King's most visceral and colloquial style, *Cujo* reexamines these themes, stripping away the veneer of supernaturalism to confront us with the mundane here-and-now of Count Chocula and Ford Pintos, baseball games and bake sales, farting and fucking, and say: reality *is* an unnatural order. You cannot explain it away as madness or drunkenness or the stuff of horror fiction. This reality has created our need for the horror story as a modern fairy tale, giving us escape or reassurance, confirming our worst expectations or simply giving us a good look at the scene of the accident. Like Donna and Tad Trenton, who are trapped in their car by the rabid Cujo, we are under siege from forces that we simply cannot understand. We are trapped by a reality as loathsome and ambiguous as the good dog gone bad, unable to believe or to find comfort in our unbelief. And the Sharp Cereal Professor's oft-repeated epigram in *Cujo* — "Nope, nothing wrong here" — is not only a summing-up of the bitter irony of the novel and its model, our reality; it also serves as a wry commentary on what we seek in horror fiction.

Cujo is an intensely-written novel told in King's characteristically effortless prose; it moves with a seemingly instinctive pace, sustaining relentless tension. It is a harrowing reading experience, uncompromising in its terror and suspense, yet imbued with humor, warmth and a deep sense of the human condition. As in his earlier novels, King evokes the horror of *Cujo* not by a concatenation of circumstances but by the exposition and understanding of characters. The aesthetics of horror — "death, destruction and destiny" — are matters of the greatest intensity and importance; they make the most rigorous demands for full expression of the human personality. King brings his characters to trial in a court of fear, and asks a question simultaneously simplistic and unreachably complex: who is this person?

He asks that question of us as well. The dark hole that snared Cujo awaits us all; when the novel's human antagonist — Steve Kemp, the layabout poet whom Donna Trenton unfortunately chooses for a lover — finally unleashes his psychotic anger upon the Trenton household, King writes: "He was down a dark hole." And when Vic Trenton learns of his wife's affair with Kemp, the image is brought home with painful clarity:

> . . . what you didn't know couldn't hurt you. Wasn't that right? If a man is crossing a darkened room with a deep, open hole in the middle of it, and if he passes within inches of it, he doesn't need to know he almost fell in. There is no need for fear. Not if the lights are off.

The hole is there, waiting, for each of us — whether we are drawn in like Cujo, descend willingly like Steve Kemp or are pushed as was Vic Trenton. This is the most chilling element of Stephen King's most disturbing novel — not the violent horror of its climax, but the stark final image that we are not unlike small animals that have died down the dark hole.

❋ ❋

What lies in wait for us, down the dark hole of death? Do the dead sing? The story of Stella Flanders, which began this exploration of the night journeys of Stephen King, would tell us that, yes, the dead sing. For although death awaits her at the far side of the Reach, it is a gentle, lovely death — hand-in-hand with those who have passed before her, singing hymns of grace. Her journey through darkness, like the journeys of *The Stand*, *The Dead Zone*, and *Firestarter*, emerges to light, renewing Doctor Van Helsing's observation in *Dracula*: "We must go through bitter waters before we taste the sweet." Her journey's end is indeed different from that of the "small animals" down the dark hole of *Cujo*, or the song greeting Carrie White in *Carrie*: "that last lighted thought carried swiftly down into the black tunnel of eternity, followed by the blank, idiot hum of prosaic electricity." Or from the fate of David Drayton in *The Mist* or Father Callahan in *'Salem's Lot*, doomed as eternal fugitives in night journeys that may never end.

As these disparate destinies suggest, the question — do the dead sing? — must go unanswered, at least for the moment. Like Stella Flanders' son, left on this side of the Reach, we can only conjecture until it is our time to know. Like the strange mist brewing about the Federal Foods Supermarket in *The Mist* —

like death and like fear itself — horror fiction must have a different meaning for every reader. Always lurking, whether sought or simply found in these night journeys, is the other side of our self and our existence — the elusive phantom of life. And the darkness, the night, the eternal negation down *Cujo*'s hole, give us access to truths that we might not otherwise seek. In "Ad Astram," William Faulkner thus wrote a fitting credo for horror fiction: "A man sees further looking out of the dark upon the light than a man does in the light looking out upon the light."

Death, destruction and destiny await us all at the end of the journey — in life as in horror fiction. And the tale of horror, like a ride on a roller coaster, serves as a full dress rehearsal of death while returning us momentarily to our childhood. The Reach *was* wider in those days. As we read these words, the Reach is shortening, and the future beckons us even as the ghosts of our past are calling us home. In the horror fiction of Stephen King, we can embark upon the night journey, make the descent down the dark hole, cross that narrowing Reach, and return again in safety to the surface — to the near shore of the river of death. For our boatman has a master's hand. . . .

Stephen King:
A Bibliography

Compiled by Marty Ketchum,
Daniel J H Levack and Jeff Levin

THIS WORK CONTAINS A CHECKLIST of the first appearances of
the fiction, non-fiction, and interviews of Stephen King. It also
contains a checklist of works about Stephen King. Only first
appearances are cited except for the books, where, when both
a limited edition and a trade edition were published, both are
cited and described. The checklist is arranged in five parts:
BOOKS, NON-BOOK APPEARANCES, INTERVIEWS, WORKS ABOUT
STEPHEN KING, and FORTHCOMING AND UNPUBLISHED WORKS.

Those interested in interviews of King or in the works written about him should consult both the INTERVIEWS and the
WORKS ABOUT STEPHEN KING sections since many of the interviews are combined pieces which also contain articles about
King or his works and many of the works about King contain
extensive quotes from him.

The compilers wish to thank Ken Shipley, Alex Berman of
Phantasia Press, Stuart David Schiff of Whispers, Ken Keller,
Stephanie Leonard, and Stephen King who supplied extensive
information and help.

Note: It has been stated that Richard Bachman is a pseudonym of Stephen King. This is not the case. Mr. Bachman lives in Bangor, Maine, and Stephen King has never used this name as a pseudonym.

Additions and corrections to the checklist are both desired and welcome. All such can be sent to:

Marty Ketchum
RR2, Box 659
Galena, Kansas   66739
USA

BOOKS

1. CARRIE
   This book has been made into a movie.
   a. Doubleday, Garden City ($5.95), 1974.
      Bound in purple cloth with gold lettering on the spine. "1974" on the title page. "First Edition" on the copyright page. Date code "P6" at inner margin of page 199.

2. CREEPSHOW
   Contents: "Father's Day"; "The Lonesome Death Of Jordy Verrill"; "The Crate"; "Something To Tide You Over"; "They're Creeping Up On You".
   This book is based on a movie written by Stephen King.
   a. Plume, New York ($6.95), 1982, paper.
      The book is a graphic adaptation of the 5 segments of the movie Creepshow. Screenplay by Stephen King; produced by Richard P Rubinstein, directed by George A Romero. Book cover by Jack Kamen. Graphic adaptation by Berni Wrightson. The format of the book is a cross between a slick art book and an EC Comic book. "First Printing, July, 1982"/"1 2 3 4 5 6 7 8 9" on copyright page.

3. CUJO
   Both a limited and a trade edition were issued.
   a. Limited edition - The Mysterious Press, New York ($65.00), 1981.
      Bound in maroon buckram with a slipcase of the same material. Lettering on the spine is in gold. There are also two dogs stamped in gold on the front cover. The book was issued without a dust jacket. There is no date on the title page. "first edition" on the copyright page. There were 750 copies signed and numbered by King. The limitation page is the last page before the rear free endpaper.

b. Trade edition - Viking, New York ($13.95), 1981.

Bound in a three-piece case with black cloth on the spine and light brown front and rear paper boards. "SK" is stamped in gold on the front board. The title is stamped in gold on the spine; and the author and publisher are stamped in copper on the spine. No date on the title page. "First published in 1981 by the Viking Press" on the copyright page.

4. DANSE MACABRE

Non-Fiction.

Both a limited and a trade edition were issued. The trade edition preceded the limited edition.

a. Trade edition - Everest House, New York ($13.95), 1981.

Bound in a three-piece case with red cloth on the spine and red front and rear paper boards. The lettering is on the spine in gold. There is no date on the title page and no indication of edition or printing on the copyright page except for "RRD281". A review slip indicates that the book was published 20 April 1981.

b. Limited edition - Everest House, New York ($65.00), 1981.

Bound in black cloth with gold and maroon lettering on the spine. Author's signature is stamped in gold on the front cover. Issued in a black cardboard slipcase and without a dust jacket. The limitation page is in the front of the book. There is no date on the title page. "First Edition" on the copyright page. The picture of King which was used on the back of the dust jacket for the trade edition is used as a frontispiece in this edition. There were 250 numbered copies, numbered 1-250, and 15 lettered copies, lettered A-O.

5. THE DARK TOWER: THE GUNSLINGER

Book 1 of the THE DARK TOWER.

As currently outlined by King, THE DARK TOWER will run about 3000 pages.

Contents: "The Gunslinger"; "The Way Station"; "The Oracle And The Mountains"; "The Slow Mutants"; "The Gunslinger And The Dark Man"; "Afterword".

a. Trade edition - Donald M Grant, West Kingston, Rhode Island ($20.00), 1982.

Approximately 10,000 copies were printed, of which approximately 1,500 were misbound, affecting the order of the signatures. Grant reportedly intends to reprint an amount equal to the number of damaged copies. It is not known if these will be distinguishable as a separate printing. Bound in brown cloth with gold lettering on the spine. There is no date on the title page. "First Edition" on the copyright page. Dust jacket, colored pictorial endpapers, black and white and color interior illustrations by Michael Whelan. The

stories have been slightly revised for this appearance.
b. Limited edition - Donald M Grant, West Kingston, Rhode Island ($60.00), 1982.

Bound in white cloth with brown lettering on the spine. There is a small decoration on the front board in brown ink. Issued in dust jacket, and in a grey-brown cloth covered box. Limitation notice is printed on the back of the front free endpaper. There were 500 copies, numbered 1-500, signed by King and the illustrator, Michael Whelan. There were also 26 lettered copies, lettered A-Z. They are otherwise identical to the numbered copies.

6. THE DEAD ZONE
   a. Viking, New York ($11.95), 1979.

Bound in a three-piece case with black cloth on the spine and black front and rear paper boards. The lettering on the spine is gold. "SK" is blind stamped on the front board. No date on the title page. "First published in 1979 by the Viking Press" on the copyright page. A review slip indicates that the book was published 16 Aug 1979. This edition has about 40,000 words less than the manuscript submitted.

7. DIFFERENT SEASONS
   Contents: "*Hope Springs Eternal:* Rita Hayworth And Shawshank Redemption"; "*Summer Of Corruption:* Apt Pupil"; "*Fall From Innocence:* The Body"; "*A Winter's Tale:* The Breathing Method"; "Afterword".
   a. Viking, New York ($16.95), 1982.

Bound in a three-piece case with dark-blue cloth on the spine and dark-blue front and rear paper boards. "SK" stamped in bronze on the front board. Title stamped in bronze on the spine; author and publisher stamped in light-blue on the spine. No date on the title page. "First published in 1982 by The Viking Press" on the copyright page.

8. FIRESTARTER
   A limited edition with two issues and a trade edition were published. Publishing priority is: first issue of the limited edition, trade edition, second issue of the limited edition. The same plates (but not sheets) were used for all three editions.
   a. Limited edition (first issue) - Phantasia Press, Huntington Woods ($35.00), 1980.

Bound in dark blue buckram with gold lettering on the spine. Issued in a slipcase of the same material. "1980" on the title page. "FIRST EDITION" on the copyright page. The limitation page is the page immediately following text page 428. The limitation pages were signed, numbered and dated by King. They were dated on three different days: 6, 7, 8 July 1980. The distribution is unknown but the copies dated the 6th go through at least copy 157, and the copies dated the 8th go down to at least copy 664. There were 750 copies.

b. Trade edition - Viking, New York ($13.95), 1980.

Bound in a three-piece case with red cloth on the spine and black front and rear paper boards. "SK" stamped in gold on the front board. Title stamped in gold on the spine; author and publisher stamped in black on the spine. No date on the title page. "First published in 1980 by the Viking Press" on the copyright page.

c. Limited edition (second issue) - Phantasia Press, Huntington Woods, 1980.

This issue was similar to "a" above except for the following. These copies were lettered, from A through Z, instead of numbered on the limitation page. All were dated 8 July 1980. This book was trimmed somewhat larger than the numbered copies. It was issued without a slipcase and without a dust jacket. The books were bound in an asbestos cloth which was then painted silver with aluminum paint. A piece of leather was inlaid in the front cover and the title and author's name were stamped in silver on the leather piece. There were 26 copies.

9. NIGHT SHIFT

Contents: "Introduction", John D MacDonald; "Foreword"; "Jerusalem's Lot"; "Graveyard Shift"; "Night Surf"; "I Am The Doorway"; "The Mangler"; "The Boogeyman"; "Gray Matter"; "Battleground"; "Trucks"; "Sometimes They Come Back"; "Strawberry Spring"; "The Ledge"; "The Lawnmower Man"; "Quitters, Inc."; "I Know What You Need"; "Children Of The Corn"; "The Last Rung On The Ladder"; "The Man Who Loved Flowers"; "One For The Road"; "The Woman In The Room".

a. Doubleday, Garden City ($8.95), 1978.

Bound in a three-piece case with black cloth on the spine and red front and rear paper boards. Gold lettering on the spine. "1978" on the title page. "FIRST EDITION" on the copyright page. Date code "S52" at inner margin of page 336.

10. 'SALEM'S LOT

This book has been made into a TV movie.

a. Doubleday, Garden City ($7.95), 1975.

Bound in a three-piece case with black cloth on the spine and red front and rear paper boards. Gold lettering on the spine. "1975" on the title page. "First Edition" on the copyright page. Date code "Q37" at inner margin of page 439.

11. THE SHINING
     This book has been made into a movie.
     a. Doubleday, Garden City ($8.95), 1977.
        Bound in a three-piece case with black cloth on the spine and tan
        front and rear paper boards. Gold lettering on the spine. "1977" on
        the title page. "FIRST EDITION" on the copyright page. Date
        code "R49" at inner margin of page 447.

12. THE STAND
     a. Doubleday, Garden City ($12.95), 1978.
        Bound in a three-piece case with black cloth on the spine and tan
        front and rear paper boards. Gold lettering on the spine. "1978" on
        the title page. "First Edition" on the copyright page. Date code
        "T39" at inner margin of page 823. This edition has about 100,000
        words less than the manuscript submitted.

13. STEPHEN KING
     This collection contains the books CARRIE, THE SHINING, 'SALEM'S
     LOT and NIGHT SHIFT.
     a. Heinemann and Octopus Books, New York, 1981.
        Bound in red paper boards with gold lettering on the spine. States
        on the copyright page that it was first published in 1981 by Heine-
        mann and Octopus books.

NON-BOOK APPEARANCES

1. "Afterword", THE DARK TOWER: THE GUNSLINGER, Donald M
    Grant, West Kingston, Rhode Island ($20.00; $60.00), 1982.
    Non-Fiction.

2. "Afterword", DIFFERENT SEASONS, Viking, New York ($16.95),
    1982.
    Non-Fiction.

3. "Apt Pupil", DIFFERENT SEASONS, Viking, New York ($16.95),
    1982.

4. "Battleground", Cavalier, Sept 1972.

5. "Before The Play", Whispers, No 17/18, July 1982.

6. "Between Rock And A Soft Place", Playboy, Jan 1982.
    Non-Fiction.

7. "Big Wheels", NEW TERRORS 2, Ed by Ramsey Campbell, Pan: 26127
    (£ 1.75), 1980, paper.

8. "The Bird And The Album", A FANTASY READER: THE SEVENTH
    WORLD FANTASY CONVENTION BOOK, Ed by Jeff Frane and

Jack Rems, The Seventh World Fantasy Convention, Berkeley, 1981. This is an excerpt, section 1 and part of section 2 of chapter 13, of the unpublished novel IT. The book was distributed as a souvenir book at the seventh World Fantasy Convention.

9. "The Blue Air Compressor", Heavy Metal, July 1981.

10. "The Body", DIFFERENT SEASONS, Viking, New York ($16.95), 1982.

11. "The Boogeyman", Cavalier, March 1973.

12. "The Breathing Method", DIFFERENT SEASONS, Viking, New York ($16.95), 1982.

13. "Carrie", STEPHEN KING, Heinnemann and Octopus Books, New York, 1981.

14. "The Cat From Hell", Cavalier, June 1977.

15. "Children Of The Corn", Penthouse, March 1977.

16. "The Crate", Gallery, July 1979.
    This story also appeared as a graphic adaptation in CREEPSHOW, Plume, New York ($6.95), 1982.

17. "Crouch End", NEW TALES OF THE CTHULHU MYTHOS, Ed by Ramsey Campbell, Arkham House, Sauk City ($11.95), 1980.

18. "Cujo", Science Fiction Digest, Vol 1 No 2, 1982.
    Condensed.

19. "Danse Macabre", Book Digest, Sept 1981.
    Non-Fiction. A condensation.

20. "Do The Dead Sing?", Yankee Magazine, Nov 1981.

21. "Father's Day", as a graphic adaptation in CREEPSHOW, Plume, New York ($6.95), 1982.

22. "The Fifth Quarter", Cavalier, 1971.
    As by John Swithen.

23. "Firestarter", Omni, July, Aug 1980.
    Two part excerpt from the novel. About a quarter of the novel. This preceded the book publication.

24. "Foreword", NIGHT SHIFT, Doubleday, Garden City ($8.95), 1978.
    Non-Fiction.

25. "Foreword", TALES OF THE NIGHTSIDE, by C L Grant, Arkham House, Sauk City ($11.95), 1981.
    Non-Fiction.

26. "Foreword", STALKING THE NIGHTMARE, by Harlan Ellison, Phantasia Press, Huntington Woods ($16.00; $40.00), 1982.
    Non-Fiction.

27. "The Fright Report", Oui, Jan 1978.
    Non-Fiction.

28. "The Glass Floor", Startling Mystery Stories, No 6, Fall 1966.
    King's first professional sale.

29. "Graveyard Shift", Cavalier, Oct 1970.

30. "Gray Matter", Cavalier, Oct 1973.

31. "The Gunslinger", Fantasy & Science Fiction, Oct 1978.
    The Gunslinger # 1.

32. "The Gunslinger And The Dark Man", Fantasy & Science Fiction, Nov 1981.
    The Gunslinger # 5.

33. "The Horror Market Writer And The Ten Bears", Writer's Digest, Nov 1973.
    Non-Fiction.

34. "The Horrors Of '79", Rolling Stone, No 307/308, 27 Dec 1979.
    Non-Fiction.

35. "How To Scare A Woman To Death", MURDERESS INK, Ed by Dilys Winn, 1979.
    Non-Fiction.

36. "I Am The Doorway", Cavalier, March 1971.

37. "I Know What You Need", Cosmopolitan, Sept 1976.

38. "I Was A Teenage Grave Robber", Comics Review, 1965.
    King's first published story.

39. "Imagery And The Third Eye", The Writer, Oct 1980.
    Non-Fiction.

"In A Half-World Of Terror"
Reprint title for "I Was A Teenage Grave Robber". Published under the reprint title in Stories of Suspense, No 2, 1966.

40. "An Interview With Myself", Writer's Digest, Jan 1979.
    Non-Fiction.

41. "Introduction", THE ARBOR HOUSE TREASURY OF HORROR AND THE SUPERNATURAL, Ed by Bill Pronzini, Barry N Malzberg and Martin H Greenberg, Arbor House, New York ($19.95), 1981.
    Non-Fiction.

42. "Introduction", FRANKENSTEIN BY MARY SHELLEY, DRACULA BY BRAM STOKER, DR. JEKYLL AND MR. HYDE BY ROBERT LOUIS STEVENSON, Signet: CE1136, 1978, paper.
    Non-Fiction.

43. "Introduction", THE SHAPES OF MIDNIGHT, by Joseph Payne Brennan, Berkley: 04567 ($2.25), 1980, paper.
    Non-Fiction.

44. "It Grows On You", Marshroots, 1975.
    Reprinted in revised form in Whispers, No 17/18, July 1982.

45. "The Jaunt", The Twilight Zone, June 1981.

46. "Jerusalem's Lot", NIGHT SHIFT, Doubleday, Garden City ($8.95), 1978.

47. "The Last Rung On The Ladder", NIGHT SHIFT, Doubleday, Garden City ($8.95), 1978.

48. "The Lawnmower Man", Cavalier, May 1975.
    There was a 21 page black and white graphic adaptation in Bizarre Adventures, No 29, Dec 1981. The adaptation was by King and the art by Walter Simonson.

49. "The Ledge", Penthouse, July 1976.

50. "The Lonesome Death Of Jordy Verrill", as a graphic adaptation of the story "Weeds" in CREEPSHOW, Plume, New York ($6.95), 1982.

51. "Man With A Belly", Cavalier, Dec 1978.

52. "The Man Who Loved Flowers", Gallery, Aug 1977.

53. "The Man Who Would Not Shake Hands", SHADOWS 4, Ed by Charles Grant, Doubleday, Garden City ($11.95), 1982.

54. "The Mangler", Cavalier, Dec 1972.

55. "The Mist", DARK FORCES, Ed by Kirby McCauley, Viking, New York ($16.95), 1980.

56. "The Monkey", Gallery, Nov 1980.
    This story was included as a separate, stapled-in, pullout booklet.

57. "The Monster In The Closet", Ladies Home Journal, Oct 1981.
    Excerpt from CUJO.

58. "The Night Of The Tiger," Fantasy & Science Fiction, Feb 1978.

59. "Night Surf", Cavalier, Aug 1974.

60. "Nona", SHADOWS, Ed by Charles Grant, Doubleday, Garden City ($7.95), 1978.

61. "Not Guilty", New York Times Book Review, 24 Oct 1976.
    Non-Fiction.

62. "Notes On Horror", Quest, June 1981.
    Non-Fiction. An excerpt from DANSE MACABRE.

63. "On Becoming A Brand Name", Adelina, Feb 1980.
    Non-Fiction.

64. "On The Shining And Other Perpetrations", Whispers, No 17/18, July 1982.
    Non-Fiction.

65. "One For The Road", Maine Magazine, March/April 1977.

66. "The Oracle And The Mountain", Fantasy & Science Fiction, Feb 1981.
    The Gunslinger # 3.

67. "Peter Straub: An Informal Appreciation", Program Book, Eighth World Fantasy Convention, 1982.
    Non-Fiction.

68. "A Pilgrim's Progress", American Bookseller, Jan 1980.
    Non-Fiction.

69. "Quitters, Inc.", NIGHT SHIFT, Doubleday, Garden City ($8.95), 1978.

70. "The Reaper's Image", Startling Mystery Stories, No 12, Spring 1969.

71. "Rita Hayworth And Shawshank Redemption", DIFFERENT SEASONS, Viking, New York ($16.95), 1982.

72. "'Salem's Lot", STEPHEN KING, Heinemann and Octopus Books, New York, 1981.

73. "'Salem's Lot", Cosmopolitan, March 1976.
    Condensation.

74. "The Shining", STEPHEN KING, Heinemman and Octopus Books, New York, 1981.

75. "The Slow Mutants", Fantasy & Science Fiction, July 1981.
    The Gunslinger # 4.

76. "Something To Tide You Over", as a graphic adaptation in CREEPSHOW, Plume, New York ($6.95), 1982.

77. "Sometimes They Come Back", Cavalier, March 1974.

78. "The Sorry State Of TV Shows" TV Guide, 5 Dec 1981.
    Non-Fiction. An excerpt from DANSE MACABRE.

79. "Stephen King's Guilty Pleasures", Film Comment, May-June 1981.
    Non-Fiction.

80. "Strawberry Spring", Cavalier, Nov 1975.

81. "Suffer The Little Children", Cavalier, Feb 1972.

82. "They're Creeping Up On You", as a graphic adaption in CREEPSHOW, Plume, New York ($6.95), 1982.

83. "Trucks", Cavalier, June 1973.

84. "Visit With An Endangered Species", Playboy, Jan 1982.
    Non-Fiction.

85. "The Way Station", Fantasy & Science Fiction, March 1980.
    The Gunslinger # 2.

86. "The Wedding Gig", Ellery Queen's Mystery Magazine, 1 Dec 1980.

87. "Weeds", Cavalier, May 1976.
    This also appears as "The Lonesome Death Of Jordy Verrill" in the
    book and movie CREEPSHOW.

88. "When Is TV Too Scary For Children?", TV Guide, 13 June 1981.
    Non-Fiction.

89. "Why We Crave Horror Stories", Playboy, Jan 1981.
    Non-Fiction. An excerpt from DANSE MACABRE.

90. "The Woman In The Room", NIGHT SHIFT, Doubleday, Garden City
    ($8.95), 1978.

There was a story called "The Float" which King sold to Knight Syndicate for
the magazine Adam. However, the story was apparently never published.

INTERVIEWS

1. "Ask Them Yourself", Family Weekly, 24 Feb 1980, 15 June 1980, 7 Sept
   1980.
   A celebrity question and answer column.

2. "Biographical Notes", Doubleday Books Publicity Department, 15 Sept
   1973.
   Mimeographed.

3. "The Dark Beyond The Door", by Freff, Tomb Of Dracula, No 4, No 5
   April, June 1980.
   A two-part interview.

4. "Filmedia: The Rest Of King", by Robert Stewart, Starship, Spring 198

5. "Flix", by Bhob Stewart, Heavy Metal, Jan, Feb, March 1980.
   A three-part article-interview in the column "Flix".

6. "Front Row Seats At The Creepshow", Twilight Zone, May 1982.

7. "Horror Teller", Horizon, Feb 1978.

8. "Interview: Stephen King", Infinity Cubed, No 5, 1980.

9. "Interview: Stephen King", by Martha Thomases and Robert Tebb
   Hightimes, No 65, June 1981.

10. "Interview . . . Stephen King" by Dan Weaver, The Literary Gui
    Monthly Selection Magazine, Dec 1978.

11. "An Interview With Stephen King", Waldenbooks Newsletter, Oct 197

12. "An Interview With Stephen King", by Joyce Lynch Dewes, Mystery, March 1981.

13. "The King Of Horror", Oui, Aug. 1981.

14. "King Of The Night", by David Chute, Take One, Jan 1979.

15. "King Of The Occult", by Lois Lowry, Down East Magazine, Nov 1977.

16. "Living In 'Constant, Deadly Terror'", by Dan Christensen, Fangoria, No 3, Dec 1979.
    Article-interview.

17. "The Night Shifter - An Interview With Stephen King", by Stephen Jones, Fantasy Media (British), March 1979.

18. "Penthouse Interview: Stephen King", Penthouse, April 1982.

19. "Riding The Crest Of The Horror Craze", by William Wilson, New York Times Magazine, 11 May 1980.

20. "'Salem's Lot", by Bill Kelley, Cinefantastique, Vol 9 No 2, 1979.
    Cover story.

21. "Shine Of The Times: An Interview With Stephen King", by Lewis Shiner, Marty Ketchum, Arnold Fenner and Pat Cadigan, Shayol No 3, Summer 1979.

22. "Stephen King", Publishers Weekly, 17 Jan 1977.

23. "Stephen King A Self Interview", Doubleday Books Publicity Department, no date.
    Mimeographed.

24. "Stephen King: Behind The Best Seller", New York Times Book Review, 23 Sept 1979.

25. "Stephen King: Behind The Best Seller", New York Times Book Review, 27 Sept 1981.

26. "Stephen King: I Like To Go For The Jugular", Twilight Zone, April 1981.

27. "Stephen King On Carrie, The Shining, Etc.", by Peter S Perakos, Cinefantastique, Vol 8 No 1, 1978.

28. "Stephen King's Court Of Horror," by Abe Peck, Rolling Stone College Papers, No 3, Winter 1980.

29. "Witches And Aspirin", Writer's Digest, June 1977.

A large number of additional interviews (but certainly still not a complete list) are known but their titles were not obtainable in time for publication of this bibliography. They are listed below by periodical and date.
Abiliene Reporter - 14 Oct 1980; American Way - Feb 1981; Bangor Daily News (Maine) - 16 Oct 1980; The Blade (Toledo, Ohio) - 5 Oct 1980; Beaver

County Times (Pennsylvania) - 14 Oct 1979; Book World - 1 Oct 1978; Boston Globe - 10 Oct 1980; Boston Herald American - Sept 1979, 3 Aug 1980; Boston Phoenix - 17 June 1980; Bowling Green News (Kentucky) - 14 Sept 1980; Burlington Free Press (Vermont) - 1 Oct 1979; Canton Ohio Repository - 9 Sept 1980; Chicago Daily News - 7 July 1977; Chronicle Telegram - 3 Oct 1980; Cleveland Press - 12 April 1979; Conta Costa Times (California) - 14 Oct 1979; Daily Nebraskan - 21 Sept 1979; Daily News (New York) - 23 Sept 1979; Detroit News - 26 Sept 1979; East/West - Oct 1980; English Journal - Feb 1980; Fort Lauderdale News/Sun-Sentinel - 28 Sept 1980; Houston Chronicle - 30 Sept 1979; Houston Post - 30 Sept 1979; Iowa City Press Citizen - 15 Nov 1980; Kennebec (University of Maine at Augusta) - April 1979; Kennebec Journal - 4 April 1977, 27 Oct 1979; Lakeland Florida Ledger - 28 Oct 1979; Lewiston Daily Sun (Maine) - 10 Jan 1980; Lewiston Journal - 2 April 1977; Lincoln Star - 20 Sept 1979; Little Professors Book Centers - Vol 1 No 3; Los Angeles Herald Examiner - 23 Sept 1979; Maine Campus (University of Maine at Orono) - April 1977, 8 Sept 1978; Middlesex News (Massachusetts) - 8 April 1979; Milwaukee Journal - 15 Sept 1980; Milwaukee Sentinel - 28 Feb 1979; Minneapolis Star - 8 Sept 1979; Morning Star Telegram (Ft Worth) - 25 Feb 1979; Morning Union - 31 Oct 1979; MS London - 9 April 1979; New Hampshire - 26 April 1977; New Kensinton Valley News Dispatch - 23 Oct 1979; New York Post - 12 March 1977; New York Times Book Review - Aug 1977, 11 May 1980; News American (Baltimore) - 16 Sept 1979; North Hills News Record - 26 Oct 1979; Patriot Ledger (Quincy, Massachusetts) - 31 Aug 1979; Peninsula Times Tribune - 2 Oct 1979; Phoenix Arizona Gazetter - 12 Oct 1979; Pittsburgh Press - 6 Sept 1979; Portland Press Herald (Maine) - 31 Oct 1979, Sept 1981; Portland Sunday Telegram - 31 Oct 1976, 29 July 1979, 28 Oct 1979; Primos Times (Pennsylvania) - 11 Oct 1980; The Red and Black (University of Georgia) - 7 Nov 1980; Rochester Democrat and Chronicle - 26 Aug 1979; Saginaw Michigan News - 11 Oct 1980; Self - Sept 1981; Shreveport Journal - 24 Nov 1978; Sky - Nov 1978; St Cloud Times (Minnesota) - 3 Oct 1980; St Petersburg Times - 4 March 1979; Sun (Baltimore) - 26 Aug 1980; Sun-Tattler (Hollywood, Florida) - 17 Sept 1981; Tampa Tribune - 31 Aug 1980; Tennessean - 5 May 1980; Toronto Sunday Star - 5 Oct 1980; Twilight Zone - May 1982; Vermont Free Press - 8 Oct 1980; Washington Post - 26 Aug 1979; Watertown Daily Times (New York) - 16 Sept 1980; Woodlands Sun (Houston, Texas) - 19 Sept 1979.

WORKS ABOUT STEPHEN KING

1. "Catching Up With The Rapidly Rising Star Of Author Stephen King: Thoughts On Books, Films, And What Went Wrong On The Shining", by Paul R Gagne, Cinefantastique, Vol 10 No 4, 1980.

2. "Checking In: Stephen King", Boston Magazine, Oct 1980.

3. "Creepshow", by Ron Hansen, Esquire, Jan 1981.

4. "Creepshow", by David McDonnall and John Sayers, Prevue, May 1982.

5. "'Creepshow' Crawlers Can Cause Creepy Cold Chills", by Jeffrey Wells, New York Post, 3 Sept 1981.

6. "Creepshow: Five Jolting Tales Of Horror! From Stephen King And George Romero", by Paul R Gagne, Cinefantastique, Vol 12 No 2/3, April 1982.

7. "Danse Macabre", by Stanley Wiater, Valley Advocate, 27 May 1981.

8. "Dark Stars Rising", by Stanley Wiater, Valley Advocate, 8 April 1981.

9. "Fantasy Books", by Fritz Leiber, Locus, No 232, April 1980.
   A long review of THE DEAD ZONE in the column "Fantasy Books".

10. "The 'Film Script As Novel' Scam", by Michael Goodwin, Boulevards, Jan 1981.

11. "For Years Stephen King's Firestarter Was Wife Tabitha; Now She Burns To Write, Too", People, 18 May 1981.

12. "Just Your Average Guy", by Stanley Wiater, Valley Advocate, 27 May 1981.

13. "The King Of The Macabre At Home", Parents Magazine, Jan 1982.

14. "Kubrick Goes Gothic", by Harlan Kennedy, American Film, June 1980.

15. "The Man Who Writes Nightmares", by Mel Allen, Yankee Magazine, March 1979.

16. "A Mild Down-Easter Discovers Terror Is The Ticket", People, 29 Dec 1980 - 5 Jan 1981.

17. "A New Definition For Ultimate Horror: The Shining", by Jim Wynorski, Fangoria, No 7, Aug 1980.

18. "On The Set Of 'Salem's Lot", by Susan Casey, Fangoria, No 4, Feb 1980.

19. "The Once And Future King", by David McDonnell, Prevue, May 1982.

20. "Patience Pays", Oakland Tribune, 5 Jan 1981.
    Very short, unbylined piece with picture.

21. "The Scariest Movie Ever Made", by Desmond Ryan, Saga, July 1980.

22. "Shadowings", by Douglas E Winter, Fantasy Newsletter, No 30, Nov 1980.
    A long review of FIRESTARTER in the column "Shadowings".

23. "The Shining", by Jim Albertson and Peter S Perakos, Cinefantastique, Vol 7 No 3/Vol 7 No 4, 1978.

24. "The Shining, Maar Schitterthet Ook?", [Dutch], by Eddy C Bertin, Rigel 76, Jan 1981.

25. "Stanley Kubrick's Horror Show", by Jack Kroll, Newsweek, 26 May 1980.

26. "Stephen King: Werelden Van Angst En Isolatie", [Dutch], by Eddy C Bertin, SF Gids, 1981.

27. "Stephen King And George Romero: Collaboration In Terror", by Stanley Wiater, Fangoria, No 6, June 1980.

28. "Stephen King Makes Millions By Scaring Hell Out Of Three Million Readers", People, 7 March 1977.

29. "Stephen King, The Master Of The Horror Novel Abandons Television And Turns To Writing For The Screen", by Paul R Gagne, Cinefantastique, Vol 10 No 1, 1980.

30. Title Unknown, [German], by Eddy C Bertin, Weird Fiction Times, No 46, 1976.

31. Title Unknown, Us Magazine, 3 April 1979.

32. "Uncrowning Of King", by Roger Smith, State of Shock, April 1981.

33. "Welke Prijs Voor De Onmenselijkheid?", [Dutch], by Eddy C Bertin, Holland SF, Vol 9 No 6, Dec 1975.

34. "Who's Afraid Of Stephen (Carrie) King?", by Carrie Carmichael, Family Weekly, 6 Jan 180.

FORTHCOMING AND UNPUBLISHED WORKS

BABYLON HERE - An early unpublished novel.

BLAZE - An early unpublished novel.

THE CANNIBALS - a novel, publication plans indefinite.

CHRISTINE - A novel to be published in 1983 by Viking.

CYCLE OF THE WEREWOLF - A graphic novel with the art by Berni Wrightson. Not yet scheduled.

GETTING IT ON - An early unpublished novel.

IT - A novel which is partially finished, but a very long way from publication.

NIGHT MOVES - A second collection of short stories, scheduled for fall 1984.

PET SEMATARY - A novel which is finished. Not yet scheduled.

"The Raft" - Due from Gallery, probably in late 1982.

SWORD IN THE DARKNESS - An early unpublished novel.

TALISMAN - With Peter Straub. Trade edition from Viking and from Coward McCann & Geoghegan jointly. There may be a limited edition.

THE TOMMYKNOCKERS - a work in progress.

"Uncle Otto's Truck" - a new short story.

"The Word Processor" - Due from Playboy, probably in late 1982.

Afterword

by George A. Romero

WE ALL HAVE FEARS, much as we may not want to admit that. Part of our contemporary sophistication demands that we behave confidently; walk right on by, don't blink an eye. Past the bum in the gutter, past the guy we make as a mugger, past the church, past the Pro-Nukes in La Guardia, we move along and we're not supposed to show that we're shook — you gotta be strong today, gotta be cool. We confess our fears only when we reach the measured safety of what we define as a "deep and meaningful relationship," and then we get points for honesty. Would we confess at all if our analysts didn't give us gold stars for doing so?

In the film, *Arthur*, Dudley Moore attends John Gielgud, who is dying. After a long and playful scene, Gielgud finally says, "Arthur, I'm afraid." It actually takes us by surprise. In stead of something that can go unspoken as a telling consequence of human arrogance.

Fear is with us all the time. We can dope it up or drown it with alcohol. We can tuck it into a drawer behind last year's designer jeans, but it comes out to sleep with us every night.

247

There are those moments in the dark when we feel its tendrils wrapping around our souls; when we feel its cold breath on the backs of our necks. We just don't talk about those times. We disown our nightmares or write them off as the results of too many Sambucas.

Come to think of it, we tend to write off many of our deeper emotions these days. We're much too hip to laugh at a clown or cry at a wedding or let our hearts swell to the beat of a passing drum and bugle corps.

But those feelings catch up with us once in a while, and a good thing, too, because if we try to survive an emotional bankruptcy we'll go insane, like sleepers deprived of dreams. We have to surrender every now and again, much as it might embarrass us, and, somehow, that surrender makes us feel good. It confirms our humanity. Those involuntary animal responses, laughing, crying, leap up from somewhere deep inside and take us totally off guard. They connect us to our origins and remind us that, while we might be a privileged specie, we are still children in this universe.

The most complex of those involuntary responses is fear, and as much as we modernists try to suppress our anxieties, our lifestyles constantly deal us new sources of horror. Once we feared thunder and death and the tiger's claw. We haven't conquered those today, yet we've added airplanes and elevators and nuclear bombs, etc.

We are ill-equipped to analyze fear because, infants that we are, we are still in fear's clutches, and our terrified viewpoint makes us incapable of defining the enemy's personality. Our individual backgrounds make us subjective. Our world makes us sublimate in order to cope. Our "fear of fear itself" makes us deny our hearts.

Can we really expect to analyze why a piece of fiction is frightening? Can we analyze why a baseball hit flies out of the park, a home run? We can examine slow-motion films of the hitter. We can study the position of his bat, mark his stance, detail the turning of his wrists. What we can't see, what we will never understand, unless we ourselves are so talented, and even then it might elude us, is the instinct at work. The natural affinity that differentiates greatness.

Is Stephen King a great writer of horror fiction? Shall we shoot slow-motion films of King at his typewriter? Shall we wire him with electrodes and inject him with pentothal? Maybe we can get him to donate his organs for dissection and analysis so that after his death we can discover something about what he was actually doing with his work.

Christ, he's Babe Ruth; he's knockin' 'em out of the park a mile, every time at bat, and we're damn lucky 'cause it's the bottom of the ninth in the last game of the play-offs between the Everytown Vidiots and the Centerville Type-Setters. Let's go Centerville!

He's talking to us, now, today. His age is five years plus-or-minus the average age of most readers who are out there responding to the recommendations of the Times and the Literary Guild. One spots half-a-dozen copies of King paperbacks on every long airplane flight, on every long beach and on every Long Island commuter train. The cat is happenin', as some say, and he's puttin' down shit that slaps five onto any of us who came up through the sixties.

Is he important? Come on, gang, who are we kidding? Is he a traditionalist? Is he a supernaturalist? Beats me, Jack, I'll have to ask him next time I see him. He tells terrific stories in an idiom that's within my grasp. His characters are clearly drawn and they feel like they've been plucked from the neighborhoods of my experience. Very often he scares the shit out of me with a few sentences.

Yes, but isn't he just re-hashing the tired old boogey-men of the past, the ones we're really not afraid of any more? The point might be that we're not afraid of them as portrayed by Bela, Boris and Lon. We're not afraid of them when they're painted with eighteenth century strokes. We would be afraid of a vampire if he got on our subway car, just as the doors closed, when there was no one else on board. We'd be afraid if we found a vampire in the fruit-cellar, or if one knocked on our door selling boxes of suspicious looking cookies.

One doesn't have to analyze the vampire. Let's study the realities, study mankind. There's no particular merit in examining any beast of fiction. Nor should any blame be attached to one who doesn't so examine. I think of the exercise as a big mox-nix, an academic pasttime akin to word-search puzzles and five-hundred-piece jig-saws — it doesn't matter if you do them, it doesn't matter if you don't. When the wolf comes out of the forest, I don't give a damn about his socio-political views, baby, I'm lookin' at his teeth, and I'm lookin' over my shoulder as I haul-ass outa there.

Now it's another thing entirely to try and analyze what the beast may represent to us, to our society at large. But even that is not the responsibility of an author to outline in his work. One hopes the author has given the topic some thought, and that he has clear opinions in his head, but explanations of that kind of sub-text can ruin the surface of an otherwise engrossing narrative.

We put our Bible in up-dated trappings; our Constitution, our nursery rhymes, our football games and our seltzer water. Why not our demons? It's the only way to keep them around. A vampire is one of the undead; he drinks the blood of the living to survive. He can be driven off with garlic, crucifix or host and he can be destroyed only by a stake driven through his heart. Do we have to tamper with that myth to make the character relevant today? What's wrong with placing him, just as tradition describes him, into today's world? That act itself makes for automatic relevance, and it serves to preserve a literary figure who might otherwise perish behind the likes of Kiss and the Dukes of Hazzard.

I eagerly enter the pages of a new Stephen King book with light-hearted joy and great expectations; not unlike the feelings I remember having as a kid entering an amusement park. Being in an amusement park is as close as most will ever come to being in a fantasy world. The geography is different, park to park, and the names of the rides change from Rye Beach to Kennywood, but the personality of those places, the world around, is constant. Familiar smells, familiar sounds, familiar thrills keep us coming back. Creatures jump at us from the shadows in the Tunnel of Fright; we are terrified as the Tornado plunges, seemingly straight down, on its rickety track. We experience the anxiety of fear and we are released by the experience. We feel, for the most part, safe in an amusement park.

Things do nibble away at our security, however, and they provide the textures which make the amusement park a place of real adventure. The clock is running. Things cost money. Some bully might smear cotton-candy all over our faces, or sneak up behind us and pop our balloons. The roller-coaster could fly off the track. We might be so heavy that we'll fall through when the floor of the Centrifuge drops away. Other boys and girls might think we're goofy.

Stephen King's books provide similar total experiences for me and, I think, for most who read them. He knows the same people I know, he's been to the same gas station, the same Seven-Eleven, he listens to the same rock and roll that's on my local a. m. band, and I know damn well he's been to an amusement park not too far from my home town.

I hear ya, Steve, and I love ya, and I'm not afraid to say it.

NOTES ON THE CONTRIBUTORS

STEPHEN KING, in just eight years, has seen 40 million copies of his books published in the United States alone. He is incontestably the most popular and best-selling horror writer in history. Movies have already been made from his novels by Stanley Kubrick, Brian De Palma and Tobe Hooper, and the rest of his novels and most of his stories have been optioned for film. King has written an original screenplay for George Romero's film "Creepshow" and has many other novels and screen treatments in the works. He lives in Maine with his wife Tabitha, also a novelist, and their three children.

PETER STRAUB is the author of several novels, including the bestsellers *Ghost Story* and *Shadowland*. He is one of the few modern horror writers to approach King in his appeal to readers and popularity among horror fans. Currently, he and King are collaborating on an epic novel of horror and fantasy to be called *The Talisman*.

CHELSEA QUINN YARBRO is a prolific author of fantasy, horror and science fiction. Her series of novels about the vampire Ragoczy, Count de Saint-Germain, which began with *Hotel Transylvania*, is especially noteworthy. Other works include *Time of the Fourth Horseman*, *Dead and Buried*, *Ariosto*, *Music When Sweet Voices Die*, and the collection of supernatural stories, *Cautionary Tales*. She lives in Berkeley, California.

DON HERRON since 1977 has been leading his Literary Walks in San Francisco, most popular among them the Dashiell Hammett tour. Two editions of his *Dashiell Hammett Tour* book have seen print. He also wrote *Echoes from the Vaults of Yoh-Vombis*, a biography of the occultist and Bigfoot investigator George F. Haas, and has contributed many articles to publications as diverse as *The Berkeley Barb*, *Nyctalops*, *Fate*, *Mystery*. He is an editor of the annual journal *The Romantist* and a founder of the Maltese Falcon Society.

FRITZ LEIBER is one of the most respected and honored figures in fantasy and science fiction. Aside from numerous awards for his fiction, he has earned the Life Achievement Award from both the Science Fiction Writers of America and the World Fantasy Convention. His work includes the sf novels *The Big Time*, *The Wanderer*, *A Spectre is Haunting Texas*, and many others; the sword and sorcery tales of Fafhrd and the Gray Mouser; and the supernatural horror books *Night's Black Agents*, *Conjure Wife* and *Our Lady of Darkness*. He is considered one of the first and greatest writers of the brand of modern horror which Stephen King has made widely popular.

BILL WARREN is a film archivist and reviewer, a regular columnist for *Fantasy Newsletter* and other professional and semi-professional publications. He has worked on *Famous Monsters of Filmland* and was Walt Lee's main assistant on his *Reference Guide to Fantastic Films*. A freelance film researcher, his book on 1950s SF Films *Keep Watching the Skies*, was recently published. He and his wife Beverly live in Los Angeles.

DEBORAH L. NOTKIN contributes a column to the science fiction magazine *Rigel*, and her reviews have appeared in the San Francisco *Chronicle*, *Locus* and many other publications. She is manager and part-owner of The Other Change of Hobbit Bookstore in Berkeley, California, which specializes in fantasy, sf and horror literature and art.

CHARLES L. GRANT is the author of a series of stories and novels set in the fictitious, haunted town of Oxrun Station, a large and growing canvas for his treatment of modern supernatural horror. He has won the Nebula Award from the Science Fiction Writers of America for best fiction of the year. He has edited numerous anthologies of horror stories, including the World Fantasy Award winning *Shadows* series for Doubleday. An omnibus of his best horror fiction, *Tales from the Nightside*, recently appeared from Arkham House.

BEN P. INDICK is a long-standing member of that Lovecraftian society known as the Esoteric Order of Dagon and has had many articles on Lovecraft and related writers published in the field. His books include *A Gentleman from Providence Pens a Letter* and *The Drama of Ray Bradbury*. An aspiring playwright, he lives in Teaneck, New Jersey with his wife Janet, an artist.

ALAN RYAN has won the John W. Campbell Memorial Award for most promising writer for his science fiction tales. He writes for the *Washington Post*, the *New York Times* and other periodicals, and also works as an editor. He has written two modern horror novels, *The Kill* and *The Dead of Winter*.

DOUGLAS E. WINTER is an attorney in Washington, D.C., an honor graduate of Harvard Law School. He has written fiction and essays in the fantasy and horror field, and serves as interviews editor for *Fantasy Newsletter*, to which he also contributes a regular column, "Shadowings." His book-length study, *The Reader's Guide to Stephen King*, will appear soon from Starmont House.

GEORGE A. ROMERO established a permanent reputation as one of the Masters of celluloid horror with his unforgettable black & white film *Night of the Living Dead*. His other films include *Dawn of the Dead*, and *Knight Riders*. He has recently collaborated with Stephen King on the movie *Creepshow*.

MARTY KETCHUM has been a science fiction and fantasy fan and collector for 15 years. He writes an occasional book review column for *Shayol Magazine*, and has loved and collected the writings of Stephen King since stumbling across *'Salem's Lot* in 1975. He lives in the woods near Galena, Kansas with his wife Sue, and their son Nathaniel.

DANIEL J H LEVACK is a collector and bibliophile, currently preparing for publication by Underwood-Miller a series of deluxe illustrated and annotated bibliographies of major authors in fantasy and science fiction. His *Fantasms*, a bibliography on the works of Jack Vance, and *PKD*, on Philip K. Dick, have appeared already. In preparation are bibliographies on Roger Zelazny, Frank Herbert, Poul Anderson, L. Sprague de Camp and others.

JEFF AND ANDREA LEVIN operate Pendragon Graphics - Typesetting & Design in Beaverton, Oregon. Together, they did the design work for *Fear Itself*, and Jeff, who has also been involved with the fantasy & science fiction field as a publisher, bookseller, bibliographer and collector helped with the bibliography.

TIM UNDERWOOD and CHUCK MILLER are publishers who specialize in hardcover fantasy and science fiction, with illustrated collector's editions that harken to the halcyon days of Howard Pyle. Under their Underwood-Miller imprint they also publish a series of annotated pictorial bibliographies, dealing with the works of major authors in the science fiction genre. They have edited a previous critical anothology on fantasy and sf author *Jack Vance* for Taplinger.

FEAR ITSELF
The Horror Fiction of Stephen King

This first edition of *Fear Itself: The Horror Fiction of Stephen King* is published in October 1982 in an edition of 5000 copies, including a special signed edition of 225 copies. The text was set in 9 and 11 point California, a type design based on W. A. Dwiggins' Caledonia typeface, on a Compugraphic EditWriter 7500 by Jeff Levin, Andrea Levin, and Steve Tambornini of Pendragon Graphics, Beaverton, Oregon. The title is set in ITC Benguiat Bold and ITC Benguiat Medium. Book design by Jeff and Andrea Levin of Pendragon Graphics. The book was printed and bound by the Book Press of Brattleboro, Vermont.